The Democracy Of God

The Democracy Of God

An American Catholicism

Robert J. Willis

iUniverse, Inc.
New York Lincoln Shanghai

The Democracy Of God
An American Catholicism

Copyright © 2006 by Robert J. Willis

All rights reserved. No part of this book may be used or reproduced by any means, graphic, electronic, or mechanical, including photocopying, recording, taping or by any information storage retrieval system without the written permission of the publisher except in the case of brief quotations embodied in critical articles and reviews.

iUniverse books may be ordered through booksellers or by contacting:

iUniverse
2021 Pine Lake Road, Suite 100
Lincoln, NE 68512
www.iuniverse.com
1-800-Authors (1-800-288-4677)

Cover design by Megan Mangum.

Cover illustration, "The First Mass on St. Clement's Island," (1984) by Ben E. Neill. Painting owned by the St. Clement's Island— Potomac River Museum, St. Mary's County, Maryland. Painting used with the permission of the Paul VI Institute for the Arts.

ISBN-13: 978-0-595-37922-4 (pbk)
ISBN-13: 978-0-595-82293-5 (ebk)
ISBN-10: 0-595-37922-2 (pbk)
ISBN-10: 0-595-82293-2 (ebk)

Printed in the United States of America

I Acknowledge Three Special Blessings:

My Life, Yearning To Grow Into One;

*My Freedom, Bestowing A Clear
Responsibility For Life And Growth;*

*My Wife, Sharing Love That Unites Me
With Her, With Myself, And With My God*

Contents

Introduction

Just as the Soviet Union dissolved in a flash, just as the Berlin Wall crumbled overnight, just as the Cold War disappeared, so has the Tridentine Catholic Church in America, a stubborn remnant of a sixteenth century council, faded to a distant recollection.

The Second Vatican Council not only threw open windows to let in fresh air; it also unlocked the doors that had held many priests and religious confined by rules and fear in a small, strictly controlled world. The exodus of the professional, religious elite began soon after.

In 1962, when Vatican II opened, 55,000 priests served the Catholic community in the United States. Over the next four decades these numbers decreased 20% by deaths and departures. New ordinations that might have filled the gap did not, decreasing by nearly half. Communities of brothers and sisters fared even worse. From 1962 to 2004 the population of brothers fell almost 50%, that of sisters an astounding 59%.[1]

As a result, the institutional heart of the American church, its parishes and schools, suffered. In 1962, most parishes had a resident priest as pastor and an elementary school. By 2004, only 83% of parishes had a resident priest as pastor, and on the average three parishes had to share an elementary school.[2]

Catholic schools have long been the crucial ground where priests and religious nourished the next generation of Catholics. But that day has passed. Consider the following telling statistics:

---

[1] *The Official Catholic Directory, Anno Domini 1962, 2002, 2004.* New York: P.J. Kenedy and Sons.

[2] *Ibid.* In 1962 the ratio of priest to parishioner was 1::171. By 2004 the ratio had grown to 1::1,521. The ratio of elementary school to parish changed from 1::1.61 to 1::3.

1

	1962	2004	Total	Change
Teaching priests	11,586	1,792	-9,794	-85%
Teaching scholastics	818	57	-761	-93%
Teaching brothers	5,016	1,195	-3,821	-76%
Teaching sisters	100,871	7,871	-93,000	-92%
Teaching laity	57,515	166,966	+109,451	+295%[3]

Priests and religious have all but disappeared from Catholic schools in America; they have turned over the task of educating Catholic children to the laity.[4]

What does the future hold? One may reasonably conclude that the task of administering parishes and teaching in schools will shift increasingly to the Catholic laity. I question, and even doubt, whether religious orders and a celibate priesthood will continue to exist in the future Catholic Church in America unless significant changes in ecclesiastical regulations concerning these vocations occur.[5]

At this juncture, the Catholic community in the United States has four options: do nothing and see what happens, become schismatic, go back to the Pre-Vatican II church, or transform.

To do nothing appears foolish. With diminishing numbers of priests, sporadic contact with the hierarchical church would result. Reception of the sacraments would become more infrequent. The reality of the church in people's lives would resemble a cultural artifact, a museum of interesting but empty structures. As in parts of Europe, Catholic life in America would change from "pray, pay, and obey" to "baptize, marry, and bury." Catholics need show up at church only on those social occasions; for the rest of life, formal religion would merit scant attention.

---

[3]   *Ibid.*, 2004. Cf. also "Frequently Requested Church Statistics, Center for Applied Research in the Apostolate (CARA), 2004."

[4]   *Ibid.* So, for example, in 2003 St. Paul's Grade School in Yakima, Washington, the place where Dominican Sisters raised me in the faith, had 351 students taught by twenty-one lay teachers <u>and no sisters</u>. Its counterpart in town, St. Joseph's Grade School, was educating 381 students with <u>one Sister of Providence</u> and twenty-one lay teachers. Although six Jesuit priests lived at St. Joseph's rectory, the Jesuit's Marquette High School <u>no longer existed</u>.

[5]   *Ibid.* Although reports vary, the median age of U.S. priests lies between fifty-seven and sixty-two, of religious sisters between sixty-five and sixty-nine. With the ordinary retirement age of these groups at seventy-one, we may expect half to the current (2004) 44,212 priests either to have died or retired by 2018, half of the 71,468 sisters to have preceded them by 2010. Since 1962 new vocations have managed a mere trickle: its 4,300 in 2004 a pale 9% of what it was then

A successful schism requires energy and imagination in it leaders. As I assess the American church, leadership exists on the extreme right and extreme left. But both groups exhaust themselves in other tasks. Those on the right inveigh constantly over the betrayal of their church, and invest their efforts in trying to get back the Tridentine church of those good, old, faith-filled days. Their unrelieved anger against, and nearly paranoid searching out of traitors among us, leaves no space for imagination or constructive change. To them, the problem rests with others. "If only *they* would repent and obey their bishops; then peace and certitude would return." And since God guides the church infallibly through its pope and hierarchy, why should one think of separating from it?

Their unnatural bedfellows on the left received a lightening blast of hope from John XXIII and Vatican II. That stimulated their energy and imagination. But then a cautious Paul VI and a determined John Paul II together tightened the reins of control, closing the doors and windows beginning to open upon the modern world. After years of striving for collaboration in church governance, most liberal thinkers have turned away in exasperation. Instead they work toward creating a freer world through governmental agencies, with international charitable organizations, in politics and health care and social service. "Let this stubborn pope," they think, "and his sycophantic entourage fiddle way while Rome burns. We tried. We have no energy left to expend in assisting a community that denies it needs help while it is slowly expiring."

Pope John XXIII called the bishops of the world to Rome in October 1962. Three years later, his successor, Pope Paul VI, having blessed their work and endorsed their decrees, sent them back to their dioceses. Almost immediately, conservative individuals and groups tried to negate the Council's decisions and new directions. Over the last forty years, they have latched on to various strategies: attending only Latin masses; relentlessly hanging on to the medieval religious garb fashionable before the Council; saying the rosary, attending benediction and forty-hours devotions in their parishes or walking the Way of the Cross; writing Rome about any perceived heterodoxy in priests or bishops or theologians; obeying scrupulously the will of God as manifested in papal decrees and declarations, episcopal guidelines, and priestly instructions as if each participated in papal infallibility. Can such efforts effectively cancel out the magisterial teachings of Vatican II?— no, at least not without a schism. Some Catholics after Vatican I, upset with the decree on papal infallibility, refused to accept it. They pulled up stakes and formed the Old Catholic Church. So too, Catholics disturbed by Vatican II, like Bishop Lefebvre and his followers, left the church in order to escape its pronouncements. No Catholic can remain a faithful church member and deny the validity of the decrees of ecumenical councils, be they perceived as too conservative (Vatican I) or too liberal (Vatican II). And no pope can overturn the work of his predecessors or previous councils, no matter his personal approval or disapproval of their official decisions.

Besides feeling the effects of the documents of Vatican II, like the "Constitution on the Church in the Modern World" which calls for the church's engagement with, and insertion into, the affairs of this earth, the American church has irrevocably changed from its Pre-Vatican II incarnation.

On July 15, 1968 Pope Paul VI in his encyclical *Humanae Vitae* rejected the advice of his family planning commission and confirmed the church's condemnation of artificial birth control. Since then, an overwhelming majority of American Catholics have disavowed that condemnation, have taken their procreative functions into their own hands, and routinely decide as couples what birth control measures are reasonable for them in their family situation. They do so without guilt and without feeling any need to confess either their decisions or their actions. They simply think the pope erred.

Since that pivotal moment in 1968, adult, educated Catholics have regained the authority of their consciences as regards their personal lives. A woman married to an abusive partner divorces and remarries and continues to receive the sacraments. For the sake of their marriage, interfaith couples take communion in each other's churches. Lifelong homosexuals joined in a loving and stable union consider themselves to be good Catholics and receive the church's sacraments. Parents no longer worry about a teenage son who occasionally masturbates, judging this to be both normal and natural. Nor do they remonstrate with a grown daughter who lives with her intended before marriage. All such instances, and others like them, happen regularly and are widespread. No matter what the church teaches, these Catholics judge that they are following the reasonable dictates of an educated conscience. Such personal freedom did not flourish in the Tridentine church before Vatican II; it does now and cannot be stopped.

Besides the failure of *Humanae Vitae* to gain the assent and obedience of the Catholic people, two other factors contribute to a growing independence from hierarchical dominance.

The Catholic school system stands as a significant achievement of the Pre-Vatican II immigrant church in America. In 1962 Catholic parishes across the country commonly had a parochial grade school or, at least, access to one. Religious women regularly staffed these institutions. In addition most cities had Catholic high schools established through dioceses or by religious orders. This network of schools played a major role in helping an immigrant population adjust to the New World, integrate into its society, and establish itself as a contributing partner in its middle class.

In the first half of the 20th Century, except in our largest cities, Catholics rarely attended institutions of higher learning except teachers' colleges. The G. I. Bill after World War II, plus an accelerating national affluence, changed that. By 1962 two hundred and seventy-eight Catholic colleges and universities were educating 337,000 students. Forty-two years later, because of the decrease of teaching priests and religious, the number of these institutions had shrunk by forty-six, while the numbers of enrolled students had increased a dramatic 222%.[6] With this advanced education, Catholics now claim their share of the country's professional class as well as the upper levels of corporate America. Immigrant Catholics, at least those of Western and Central European extraction, no longer look to the church with its priests and religious for upward mobility.

Prior to the 1960's, one assumed that the church's clergy were more finely educated than the majority of Catholic laity, certainly in theology and philosophy. Today, many clergy have the same education they had in the Pre-Vatican II church while increasing percentages of their parishioners hold professional and doctoral degrees, even in theology and philosophy. A better-educated laity, one superior in its education to that of many of the clergy, no longer unquestioningly accepts "what father says" as correct or true. The laity still listens to what the church's representatives teach, but it more often reserves to itself decisions about the relevance and application of those teachings.

Before Vatican II, the personal and social distance maintained between clergy and laity reinforced the moral hegemony of the clergy. At mass the priest stood before and above the congregation, with his back to it. Latin prayers and fine ceremonial robes added to his mystery. In Confession the priest spoke quietly and impersonally from behind a screen in a dark chamber. Outside sacramental settings the priest routinely wore a roman collar, a clerical habit or a dark suit. Even on occasions when a priest joined a family at its home in celebration of a baptism or a marriage, he attended in clerical garb and maintained a professional demeanor. In general, laity knew next to nothing about the personal lives of their priests. Given their status in the church, the ceremonies surrounding them, and their constant urging of others toward a life of holiness, most laity presumed, for lack of other data, that their priests led holy, moral, prayerful and dedicated lives.

After Vatican II, many of the barriers between clergy and laity disappeared. With closeness came familiarity, with personal relationships the mysteries of church life and the illusions about clerical holiness dissolved. Depending upon one's circumstances and opportunities to interact with priests and religious, one came to recognize that they lived their calling as laypeople do theirs: sometimes well, other times not; often joyfully, often not; on occasion prayerfully, on occasion with only external forms of prayer; with moral integrity or its absence.

---

[6]   *Ibid.*

If Catholics previously had reasons to disavow accusations concerning the suspicious behavior of their clergy, the revelations in 2002 of sexual crimes against children in the United States and around the world make such disavowals and denials now horrifyingly naïve. Priests and bishops did molest thousands of teen-aged, and younger, boys and girls. Their actions were predatory, immoral, and criminal. At least as disturbing has been the ineffective and weak-kneed response of diocesan and religious superiors. A favorable light portrays them as terrible managers of people; a harsh spotlight exposes them as complicit in crime for allowing sexual predators to continue to prey on the church's children.

That clerics, from popes to priests, may be scoundrels can come as no surprise to anyone familiar with church history. In his recent recounting of the development of the Catholic Church in the United States, Charles Morris does not hesitate to paint, for example, Cardinal William O'Connell of Boston in stark, lurid, scandal-drenched red:

> On a personal level, O'Connell was an irreligious hypocrite, lacking honesty or integrity, naturally ambitious and endlessly self-aggrandizing, a kind of Gilded Age buccaneer of churchmen, who ran his diocese like a Cornelius Vanderbilt or a Jay Gould....
>
> Much more so than his fellow bishops, O'Connell was a man of the boardroom and the country club rather than of the church. He showed little interest in religion, rarely said daily Mass, and rushed through services at a pace that sometimes scandalized onlookers.... When he arrived from Rome for his first episcopal assignment in Portland, Maine, he brought an Italian valet and his family, a coachman, and Italian music master. In Boston he built a succession of ever grander houses, finally settling in a Renaissance *palazzo* in Brighton, complete with a private golf course.... O'Connell had an oceanside summer estate, Villa Santa Croce, in fashionable Marblehead, and a winter home in the Bahamas, whence he sent his flock encouraging words during one of the cruelest winters of the Depression. He sported a gold-headed cane, tooled around in a customized Pierce Arrow, was a connoisseur of fine wines, and spent so much time traveling to the Caribbean or to Europe that cynics called him "Gangplank Bill."
>
> O'Connell was dishonest. When he left Portland for Boston, he took $25,000 of diocesan funds with him. (He returned the money without comment when his shocked successor called him to account.) He commingled his own and archdiocesan monies and lavished benefits upon his relatives. He appointed his nephew, James O'Connell, chancellor of the archdiocese almost as soon as the young man was ordained, and then

stood by for more than a decade while James divided his time between his duties in Boston and his real estate business and wife (a divorcee) in New York....

O'Connell's personal ambition was boundless. He was not on anyone's list to succeed either to the Portland or to the Boston sees but engineered the appointments through his friend, [Cardinal] Merry del Val. When the Boston appointment was open, he did not hesitate to spread calumnies against his predecessor and the other candidates to secure the see for himself....

A dreadful human being and a bad priest, he was undeniably a successful cardinal.[7]

When one compares O'Connell's recent successor, Cardinal Bernard Law, with "Gangplank Bill," Law comes off as incompetent, a bit proud and slightly stupid, a well meaning company man who put the defense of orthodoxy and church power ahead of his Christian and priestly duties. Like O'Connell, Law let ambition and position drive him, instead of his duties to the people of Boston. However, I have heard no one accuse him of being either a dreadful human being or a bad priest. Some, indeed, have called him undeniably an unsuccessful cardinal.

Many commentators on the current church scene in America bemoan it in dire terms. Jay Dolan, professor emeritus of history at the University of Notre Dame, notes in a postscript to his book, *In Search of an American Catholicism*:

Since I completed work on this book in the fall of 2001, a major scandal has torn apart the American Catholic community.... The magnitude of the crisis is clear, and there is no question, whatever the ultimate outcome of the Vatican meetings, that it will take time and great effort to restore the hierarchy's credibility.[8]

George Weigel, a theologian and Senior Fellow of the Ethics and Public Policy Center in Washington, D. C., introduced his work, *The Courage to be Catholic*, with these sober words:

In the first months of 2002, the Catholic Church in the United States entered the greatest crisis in its history. When Lent began on February

---

7   Morris, Charles R. *American Catholic*. New York: Vintage Books, 1997, pp. 120-123.

8   Dolan, Jay P. *In Search of an American Catholicism*. New York: Oxford University Press, 2003, p. 257.

13, the penitential ashes imposed that day on millions of Catholics felt leaden. Something had gone desperately wrong. Something was broken. Something had to be fixed.[9]

In March 2003 the Thomas More Center at Yale University held an academic conference in response to the revelations of sexual abuse by priests and of episcopal complicity. Afterwards, Francis Oakley and Bruce Russett edited the proceedings as *Governance, Accountability, and the Future of the Catholic Church.* In their introduction the editors noted:

> First, none of the contributors is at all disposed to underestimate the sheer gravity of the crisis that the scandal of clerical sexual abuse and its inept and disgraceful handling by many in church leadership positions has helped precipitate...."
>
> That said, and in the second place, the acknowledged gravity of the sexual abuse crisis itself and its mishandling by so many bishops at home and abroad is widely seen by the contributors to spring from the further fact that it is grounded in, builds upon, reflects, and certainly discloses long-established pathologies in the clerical culture, in our modern structure of ecclesiastical governance, and in the well entrenched and almost instinctive mode of ecclesiological thinking prevalent among so many of our church's leaders.[10]

Finally, Peter Steinfels, a long-time senior religion correspondent for the *New York Times* and former editor of *Commonweal*, begins *A People Adrift* with this trenchant observation: "Today the Roman Catholic Church in the United States is on the verge of either an irreversible decline or a thoroughgoing transformation."[11]

Diverse commentators explain the crisis differently; all appear to agree that one has us in its grip. In its deepest and most critical aspect, I would describe it as follows: In a Post-Vatican II church, an educated American laity questions, doubts, and even denies the moral authority of the church hierarchy to shape their lives and those of their families. Clergy who pretend that an immigrant, Tridentine church still exists in America appear to be ignorant, arrogant, or desperate to their co-religionists. Those who treat their parishioners as children just off the boat earn

---

[9]   Weigel, George. *The Courage to be Catholic.* New York: Basic Books, 2002, p. 1.

[10]   Oakley, Francis & Russett, Bruce (eds.). *Governance, Accountability, and the Future of the Catholic Church.* New York: Continuum, 2004, p. 9.

[11]   Steinfels, Peter. *A People Adrift.* New York: Simon and Schuster, 2003, p. 1.

heartfelt disdain. Those who deny the crisis or judge that it will pass harmlessly away seem to the thoughtful to be disingenuous, feckless, silly, or all three. To do nothing is to die; to separate from the church is to lose the worthwhile and to join in its death; and to strive to turn back the years to a romanticized Tridentine church courts failure. The church must address the crisis in ecclesiastical governance and change it in order to restore the moral authority and credibility of its hierarchical structure.

Pope John Paul II displayed little understanding of the American experience. He grew up in a Poland ravaged by two world wars and tyrannized by Soviet Communism. He understood resistance, preserving Catholic orthodoxy, and international diplomacy. He also knew much about control. Indeed, he ran the church like any number of past European monarchs. Ironically, he oversaw an international bureaucracy calculated to maintain the party line that would draw admiration and envy from many Cold War Communist commissars. In the United States, he fashioned a church even big brother might emulate: he handpicked cardinals proven loyal to him and to his brand of strict orthodoxy; his American nuncio and the cardinals guided his choice of archbishops, educated in Rome, and bishops of demonstrated obedience to Rome and of a clear conservative bent; theologians faced the scrutiny and interrogation of the infamous Holy Office; professors in Catholic colleges and universities must publicly profess their orthodoxy; right-leaning Catholic groups found in the Vatican ready ears for their complaints about priests or theologians or bishops who question orthodoxy or dare to explore what others consider heterodox. John Paul II aped well monarchical rulers who through legions of functionaries insure compliance with the ruler's mandates and desires. One wonders how, given his life and training and experience, he could have begun to understand a country like ours that soundly rejected all monarchical governance and placed its faith, trust, and authority in the people themselves.

Since his installation in 1978, John Paul II appointed every living American cardinal save one, Luis Aponte Martinez, retired, from Puerto Rico. Of forty-one serving archbishops, he elevated all but two, William Borders and Elden Curtiss. All currently serving bishops owe their consecration to Paul VI or John Paul II.[12]

Direct ties with Vatican II have weakened. Only thirteen of the living hierarchy attended: one cardinal, four archbishops, and seven bishops. All these men

---

[12]   *Ibid.* One bishop, Phillip Hannon, was elevated to the bishopric by Pius XII, three (Ignatius Strecker, Raymond Hunthausen, and Charles Salatka) by John XXIII, and four (Eusebius Beltram, William Borders, Daniel Cronin, and Elden Curtiss) by Paul VI. Of the 375 bishops in 2004, 87% of them owed their consecration to John Paul II, 12% to Paul VI, and the remaining 1% to John XXIII and Pius XII.

have retired. No member of the currently active American hierarchy participated in the discussions and registered votes at the Second Vatican Council.[13]

Given John Paul II's mode of governance, need anyone doubt that the current American hierarchy reflects his moral conservatism, social activism, strict orthodoxy, and European political tendencies? In order to transform the current mode of ecclesiastical governance in the United States, three changes must occur: Benedict XVI must come to understand the uniqueness of the American experience; the American hierarchy must give up being pseudo-Roman and instead dare to be American; the Vatican must allow and bless modes of church governance in America consistent with, and in harmony with, the American social and political experience.

Which brings us to the task of this book.

The church in America must transform, but how? A significant part of an answer may be found in the American political experience that entailed, in its inception, rejecting and separating from the aristocratic, monarchical world of post-medieval Europe, and secondly, fashioning for itself a unique sort of representative democracy.

In order to illuminate the American political experience, I rely principally on a classic work on the American political experiment: *Democracy in America* by Alexis de Tocqueville. A member of the former French aristocracy, Tocqueville came to the United States in 1830. His country, since its own revolution in 1789, had not settled comfortably into a representative form of government, but had, instead, shuffled back and forth between the extremes of revolutionary democracy, Napoleonic dictatorship, and traditional monarchy. Tocqueville came here to learn about our young but successful and growing democracy, and to contrast it with the political experimentation at home. He also desired "to observe the future society of 'almost complete equality of social conditions' toward which he believed Europe was moving inexorably."[14]

I have chosen this work as the basis of an exploration of the unique American political experience for these reasons:

- Its sheer excellence, considered still "the best book ever written on democracy and the best book ever written on America."[15]

- Tocqueville and his companion, Gustave de Beaumont, spent nine months touring the United States in 1830-1831. They visited throughout the

---

[13] All figures are taken from *The Official Catholic Directory, Anno Domini 2004*.

[14] Tocqueville, Alexis de. *Democracy in America*. Harvey C. Mansfield & Delba Winthrop (eds.). Chicago: University of Chicago Press, 2002, p. xl.

[15] *Ibid.*, p. xvii.

states, from New England to the northwestern frontiers, from Canada to New Orleans, from the southeastern original colonies to the mid-Atlantic core. They spoke with our citizens about the nation and its political system. They gained access to many prominent men involved in government and law, like John Quincy Adams and Andrew Jackson, James Kent and Francis Lieber, Daniel Webster and Sam Houston, Roger Taney and Charles Carroll. Using his daily journals Tocqueville published his working notes from these meetings under the title *Journey to America*. But his great work, *Democracy in America*, appeared as two volumes in 1835 and 1840. By that time, the Catholic Church here had become hierarchically organized, the American church of Charles Carroll, Archbishop John Carroll and Bishop John England was being swept aside by the Rome-oriented one of Baltimore archbishops Ambrose Marechal, Samuel Eccleston and their suffragan followers. The first wave of European immigration, the peasant Irish, had begun and was accelerating. These people and their priests brought their brand of Catholicism with them. They and subsequent immigrant bands—Germans in mid-century, Italians on the eve of the 20th Century, and refugees from Central and Eastern Europe in its first three decades—succeeded in transforming the American church into their own European version.

- Tocqueville not only details what is unique about America's experience and governance; he also contrasts those details with the aristocratic European experience and monarchical form of governing. This addresses my goal of distinguishing between the present "Roman Church in America" and a transformed "American Catholic Church."

I present four aspects of American democracy as described by Tocqueville: the separation of church and state, administrative decentralization, the sovereignty of the people, and the equality of citizens. In each chapter I contrast the American way with the monarchical and aristocratic form of European governance. Then I indicate how the current church in the United States, one ruled by a European pope surrounded by a European Vatican, and dominated by an American hierarchy governing like medieval lords, acts at odds with the American social and political milieu. Finally, I suggest directions for changing our Roman church into an American one.

Before entering that discussion, it makes sense to address one current, ready, almost flippant objection to this enterprise. How often does one hear the dismissive comment that "the Catholic Church is *not* a democracy"? It tends at the same time to affirm and silently to maintain: "The Catholic Church *is* a monarchy." But herein lies, precisely, the question: in those sentences what do "is not a democracy" and "is a monarchy" mean?

Perhaps it means that the church, unlike the United States, has no constitution. Isn't the New Testament the agreed-upon constitution of the Early Church as to the life and teaching of Jesus Christ? But surely this "deposit of faith," closed with the death of the last direct witness to Christ's earthly sojourn among us, cannot be amended as a constitution can. Yes, it can; the whole of church history—its councils, its encyclicals, its theological debates, its infallible declarations—are the work of Catholic people trying to understand more deeply and fully and from new angles the meaning of that original deposit. As a dogma professor remarked, "The Early Church offers us the original sentence—subject, act, object—about the Divine Revelation. Tradition, that is, the ongoing life of the church, furnishes us with the adjectives, adverbs, prepositional phrases which fill out and make clear the basic message."

But surely the Roman pontiff is more like a European king than an American president?—in practice, yes; of necessity, no. Monarchs tend to consider themselves the embodiment of the nation, even proclaiming themselves above the law because obedience to them equals obedience to the law. But Catholic theology makes abundantly clear that Christ embodies the church, the pope does not. The pope subjects himself to Christ, His church, to dogma and revelation and tradition just as any other Catholic does. The pope, "the servant of the servants of God," waits upon the church: he does not own it nor does it belong to him.

Unless otherwise indicated, throughout this book I use the terms "hierarchical" and "hierarchy" in a global fashion to indicate a governing system opposed to a democratic one. I do not intend to imply that every pope or cardinal, bishop or priest, acts in that fashion. For example, people around the world loved John XXIII in a special way because he refused to govern like a European king out to shape for himself a worldwide kingdom.

American bishops fall into predictable categories. Some—like the nineteenth century Bishop John England—while remaining faithful to the Church do not hesitate to confront Rome and their fellow bishops for the sake of Christ and his people. Others, realizing the overwhelming power of the clerical political system, refuse to get caught up in it. They resign themselves to a lifetime out of the limelight, auxiliary bishops with slight chance of advancement. They content themselves to be pastors of their people, giving them the leadership of a holy and dedicated life. While one might wish they would, for the sake of the church at large, speak out against a self-serving and self-perpetuating hierarchy, one also understands the pain and frustration of being held in the grip of a system too large and powerful to resist. Still others, hoping to rise within the hierarchical ranks, bow to the wishes of their episcopal betters; they know well that successful politics demand that they curry the favor of, not challenge the actions of, the current church aristocracy. They merit, at best, pity. Finally, some bishops rule like venal followers of the likes of Cardinal O'Connell; others spout the party line and protect themselves like surrogates of Cardinal Law; most of these movers and shakers model themselves after their lordly forbears in the royal courts of Europe. As the price of the transformation of the American church, these people must be willing to die for Christ and His` Church. If death itself doesn't take them, they must change or resign.

Crises often lead to change; disasters offer opportunities for new, even unsuspected, growth. The monarchical Catholic Church in America is suffering serious shocks as the extent of its failure is revealed. Church members feel the pain, deeply. At the same time, this may be the moment in God's Providence when the American church throws off its historical linkage to monarchy and embraces a new Christian democracy. Could not this be the gift of American Catholicism to the whole church?

Let us now explore how the Roman pontiff in our time, in union with his American bishops, might best lead the People of God in America into a future of hope and growth.

Chapter One:
Seeds of an American Catholic Church

I. European Catholics Immigrate to the Colonies

By the time Alexis de Tocqueville visited the United States in 1830-1831, Catholic pioneers had been settled in the former English colonies for nearly two hundred years. Lord Baltimore's Maryland and William Penn's Pennsylvania accepted the presence of Catholics and their clergy. The other colonies—notably New Jersey and Virginia—had a fractional Catholic minority but their laws restricted the establishment of Catholic churches.

With a grant of land from Charles I to the First Lord Baltimore, George Calvert, his son, Cecil Calvert, established a colony in March 1634 at St. Mary's, between the Potomac River and Chesapeake Bay. Catholics numbered about a third of the two hundred settlers. With them journeyed two Jesuit priests, Andrew White and John Altham. All hoped to escape the restrictions of the penal laws enacted to secure conformity to the established Church of England, especially since they knew that the Calverts would insist from the beginning on religious toleration and the separation of Church and State in their new colony. Although this freedom waxed and waned over the next century and a half, by 1763 Richard Challoner, Vicar-Apostolic in London with jurisdiction in the English colonies, reported to the Reverend Dr. Stoner, the English clergy agent in Rome, that 16,000 Catholics were living in Maryland. Twelve Jesuit priests ministered to them.[1] On March 1, 1785 the Prefect-Apostolic for the United States, John Carroll, gave that number as 15,800.[2]

---

[1]   Guilday, Peter. *The Life and Times of John Carroll*. Vol. I. New York: The Encyclopedia Press, 1922, p. 60. For a summary overview of early Catholic history in America, cf. England, John. "American Catholicity," *The Works of Right Rev. John England, Vol. II*. McElrone, Hugh P. (ed). New York: P. J. Kenedy, 1894, pp. 329-377.

[2]   *Ibid.*, Guilday, p. 225. Cf. Hanley, Thomas (ed.). *The Letters of John Carroll*. Vol. I, "Report for His Eminence Cardinal Antonelli on the condition of religion in the sections of the United States of America," March I, 1785, pp. 179-185.

Nearby Pennsylvania, established in 1681 by a Quaker, William Penn, in its founding constitution guaranteed freedom of conscience. In a new Charter of Liberties in 1701 the Pennsylvania colony assured liberty of conscience to all who acknowledged one, almighty God, creator and ruler of the universe, and full civil rights to all who believed in Christ. Challoner placed the number of Catholics in that colony by 1763 as 6,000-7,000, including four Jesuit missionaries;[3] in 1785 Carroll settled on a Catholic population of 7,000.[4]

Because of civil and religious restrictions against Catholics and their worship, before the Revolutionary War only a scattering of adherents lived in Virginia and New Jersey, and virtually none in the remainder of the original English colonies. No priests served the Catholic people except the Jesuits in Maryland and Pennsylvania.

Although the population numbers in the early years in America should be treated as estimates, in 1770 approximately 2,205,000 people lived in the original thirteen colonies, a majority in Virginia (and Kentucky)—450,000—and 309,000 in Massachusetts. With around 22,000 members in English America, Catholics made up just over 1% of the population.

Despite the religious intolerance they suffered, when the revolution broke out, Catholics joined their fellow colonists in the struggle against England. One may attribute this readiness to a common desire to get out from under English tyranny; one also suspects that they hoped in this way to prove their loyalty and thus earn greater space and freedom for the practice of their religion. In his biography of John Carroll, Peter Guilday mentions some of the prominent contributors to the rebel cause:

> ...Commodore John Barry, the Father of the American Navy; General Stephen Moylan, "Muster-Master General of the Army of the United Colonies," and the Colonel of the Light Horse Dragoons; Colonel John Fitzgerald, aide-de-camp and secretary to General Washington; Thomas FitzSimons, a Catholic signer of the Constitution; George Meade, Dr. Joseph Cauffman, Colonel Francis Vigo, Orono, and the most romantic figure of adventure during the whole war, Timothy Murphy. The names of two foreign officers, probably Catholic, in the American Army are well known: Count Pulaski and Kosciuszko. Lafayette, though born a Catholic, neglected his faith until on his deathbed.[5]

---

[3]   *Ibid.,* p. 60. Cf. Hanley, p. 181.

[4]   *Ibid.,* p. 225. Cf. Hanley, p. 179

[5]   *Ibid.,* p. 86.

One must also include members of the Carroll dynasty of Maryland: Daniel, Charles, and John.

II. The Carrolls and the Establishment of the American Episcopacy

Daniel Carroll, son of a prominent Maryland planter, served as a member of the Continental Congress. In 1781 he signed the Articles of Confederation. As a delegate from Maryland, he took an active role in the Constitutional Convention. He and Thomas FitzSimons, both Catholics, signed the new Constitution.

Charles Carroll of Carrollton (his father, also Charles, lived in Annapolis) was born in Annapolis on September 19, 1737. He and his cousin, John, spent a year studying together at a clandestine Jesuit school at Bohemia on Harmon's Manor, Cecil County, Maryland. They both continued their education at the Jesuit College at St. Omer's in French Flanders from 1748-1753. Charles later pursued a degree in law at the College Louis Le Grand in Paris, while John entered the Society of Jesus. The latter studied philosophy and theology at Liege and, in 1769, was ordained to the Catholic priesthood.

Immediately prior to the American Revolution, Charles Carroll, having returned from Europe in 1765, lived at Carrollton in Frederick County, Maryland. He publicly debated the jurist Daniel Dulaney concerning taxes imposed on the colonists by its English governor without their consent. He became well known and regarded for his defense against "taxation without representation." He also was involved in the public outcry about the "Peggy Stewart."

A resident of Annapolis, Anthony Stewart, owned a ship named after his daughter, Peggy. In October of 1774 it dropped anchor in Annapolis Harbor, loaded with 2,000 pounds of tea. The owner secretly agreed to pay the taxes on tea imposed by the Stamp Act, contrary to a non-importation agreement in the colony. When word leaked out, an outraged mob forced Stewart to ground his vessel and burn it on the threat of being hanged. The names of the patriots, including Charles Carroll, were published with their permission in the *Maryland Gazette.*

The next year he served on the first "Committee of Safety" in Annapolis. In 1776 he became the only Catholic to sign the Declaration of Independence. Earlier that year he had traveled with Benjamin Franklin, Samuel Chase, and his cousin, John Carroll, at the behest of the Continental Congress to Quebec. He enlisted John because of his priesthood and his knowledge of French in an attempt to persuade the Catholics in Quebec to join the revolutionary cause. Where the English colonies in America had only 22,000 Catholics, "The Province of Quebec, where most of the Canadians were living, contained about 150,000 Catholics to only some 360 Members of the Church of England."[6]

---

[6]   *Ibid.,* p. 97.

Unfortunately, the trip was doomed to failure from the beginning. In 1774 George III had, in the Quebec Act, granted freedom of religion to the Catholics of that Province. He hoped thereby to forestall any union between his Canadian and American subjects against him. In response the Continental Congress had raised an indignant and intolerant howl. In an Address to the People of Great Britain, Friday, October 23, 1774, it passionately exclaimed:

> ...That we think the Legislature of Great Britain is not authorized by the constitution *to establish a religion, fraught with sanguinary and impious tenets,* or, to erect an arbitrary form of government in any quarter of the globe.... And by another Act the Dominion of Canada is to be so extended, modelled, and governed, as that by being disunited from us, detached from our interests, by civil as well as religious prejudices, that by their numbers swelling with Catholic emigrants from Europe, and by their devotion to Administration, so friendly to their religion, they might become formidable to us, and on occasion be fit instruments in the hands of power, to reduce the ancient free Protestant colonies to the same state of slavery with themselves.... *Nor can we suppress our astonishment that a British Parliament should ever consent to establish in that country a religion that has deluged your island in blood, and disbursed impiety, bigotry, persecution, murder and rebellion through every part of the world.*[7]

Can one imagine that the conciliatory words now offered the Canadian Catholics from that same Congress would be met with anything better than intense suspicion? Indeed, the Catholic bishop, Jean Briand, had all but ordered his priests to offer scant hospitality to the American priest. He knew how the Catholic population was systematically mistreated in the rebellious colonies; he also had undoubtedly learned of the Continental Congress' tirade over the Quebec Act. Why should he, especially now that the Crown had bestowed on his people religious freedom, counsel them or encourage them to throw in their lot with their bigoted Protestant neighbors to the south? As actions speak so loudly, one need only mention that Bishop Briand, on the anniversary of Benedict Arnold's failed mission against Canada, ordered a *Te Deum* to be sung on December 31, 1776 in gratitude to God for their delivery from the American forces.

John Carroll returned to Philadelphia on June 11th of that year. He and his fellow commissioners had accomplished little. Congress now understood that it could hold out no hope for assistance in their cause against England from the

---

[7]   *Ibid.,* p. 80. Cf. *Journals of the Continental Congress 1774-1789,* Vol. I., pp. 81-89, 115-120.

king's Canadian subjects. Carroll's trip succeeded only in making of the elderly Benjamin Franklin a new friend because of Carroll's kindnesses and attention to him.

Carroll had gone to Quebec as an ex-Jesuit. On July 21, 1773 Pope Clement XIV, bowing to pressure from the Bourbon courts of Spain and Portugal, Italy and France, issued a brief of suppression of the Society of Jesus. Carroll himself had been in Rome during the days leading up to this violent act. Dismayed and disturbed, he made his way back to Maryland. He and twenty other ex-Jesuits affixed their signature the next year to the Act of Submission sent by Rome to America.

Although still a young man, John Carroll already had deep personal experience of religious bigotry, of the sanctity of one's own conscience in matters of religion, of the devastating effects on religion that came about when Church and State were joined in an unholy marriage. As a child he had to practice his faith in secret and endure the hostility of an anti-Catholic government; as a newly ordained priest he suffered the destruction of the order to which he had consecrated his life because of the undue influence of European Catholic governments on his church; as a dedicated patriot he had been rebuffed by the Catholic church-government coalition in Canada incensed with a Protestant one in America. These experiences would have a perceptible influence on him as a priest and bishop in his new country for the remainder of his life.

According to the Brief of Suppression, *Dominus Ac Redemptor*, the former Jesuits were commanded to pursue the following course: if priests, to join another religious congregation or to present themselves to a bishop for diocesan service; if scholastics or brothers, to return to lay life or to look for another avenue of church work, according to one's preferences; to leave properties owned by the former Society and to turn them over to the proper ecclesiastical authorities. The unique situation in the English colonies in America made much of this impractical. Indeed, no other religious congregations operated in these regions to which a former Jesuit might apply; nor could one turn to a diocesan bishop for incardination as none had yet been appointed nor any diocese been formed. So the Jesuit missionaries simply stayed in place and assisted the Catholics of Maryland and Pennsylvania as previously. Their superior in London, Fr. John Lewis, continued by default to oversee them, their work, and the properties of the defunct order. John Carroll decided to sever all religious links with his erstwhile superior, considering himself both free of his vow of obedience and of any allegiance to a London overseer. Since he took this action, since he chose to live with his aging mother instead of continuing to live with former Jesuits and to move at the command of his former superior, Carroll forfeited any share of revenues from the suppressed group's estates. He remained a priest but one bereft of any order, any diocese, or any community. He could minister to his fellow Catholics in Maryland, but he did so entirely on his own.

Even before the end of the War, religious liberty grew in the colonies. By February 28, 1779, John Carroll could write to his friend, and former Jesuit comrade, Fr. Charles Plowden about the dawning of toleration

> You inquire how congress intend to treat the Catholics in this country. To this I must answer you that congress have no authority or jurisdiction relative to the internal government, or concerns of the particular states of the Union; these are all settled by the constitutions and laws of the states themselves. I am glad, however, to inform you that the fullest and largest system of toleration is adopted in almost all the American states; public protection and encouragement are extended alike to all denominations, and Roman Catholics are members of congress, assemblies, and hold civil and military posts, as well as others.[8]

Complete religious freedom came inevitably but slowly. The Federal Government would not assure it until 1791 when the first Amendment to the Constitution firmly removed any formal linkage between Church and State: "Congress shall make no law respecting an establishment of religion or prohibiting the free exercise thereof." This amendment, however, did not prohibit individual states from enacting or continuing existing laws touching on religious liberty. The following chart summarizes these restrictions in the thirteen original colonies:

State	1787	Religious Freedom
Rhode Island	No legal restrictions	1635
Pennsylvania	One eternal God	1681
Virginia	No legal restrictions	1786
South Carolina	Only Protestantism	1790
Georgia	Only Protestantism	1798
New York	No minister in public office	1806
Connecticut	Only Protestantism	1818
New Hampshire	Only Protestantism	1819
Delaware	Only Christian	1831
Massachusetts	Established Religion	1833
North Carolina	Only Protestantism	1835

---

[8]   *Ibid.*, p. 110. Cf. Rock Creek, February 28, 1779, in the *United States Catholic Miscellany*, Vol. III (1844), pp. 367-368. Cf. Georgetown University Library, Special Collections, Archives, Maryland Province, Society of Jesus, Box: 57, Fol.: 4, Carroll-Plowden Correspondence (1) [202 B1-9] 1779-1785. Cf. also Hanley, *op. cit.*, pp. 51-55.

New Jersey	Only Protestantism	1844
Maryland	Only Christian	
	No minister in public office	1961[9]

By the time of the ratification of the First Amendment, government, both federal and state, assured freedom of religion to Protestant Christians. For Catholics assurance came in dribs and drabs over the next half century. However, by 1820 ten of the thirteen original colonies no longer placed legal barriers to the practice of Catholicism. The stage for refugees from revolutionary France and from Ireland still suffering under the penal laws was prepared.

For all these possibilities, the state of the Catholic Church in America remained precarious. It lacked both organization and effective leadership. John Carroll assessed the stagnant situation insightfully in a letter to Fr. Plowden on February 20, 1782:

> The clergymen here continue to live in the old form. It is the effect of habit, and if they could promise themselves immortality, it would be well enough. But I regret that indolence prevents any form of administration being adopted, which might tend to secure to posterity a succession of Catholic clergymen, and secure to these a comfortable subsistence. I said, that the former system of administration (that is, everything being in the power of a Superior) continued. But all those checks upon him so wisely provided by former constitutions are at an end. It is happy that the present Superior [Father John Lewis] is a person free from every selfish view and ambition. But his successor may not [be]. And what is likewise to be feared, the succeeding generation, which will not be trained in the same discipline and habits as the present, will in all probability be infected much more strongly with interested and private views. The system, therefore, which they will adopt, will be less calculated for the publick or future benefit, than would be agreed to now, if they could be prevailed upon to enter at all upon the business. But ignorance, indolence, delusion (you remember certain prophecies of re-establishment) and above all the irresolution of Mr. Lewis, put a stop to every proceeding in this matter.[10]

---

9   Cf. *Ibid.*, p. 111, 114.

10   *Ibid.*, p. 164. Cf. Hughes, Thomas. *History of the Society of Jesus in North America, Colonial and Federal*, Vol. 1, Part II, 1907, p. 609. Cf. also Hanley, *op.cit.*, pp. 63-67. Cf. also Georgetown University Library, Archives of the Maryland Province of the Society of Jesus, Special Collections, Box: 57, Fol.: 4.

With his former compatriots lacking direction and his erstwhile superior showing his age, with a sentimental and listless waiting for the Society's restoration infecting his fellow priests, and with immigration from Europe on the rise, Carroll knew that something must be done, and quickly. With Catholic immigrants would come attendant priests, both from orders and dioceses, who soon would begin to organize the church according to their European experience. If a truly American church were to be created, the American ex-Jesuits must do it now.

Carroll drew up a Plan of Organization in 1782. It undoubtedly stimulated a meeting in November 1783 called by Father Lewis. Six delegates from Pennsylvania and Maryland met with him at the old Jesuit residence at Whitemarsh, not far from Georgetown.

One of the results of the meeting came in the form of a Committee of Five charged with drawing up a Petition to the Holy See. It should request from Pius VI the naming of Fr. John Lewis, their former religious superior, as ecclesiastical superior in the United States. Specifically, it should further ask that he be delegated the right to ordain, to bless holy oils, and to administer the Sacrament of Confirmation.[11]

Because of subsequent worries by some of the clergy that the initial petition lacked a sufficiently respectful tone, a second committee was deputed to fashion a follow-up petition. John Carroll sent this new request to the pope. In it the committee asked that the clergy be granted the right to elect their own superior; moreover, it stressed that the United States Government would not permit the presence of a bishop in the country.

In an accompanying letter addressed to Cardinal Vitaliano Borromeo, a cardinal with influence at *Propaganda*, dated November 10, 1783, Carroll set out the opinion of the American clergy relative to the establishment of a Catholic hierarchy in the United States. He stressed a theme to be heard continually: do nothing that would appear as some form of foreign dominance:

> You are not ignorant that in these United States our religious system has undergone a revolution, if possible, more extraordinary than our political one. In all of them free toleration is allowed to Christians of every denomination; and particularly in the States of Pennsylvania, Delaware, Maryland, and Virginia, a communication of all civil rights, without distinction or diminution, is extended to those of our religion. This is a blessing and advantage which it is our duty to preserve and improve,

---

[11]   Clergy's Petition to the Pope, 1783. Propaganda Archives. Scritture Riferite nei Congressi, America Centrale. Vol. II, Fol. 238. Cf. John Carroll Papers, transcript. Catholic University of America Archives. Cf. also Hanley, *op.cit.*, pp. 68-69.

with the utmost prudence, by demeaning ourselves on all occasions as subjects zealously attached to our government and avoiding to give any jealousies on account of any dependence on foreign jurisdictions more than that which is essential to our religion, an acknowledgment of the Pope's spiritual supremacy over the whole Christian world. You know that we of the clergy have heretofore resorted to the Vicar-Apostolic of the London District for the exercise of spiritual powers, but being well acquainted with the temper of Congress, of our assemblies and our people at large, we are firmly of opinion that we shall not be suffered to continue under such a jurisdiction when ever it becomes known to the publick. You may be assured of this from the following fact. The clergy of the Church of England were heretofore subject to the Bishop of London, but the umbrage taken at this dependence was so great, that notwithstanding the power and prevalence of that sect they could find no other method to allay jealousies, than by withdrawing themselves as they have lately done, from all obedience to him.

Being therefore thus circumstanced, we think it not adviseable in us, but in a manner obligatory, to solicit the Holy See to place the epis-copal powers, at least those such as are most essential, in the hands of one amongst us, whose virtue, knowledge, and integrity of faith, shall be certified by ourselves. We shall annex to this letter such powers as we judge it absolutely necessary he should be invested with. We might add many very cogent reasons for having amongst us, a person thus empowered, and for want of whom it is impossible to conceive the inconvenience happening every day. If it is possible to obtain a grant from Rome for vesting these powers in our Superior *pro tempore*, it would be most desirable.[12]

Rome acted promptly, if not exactly as the Americans wished. On June 9, 1784 the *Congregatio de Propaganda Fide* announced the appointment of Father John Carroll as Prefect-Apostolic of the United States.[13]

Carroll felt unsettled by this appointment. He did not like being appointed instead of being elected by his fellow clergy; he knew that control by *Propaganda* in Rome would not sit well with Americans; he bridled at the limited power

---

[12] *Ibid.*, p. 172. Cf. Associated Archives at St. Mary's Seminary and University, Archdiocese of Baltimore Archives, Special Case C-A4. Cf. also Hanley, *op. cit.*, pp. 80-81.

[13] Agonito, Joseph. *The Building of an American Catholic Church: The Episcopacy of John Carroll*, p. 18.

granted him to shape as needed the American church. In a letter on February 17th of the succeeding year to his friend and former Jesuit in Rome, Father John Thorpe, he spelled out his concerns:

> ...and of thanking you most cordially for your active and successful endeavors to render service to this country. I say successful, not because your partiality, as I presume, joined to that of my old cheerful friend Dr. Franklin suggested me to the consideration of his holiness; but because you have obtained some form of spiritual government to be adopted for us. It is not indeed quite such as we wish; and it cannot continue long in its present form. You well know, that in our free and jealous government, where Catholics are admitted into all public councils equally with the professors of any other Religion, it will never be suffered that their Ecclesiastical Superior (be he a Bishop or Prefect-Apostolic), receive his appointment from a foreign State, and only hold it at the discretion of a foreign tribunal or congregation. If even the present temper, or inattention of our Executive and legislative bodies were to overlook it for this and perhaps a few more instances, still ought we not to acquiesce and rest quiet in actual enjoyment; for the consequence, sooner or later, would certainly be, that some malicious or jealous-minded person would raise a spirit against us, and under pretense of rescuing the State from foreign influence and dependence, strip us perhaps of our common civil rights. For these reasons, every thinking man amongst us is convinced, that we neither must request or admit any other foreign interference than such, as being essential to our religion, is implied in the acknowledgment of the Bishop of Rome being, by divine appointment, head of the universal Church; and the See of St. Peter being the centre of ecclesiastical unity.[14]

John Carroll held the office of Prefect-Apostolic for five years. In his letter of acceptance on February 27, 1785 to Cardinal Leonardo Antonelli, he addressed straightforwardly the question of appointing a bishop. He suggested that Rome act now; he prayed that the pope in his wisdom would allow the Americans to select one of their own:

---

[14]   Guilday, *op. cit.,* pp. 208-209. Cf. Georgetown University Library, Special Collections, John Gilmary Shea Papers, transcript: Box: 23, Fol.: 10 Carroll, John—Correspondence. Cf. also Hanley, *op. cit.*, pp. 162-166.

While the matter stands thus, the Holy Father will decide and you, Most Eminent Cardinal, will consider whether the time is now opportune for appointing a bishop, what his qualifications should be, and how he should be nominated [appointed]. On all these points, not as if seeking to obtain my own judgment but to make this relation most simple, I should note a few facts. First, as regards the seasonableness of the step, it may be noted, that there will be no excitement in the public mind, if a bishop be appointed, as Protestants think of appointing one for themselves: nay, they even hope to acquire some importance for their sect among the people from the episcopal dignity; so too we trust that we shall not only acquire the same, but that great advantages will follow; inasmuch as this church will then be governed in that manner which Christ our Lord instituted. On the other hand, however, it occurs that as the Most Holy Father has already deigned to provide otherwise for conferring the sacrament of confirmation, there is no actual need for the appointment of a bishop, until some candidates are found fitted to receive holy orders; this we hope will be the case in a few years, as you will understand, Most Eminent Cardinal, from a special relation which I propose writing. When that time comes, we shall perhaps be better able to make a suitable provision for a bishop, than from our slender resources we can now do.

In the next place, if it shall seem best to his Holiness to assign a bishop to this country, will it be best to appoint a Vicar-Apostolic or an ordinary with a See of his own? Which will conduce more to the progress of Catholicity, which will contribute most to remove Protestant jealousy of foreign jurisdiction? I know with certainty that this fear will increase, if they know that an ecclesiastical superior is so appointed as to be removable from office at the pleasure of the Sacred Congregation for the Propagation of the Faith, or any other tribunal out of the country, or that he has no power to admit any priest to exercise the sacred function, unless that Congregation has approved and sent him to us.

As to the method of nominating a bishop, I will say no more, at present, than this, that we are imploring God in his wisdom and mercy to guide the judgment of the Holy See, that if it does not seem proper to allow the priests who have laboured for so many years in this vineyard of the Lord to propose to the Holy See, the one whom they deem the most fit, that some method will be adopted [let them at least decide upon some way of nominating a bishop] by which a bad feeling may not be excited among the people of this country, Catholic and Protestant.[15]

He no longer hesitated about having a bishop; the process of nomination concerned him more. The American priests who know each other, the needs of the Catholic people, and the temper of the young country's democracy, should be intimately involved in it.

The Cardinal responded almost immediately that *Propaganda* had every intention of acting in line with the wishes of the American clergy and the general sentiments of independence in the new republic.[16]

In November 1786 a Second General Chapter was held at Whitemarsh.[17] After some continuing opposition to having a bishop had been overcome, a Committee of Three, including Carroll, was appointed to draft a "Clergy Petition for a Bishop" to be sent to Pope Pius VI. It appears that John Carroll essentially wrote it. In the petition he specifically asks for a bishop elected by the priests of America:

> Therefore, Most Holy Father, we express in the name and by the wish of all, our opinion that the political and religious condition of these States requires that form of ecclesiastical government by which provision may be most efficaciously made in the first place for the integrity of faith and morals, and consequently for perpetual union with the Apostolic See, and due respect and obedience toward the same, and in the next place, that if any bishop is assigned to us, his appointment and authority may be rendered as free as possible from suspicion and odium to those among whom we live. Two points, it seems to us, will contribute greatly to this end; first, that the Most Holy Father, by his authority in the Church of Christ, erect a new episcopal see in these United States, immediately subject to the Holy See; in the next place, that the election of the bishop, at least for the first time, be permitted to the priests, who now duly exercise the religious ministry here and have the care of souls. This

---

[15] *Ibid.,* pp. 221-222. Cf. Propaganda Archives. *Scritture Riferite nei Congressi, America Centrale,* Vol II, Fol. 306. John Carroll Papers, transcript. Catholic University of America Archives. Cf. also Hanley, *op. cit.,* pp. 169-179. Inserts in text are taken from this edition and translation.

[16] Agonito, *op. cit.* p. 27. Cf. Antonelli to Carroll, July 23, 1785. Propaganda Archives. Letters della S.C., Vol. 246, Fol. 437. Guilday Transcripts. Catholic University of America Archives.

[17] Cf. Hanley, *op. cit.* pp. 226-234.

being established, your most vigilant wisdom, Most Holy Father, after hearing the opinions of our priests of approved life and experience, and considering the character of our government, will adopt some course, by which future elections may be permanently conducted.[18]

Carroll sent the petition on March 18, 1788; Cardinal Antonelli replied affirmatively for Pius VI on July 12th of that year:

Inasmuch as all the labourers in this vineyard of the Lord agree in this, that the appointment of one bishop seems absolutely necessary to retain priests in duty and to propagate more widely piety and religion—a bishop who can preside over the flock of Catholics scattered through these States of Confederate America, and rule and govern them with the authority of an Ordinary, Our Most Holy Lord Pope Pius VI with the advice of this holy Congregation, has most benignly decided that a favorable consent should be given to their vows and petitions. By you, therefore, it is first to be examined in what city this episcopal see ought to be erected, or whether a titular bishop only should be established. This having been done, his Holiness as a special favour and for this first time, permits the priests who at the present time duly exercise the ministry of the Catholic religion and have care of souls to elect as bishop a person eminent in piety, prudence, and zeal for the faith, from the said clergy, and present him to the Apostolic See to obtain confirmation. And the Sacred Congregation does not doubt that you will discharge this matter with becoming circumspection, and it hopes that this whole flock will derive not only great benefit but also great consolation from this episcopate. It will be then for you to decide both the proper designation of a See and the election of a bishop, that the matter may be further proceeded with.[19]

The clergy met again at Whitemarsh. They decided that a bishop with ordinary jurisdiction, rather than a titular bishop, would be most fitting in their situation.

---

[18]   *Ibid.,* p. 348. Cf. Propaganda Archives, *Scritture Riferite nei Congressi, America Centrale,* Vol. II, Fol. 358. Cf. also John Carroll Papers, transcript. Catholic University of America Archives.

[19]   *Ibid.,* p. 352. Cf. Propaganda Archives, Atti (1789) ff. 369-378. Cf. also, Associated Archives at St. Mary's Seminary and University, Archdiocese of Baltimore Archives, Case 9A-G1.

They selected Baltimore, centrally situated in Maryland, as the episcopal see. John Carroll received twenty-four affirmative votes, Ignatius Matthew and Henry Pile two each, and three electors did not record their choices. The pope with the concurrence of the cardinals at *Propaganda* accepted the decisions of the American clergy. In his brief *Ex hac apostolicae* Pope Pius VI created John Carroll bishop of Baltimore with jurisdiction over all the current territory of the United States.

In March 1791 the clergy of the diocese met at John Carroll's residence in Baltimore in its first diocesan synod. They addressed the important question, among other things, of episcopal succession should any injury or death visit their bishop. The synod decided to request from *Propaganda,* either the creation of a suffragan diocese with its own bishop, or the elevation of one of their own to the coadjutor position. After discussion in Rome, the Holy See decreed that a coadjutor to Bishop Carroll was needed. In his letter of September 29, 1792 to John Carroll, Cardinal Antonelli suggested a democratic nomination process:

> This Sacred Congregation, therefore, with the express sanction of His Holiness, enjoins Your Lordship to consult with the older and more prudent priests of the diocese and to propose any priest in the American mission, whom you think fit and capable; the Holy Father will then appoint him coadjutor with all necessary and seasonable faculties.[20]

In order to forestall any problems with the young American republic, and to blunt any public criticism against the intrusions of a foreign power, once again Rome allowed the American clergy to select its own bishop.

In May 1793 his fellow priests chose Father Laurence Graessl of Philadelphia, a native of Bavaria and a former Jesuit, to assume the role of Carroll's coadjutor. Unfortunately, before his consecration, he died in Philadelphia that October, victim of the plague. The pope and his advisors, unaware of his death, appointed him Bishop of Samosata and coadjutor of Baltimore. Subsequently, with the advice of the older clergy, Carroll proposed in his stead Father Leonard Neale, pastor of St. Mary's Church in Philadelphia. In April 1795 he became Bishop of Gortyna and the long-sought coadjutor for the Baltimore diocese.

As early as 1792 John Carroll wished his diocese to be divided. He urged this because of its vast distances; because of the slow pace of communications between the United States and the Vatican, one that would be most troubling should he

---

[20]   Guilday, Peter. *The Life and Times of John Carroll*, Vol. II. New York: The Encyclopedia Press, 1922, p. 445. Cf. Propaganda Archives. Letters della S.C., Vol. 262, Fol. 558. Cf. also Guilday Transcripts, Catholic University of America Archives.

suddenly die; and because with new dioceses more priests might be attracted to assist in building up the church in America.

After Pius VII assumed the pontificate, the new prefect of the *Congregatio de Propaganda Fide*, Cardinal Stefano Borgia, informed Bishop Carroll of the Holy See's intention of creating four or five suffragan dioceses in the United States. He asked that Carroll send a memorandum to the congregation suggesting names of possible episcopal sees, the physical limits of each diocese, the means of sustenance for each bishop, and the names of priests worthy to occupy the new positions.

On November 23, 1806[21] Carroll proposed dioceses in Boston, New York, Philadelphia, and Bardstown, Kentucky. He nominated John Cheverus for Boston, Michael Egan for Philadelphia, and Joseph Flaget for Bardstown. As for New York he could not conscientiously nominate any priest currently serving there. Rome accepted his suggestions, set about erecting sees and filling episcopal chairs, but with the addition of Fr. Richard Luke Concanen, an Irish Dominican dwelling in Rome, selected for the New York diocese. On April 8, 1808 Pius VII created Baltimore as a metropolitan see, with four suffragan dioceses and bishops, by his briefs *Ex debito pastoralis officii* and *Pontificii muneris*. A hierarchical church organization now existed in America.[22]

From his initial interactions with Rome concerning the establishment of an American Catholic Church, John Carroll sought to balance two opposing realities. In the first place, in a people recently separated from the dominance of Great Britain, he shared his fellow citizens acute sensitivity about any perceived interference of a foreign power. Recognizing also that Catholics in this new nation lived among, and were surrounded by, a Protestant majority, he judged it essential to avoid inflaming their suspicions about Roman jurisdiction over Americans. To these ends Carroll sought for and obtained the limiting of Englishman John Lewis's religious authority, the removal of the control of the Congregation for the Propaganda of the Faith, and the right of the American clergy to nominate their bishops. This latter concession, however, did not endure, even during the final years of Carroll's episcopacy. He also persuaded the Holy See to agree to a change in the oath that a bishop-elect recited as part of his consecration. This phrase, as had been granted in Ireland, was deleted: "I will to the utmost of my power seek out and oppose schismatics, heretics, and the enemies of our Sovereign Lord and his successors."[23] Rome recognized that in America, to a people jealous for its independence, it must allow ecclesial latitude.

---

21   Cf. Hanley, Thomas. *The John Carroll Papers*, Vol. II, p. 537.

22   Agonito, *op. cit.*, pp. 47-48.

23   *Ibid.*, p. 45.

At the same time, Carroll saw the danger of the church separating from the spiritual authority of the pope. Although he firmly opposed any temporal intervention of pope and Vatican into the internal life of the Catholic community here, he considered it absolutely essential that papal authority be recognized in spiritual matters affecting the Catholic community worldwide. For him, Rome acted appropriately when it pronounced on faith and morals; it acted at least unwisely, and certainly imprudently, if and when it tried to tell Americans how to run their national church. One needs little imagination to surmise how Archbishop Carroll would react today to the pervasive intrusions of recent popes and their bureaucratic surrogates into the life of American Catholicism: you will pray with these words in your liturgy; your professors will take loyalty oaths to Rome; your seminaries will not take in homosexual candidates; your magazines and newspapers will fire editors who don't write as apologists for current Roman discipline; you will discipline wayward priests in ways we approve; you will not talk about married or women priests; you will threaten with ecclesiastical penalties Catholic politicians who refuse to bear the public burden of enforcing church positions. He would, I submit, merely say: "I think not." And what would he feel for his sychophantic episcopal descendents except dismay and, perhaps, pity.

During John Carroll's tenure and those of his successors, homegrown challenges to episcopal authority of varying severity cropped up. In discussions about these troubles in the early days of the church in the United States, "trusteeism" comes off as the principal culprit. Indeed, it has become a shibboleth that is raised by succeeding generations of clerics against any and all lay participation in church governance. Usually the equating of "trusteeism" and "lay participation" comes out of ignorance about the shape that lay adventurism took in those times.

III. Trusteeism and Schism in the Early American Church

A typical crisis of trusteeism occurred in Charleston, South Carolina, during the final period of John Carroll's bishopric. It continued through the reigns of his two successors, Leonard Neale and Ambrose Marechal. It came to a peaceful resolution through the strength, imagination, and diplomacy of Charleston's first bishop, John England. Let us look closely at the progress of this disturbance so as to understand better its causes, its severity, and the stage it prepared for Bishop England's episcopacy.

In 1790 the Catholic congregation of Charleston sought incorporation under the laws of South Carolina. Most usually, the legislative act incorporated a board of trustees; in this instance, however, the legislature saw fit to incorporate the members of the church. This action laid a seedbed for dissent as the corporation itself now had to answer to various factions within the congregation. The corporation owned a lot and a small, renovated wooden church that had once been used by the city's Methodists; the congregation numbered less than five hundred members, principally Irish middle-class immigrants, and no pastor (Fr. Keating, the renovator of the old church, had left for Philadelphia in 1790, with no replacement in sight).

In 1793 Bishop Carroll sent Father Simon Felix Gallagher, D. D., a priest of the diocese of Dublin and a graduate of the University of Paris, to the Charleston congregation. He came with the approbation of his superior, Archbishop Troy. He became noted for his eloquence, intelligence, culture, and, sadly, his fondness for spirits. Following complaints from the trustees, Carroll finally declared to Dr. Gallagher, after meeting with him in Washington D. C. in 1801, the following:

> But at my return to Baltimore, I was mortified by the recital of your excesses here, immediately after your own return from our conferences. The knowledge of these excesses was communicated by those who had been eye witnesses to them, and had previously manifested a particular attachment to you, during your abode here. Since your return to Charleston, I scarce ever hear you mentioned by a Catholic or a Protestant, especially the latter who, tho' they give you credit for your uncommon talents, do not add some remarks on that intemperance, which, if it be as habitual, as it is represented, must destroy in great measure the effect of your discourses, and other ministerial duties. This has suggested to me the propriety of some other arrangement, not altogether such, as I would wish, but as circumstances enable me to make.... If you be disposed to relinquish your pastoral care, I will appoint Mr. Ryan to succeed you: but remaining Principal of the College, I flatter myself, that you would go often into the pulpit, and devote to God's honour the exercise of your abilities.[24]

Gallagher rejected this request for his resignation. Instead, he appealed his case to *Propaganda*. After an exchange of letters, that body ruled that Bishop Carroll had all the requisite authority to deal with Dr. Gallagher as he saw fit.

When Gallagher left Charleston for a time because of ill health, his bishop sent Father LeMercier, founder of the church in Savannah, to take his place. The trustees refused to accept him as any more than a temporary pastor filling in till Gallagher should return. When Gallagher reappeared and found LeMercier, in

---

[24]   Guilday, Peter, *The Life and Times of John England, 1786-1842*. Vol. I: New York: The America Press, 1927, pp. 145-146. Cf. Hanley, *op. cit,* Vol. II, pp. 354-355.

protest he opened a public chapel in his house. The small congregation now was even physically divided. Le Mercier went back to France in 1806.

The trustees then requested that Dr. Gallagher be reinstated as pastor. Bishop Carroll acquiesced that December. All seemed to go well until the trustees passed a resolution, adopted during one of the pastor's periodic absences, that declared the following: "The clergyman shall not be entitled to a vote, neither to be present at any of the meetings of the Vestry; all communications from him to the Vestry to be in writing, and their answer to him in like manner."[25]

Dr. Gallagher publicly confronted the trustees with their invasion of his pastoral authority. He also notified Carroll of the problem; the bishop responded directly to the trustees with an admonition of his own.

The situation quieted down until in 1812, a young French priest, Joseph Picot de la Cloriviere, came to St. Mary's as assistant pastor. This occurred both because of Gallagher's frequent requests for assistance and because of his continuing struggle with alcoholism.

Although the Irish congregation did not take well to being directed by a French priest, he and Gallagher appear to have gotten along reasonably well. Then in 1814, when news of the Bourbon restoration reached him, the young priest-nobleman decided to return to France. Because of this departure, Father Robert Browne, an Irish Augustinian priest stationed in Augusta, Georgia, came to assist Dr. Gallagher.

Problems erupted anew when Fr. Cloriviere, reconsidering his decision, returned to Charleston in November 1815, and Archbishop Carroll died on December 3rd. Fr. Browne, in Gallagher's current absence and echoing the feelings of the trustees, publicly expressed displeasure at the French priest's reappearance and continued presence. Cloriviere, in turn, wrote to Fr. Tessier, the vicar-general of the diocese, about the ominous situation developing in the Charleston church.

Archbishop Neale, Carroll's successor, took prompt action. He wrote to Charleston, reaffirmed Cloriviere's appointment there, and directed Browne to return to Augusta. After promising to comply, Browne stayed on at St. Mary's. The circumstances became so fractious that Cloriviere gathered some of the polarized congregation around him in a small, separate chapel.

Gallagher returned on February 2nd. Straightway he tried physically to eject Cloriviere from the church vestry, saying he had no right to be there. His arguments centered on Cloriviere's previous departure for France, the *exeat* signed by Archbishop Carroll, the appointment of Browne as his new curate, and Cloriviere's resumption of his position without Gallagher's knowledge or approval. He clearly

---

[25] *Ibid.,* p. 151.

dismissed Carroll's acceptance of the Frenchman's return and Neale's subsequent intervention in his favor.

Again, Archbishop Neale responded strongly. He revoked the faculties of both Gallagher and Browne; he appointed Cloriviere as sole pastor of St. Mary's. Gallagher now gathered around him influential friends among the trustees, took possession of the church register, ordered Cloriviere to leave the place for good, and forbade him to operate a separate chapel in the city. He and Browne, both suspended, declared themselves co-pastors, and penned a new petition for Rome. In it Gallagher claimed his canonical appointment as a *parochus* (pastor) as the basis of his appeal to a higher ecclesiastical court. Browne forthwith took their claim to Rome.

Propaganda, accepting Gallagher's argumentation, agreed to hear the case. It requested relevant documents from all interested parties. In the meantime, at the prefect's solicitation the pope ordered the reinstatement of the two clergy, the removal of all censures and irregularities, plus the immediate departure of Fr. Cloriviere from Charleston. These well-intentioned but questionable actions were devised to bring a measure of peace to the troubled church community. Browne left immediately for Charleston, official documents in hand.

During this period Dr. Gallagher had met personally with Archbishop Neale. He admitted to him his guilty opposition to legitimate church authority and his part in the growing schism in Charleston. As conditions of his repentance he agreed to the following: 1) He would never again exercise any religious faculties in Charleston; 2) he would go straightway to New York, place himself under the authority of Bishop Connolly, and make an eight-day retreat; 3) he would write a public letter, forwarded first to Neale, to be read in Charleston acknowledging his misconduct and penitence. In his letter to Cloriviere concerning the resolution of the Gallagher troubles, the archbishop appointed him as "my Grand Vicar for the Carolinas and Georgia; but you must place no priest any where without my prior knowledge and consent. Should Rev. Mr. Browne return you must grant him no powers, not even to say Mass."[26] He also placed an interdict on St. Mary's until that time when Cloriviere is accepted as pastor and is truly independent of all intrusions from the trustees.

Where did the trustees stand in the midst of this clerical wrangling? In October 1816 Edward Lynch wrote for the congregation to the archbishop about the troubles swirling around it. After dismissing all accusation against Gallagher and Browne as erroneous and based on misrepresentations, he states clearly and for the record the reasons for standing against the episcopal directives:

---

[26]   *Ibid.*, p. 198.

They beg leave to state that the Catholic Congregation of Charleston are chiefly composed of natives of Ireland and of course more closely attached to Clergy of their own Nation where found worthy, and that their priests are solely supported by their voluntary contributions, that they have an insurmountable personal dislike to the Rev. Mr. Cloriviere, that none but a person capable of preaching clearly and distinctly in the English language will suit them nor do they think him calculated for the Pastoral care of this Church—to be plain they do not respect him nor can they receive or support him as their Pastor—I am convinced they would pay all due submission to your pastoral authority except that of placing over them a priest whom they do not love or esteem; should they ultimately be deprived of the Pastor of their affections, I much fear many of the flock will go astray and seek and enter strange folds from which it will be hard to bring them back—indeed some are already inclined to do so, and which actually took place on a former unhappy dissension in the Church....[27]

Before resuming the twisted path of the Charleston uprising, it may be well to summarize our discussion so far about trusteeism in early Catholic America. By civil incorporation lay trustees owned the temporal goods of the church. Given this fact, many trustees sought to instill a European practice, *Jus patronatus*, by which one who owns the land, or builds the church, or pays for its upkeep and personnel, has "the right to *present* the name of a person for pastor to the ecclesiastical superior for his approbation." In practice they tended to consider the bishop's "approbation of their choice as a formality."[28] Indeed, very often trustees and congregation predated the presence of a pastor, and had responsibility for the church's nascence without clerical assistance or oversight. The roles of trustees in safeguarding the church's material assets were rarely spelled out vis-à-vis the spiritual authority of pastors and bishops. Intrusions into pastoral and episcopal authority did, as a result, occur, but rarely without the connivance of a dissident cleric. When trustees joined in an ecclesiastical rebellion, their attachment to, or opposition to, given priests often came from a longing for one's native land or from national and racial prejudices against foreigners.

Armed with the decision from *Propaganda*, Gallagher and Browne returned to St. Mary's and resumed their roles as co-pastors. Cloriviere, having heard from the archbishop that he should maintain the interdict on the church, should stay put

---

[27]   *Ibid.*, p. 199.

[28]   Agonito, *op. cit.*, pp. 117-118

in Charleston, should gather all relevant documentation concerning their present and previous actions, and that he should have nothing to do with them so as to avoid appearing to accept their return, did as ordered. Meanwhile, Neale wrote forcefully to Rome about the undermining of his authority. He asserted that he could only hope that the Congregation's decisions and papal directives were based on misrepresentations. He also began sending all relevant information concerning the case. At first the Congregation complained that Neale had been negligent in not sending such previously (he had assumed Carroll's position at age sixty-nine, had this situation thrust upon him at age seventy, and died at age seventy-one). Finally, after reviewing his tardy but extensive dossier, it accepted its error and reversed its decisions. Unfortunately, the old archbishop, astonished at and hurt by the actions of the Holy See, expired before the reversal and expressions of regret could reach him.

His successor, Ambrose Marechal, counseled Cloriviere to stay on in Charleston. When the rescript arrived from Rome reversing *Propaganda's* prior position, he forwarded it with letters of his own to the two rebellious priests. Both attacked the authenticity of the papal document. Browne, however, made a show of submission but one calculated to secure a reappointment to St. Mary's. Marechal firmly rejected any efforts by either of them to remain in Charleston as active priests.

There followed an exchange of letters between the trustees and the archbishop. The former argued at length for the removal of Cloriviere; they did not continue their efforts toward the reinstatement of their former pastors. As for those two, Marechal simply gave up corresponding with them. The church was under an interdict, both priests were suspended, and he held out little hope for their repentance. It would now simply be up to God.

The trustees petitioned Rome for the removal of Cloriviere and the creation of a new diocese in the south, one separated from the "Baltimore junta." They suggested as a likely candidate for the new bishopric an Irish Dominican, Thomas Carbry. At the same period, the Norfolk trustees were seeking the separation of Virginia from Baltimore with the same man as their choice for bishop.

Marechal sent two Jesuits, Father Benedict Fenwick, future bishop of Boston, and Father James Wallace to Charleston to take charge of the situation. (Pius VII had restored the Society of Jesus as a world order in 1814.) They arrived there on November 7, 1818. They succeeded in barring Gallagher and Browne from any further overt rebellion. They also prevailed upon Marechal to remove Cloriviere, as his presence could never lead to peace. He did so. The unfortunate French priest left Charleston, to the trustees' delight, in December. He became chaplain of a Visitation Sisters convent in Georgetown the next month. He died there in 1826.

When Rome failed to create a new diocese, the schismatic trustees attempted one last gambit. On January 4, 1819 they sent a letter to Fr. Carbry, then in New

York. He, in turn, forwarded it to an Irish Franciscan, Fr. Richard Hayes. He had lately been accused in Rome of disloyalty to the pope because of Hayes' efforts to defeat any concordat between London and Rome that would exchange the king's veto of any nominee for bishop in Ireland for the religious freedom of the Irish Catholics.

The letter begins with a compassionate understanding of Hayes' troubles with the Holy See. It then turns to a plan of action that could profit him and the persecuted Catholics of Charleston:

> Under this conviction I [says the writer] shall hazard to submit to your consideration a plan, which will enoble [sic] your misfortunes, and cover your enemies with humiliation and disgrace, trusting that your mind is too exalted to stoop to the pitiful alternative of courting the favour of your persecutors by treating confidence with perfidy, in divulging indiscreetly a proposal which might prematurely alarm the prejudices of the public against persons unknown to you, whose wish it is to raise you above unmerited humiliation, to support the cause of suffering religion, and likewise to overturn a system of ecclesiastical tyrrany [sic], which a cabal of unprincipled French churchmen are endeavoring to establish in this country, not less derogatory to individual rights than opposed to the laws and constitution of the United States....
>
> Here it is then: *On receipt of this letter to proceed to Utrecht in the most secret manner, carrying testimonials of good conduct from some of the clergy, and to have yourself consecrated Bishop of South Carolina in North America, by the Prelate of that city or church, and to set out for that state as soon as possible.* On your arrival in America your expenses shall be made good to you, but you must agree to consecrate other Bishops, when settled in this country, otherwise any salary may be doubtful. At the first blush, this proposal may appear singular and even extravagant, but on maturely consulting religion and reason, it may not appear altogether strange or novel in the Christian church.[29]

Hayes immediately denounced the proposed schism to his superior, Archbishop Troy of Dublin. He then wrote both Pius VII and the prefect of *Propaganda Fide*, Cardinal Litta, revealing the plot and disclaiming any part in it.

Rome acted with deliberate speed. On June 18, 1820 the pope erected a new episcopal see, centered at Charleston, for the two Carolinas and Georgia. It chose

---

[29] *Ibid.*, pp. 273-274.

as its bishop, John England, an Irish priest, a long-time friend of Fr. Hayes, and himself a strong proponent of church rights in Ireland. If nothing else, the plot did accomplish one goal of the Charleston trustees: they would no longer need to deal with a "French cabal" in Baltimore. Now an Irishman, one of their own, would take on Gallagher, Browne, and their lay supporters. Unwittingly, Rome was also giving to the American church a determined advocate of democratic government within its monarchical structure.

IV. Bishop John England and an American Diocesan Constitution

Thomas England worked as a surveyor in County Tipperary. A job took him to the Lordan family home in nearby County Cork. He met a daughter, Honora, who, after overcoming some parental opposition, married him on April 15, 1785. Seventeen months later, on September 23, 1786, their first child, John, joined them[30]. He would be the oldest of ten children born to this couple in County Cork.

The Catholic Relief Bill of 1793 removed previous prohibitions against Irish Catholics practicing in various professions. John at age fourteen thought he would like to study law; indeed, for two years he apprenticed with a local barrister. The call to the church, however, proved stronger. He enrolled at the recently opened St. Patrick's College in County Carlow, the seminary being used by Bishop Francis Moylan to prepare students for service in the Cork diocese. After completing five years of philosophical and theological studies, the earnest seminarian presented himself to Dr. Moylan in St. Mary's Cathedral for ordination on October 11, 1808.

He worked in various capacities in the diocese at his bishop's request. He offers this summary statement of the positions he held:

> During this period [he writes], I successively held the following situations, all the duties of which I regularly discharged: the chaplaincy of the city prisons; that of the Presentation Convent of nuns for the education of poor children; that of the Magdalen Asylum; the lectureship of the Cathedral; the superintendence of the diocesan seminary, and teacher of philosophy and theology therein; inspector of the poor schools of the city, which contained upwards of two thousand boys; and secretary to the Fever Hospital; and was on the committee of several

---

[30] In order to reduce the unintentional confusion occasioned by the England family name, throughout this chapter I will name the boy John, the priest Father or Father John, and the prelate Bishop or Bishop John.

charitable institutions. Many of these situations I held together, and was during the entire period secretary to the diocese, and secretary to the Board of Examiners of Candidates for Holy Orders.[31]

Of special interest, however, are activities engaged in that prepared him for his ministry in the United States. They may be grouped under four headings: religious liberty, separation of church and state, voluntaryism, and the nature of the church.

Father John grew up in a Catholic Ireland suffering under intolerant penal laws. They curtailed civil and religious rights in order to protect and to maintain the primacy of the Church of England. Because of the union of church and state in the British Empire, to follow the Catholic, rather than the Anglican, religion created suspicions relative to one's loyalty to the Crown.

During the late eighteenth and early nineteenth centuries, a great controversy sprang up over the question of civic loyalty versus religious freedom. Forces within the British Parliament were prepared to allow the free practice of the Catholic religion in Ireland as long as they could receive assurances that loyalty to Rome did not necessitate disloyalty to London. The argument centered on a *quid pro quo*: if Rome would grant the king the power to veto any nominee to a Catholic bishopric in Ireland, then London, the fear of disloyalty abated, would allow Irish Catholics religious freedom.

Some within the hierarchies of both Ireland and England saw no opposition between such assurances and the practice of Catholicism. Father's own bishop, Dr. Moylan, was numbered among them. Yet, after 1813 Moylan allowed his young priest to be the proprietor of the *Cork Mercantile Chronicle* with the express purpose of presenting to the nation the views of the anti-vetoists.

Father John kept his readers informed of the give and take of ecclesiastical maneuvers in England, Ireland, and Rome while he consistently opposed any intrusion of civil authority into the realm of religion. For him a person freely chose to follow a given faith. Moreover, he had the inalienable right of obeying the dictates of conscience in faith and morals without any interference from secular authority as long as civil order was not thereby disturbed. For example, on April 19, 1816 he co-signed this resolution of the Cork Catholic Aggregate meeting:

That unalterably attached to the principles of Religious Liberty, and sympathizing with those who suffer on the score of conscience, we would deem ourselves unworthy of that Freedom, which as Irishmen

---

[31]   *Ibid.*, pp. 83-84.

and Catholics, we demand, did we not thus publicly express our unqual-
ified abhorrence, and detestation of the late cruel persecution of the
Protestants in France, a persecution as inconsistent with every principle
of justice, and liberal policy, as contrary to the sacred and inalienable
rights of humanity.[32]

It echoed the tolerant words of Arthur O'Leary: "In the course of this work,
I intend to make Toleration a citizen of the world, instead of confining it to one
kingdom or province. I am not an able, neither am I a partial advocate. I plead
for the Protestant in France, and for the Jew in Lisbon, as well as for the Catholic
in Ireland."[33] It recalls as well the fighting ones of a fellow Cork patriot, Daniel
O'Connell, who advocated "the eternal right to freedom of conscience, a right
which, I repeat it with pride and pleasure, would exterminate the Inquisition in
Spain and bury in oblivion the bloody orange flag of dissension in Ireland."[34]

Father John would leave his homeland before O'Connell successfully won the
battle for Catholic Emancipation in 1829—without the Veto.

In November 1215 the church hierarchy and representatives of many kingdoms assembled in Rome in the Fourth Lateran Council. It would mark the high
point of medieval papal legislation. In a time when church and state were virtually one, the council saw fit to confirm Frederick II as emperor of the West, to
grant Simon de Montfort part of the conquered Toulouse region because of his role
in fighting Albigensianism, and to confirm Innocent III's prior rejection of the
Magna Carta as invalid because of its being extorted from King John.[35] Because of
the heresies of the Albigenses and Waldenses, the council reaffirmed the canons of
the previous Lateran councils concerning the duty to stamp out heresy. In its third
canon it directly obliged secular rulers to assist the church in this task at the risk
of forfeiting their secular rule. Indeed, this council laid the theological basis, along
with the bull *"Excommunicamus"* of Gregory IX, for the organized crusade against
heresy we know simply as "the Inquisition."[36]

---

[32]   Carey, Patrick. *An Immigrant Bishop: John England's Adaptation of Irish Catholicism to
American Republicanism.* Yonkers, New York: U. S. Catholic Historical Society, 1982,
p. 49. Cf. *Cork Mercantile Chronicle, April 19, 1816.*

[33]   *Ibid.,* pp. 47-48. Cf. O'Leary, Arthur. *Miscellaneous Tracts,* 2nd Edition. Dublin: John
Chambers, 1781, p. xv.

[34]   *Ibid.,* p. 48. Cf. O'Connell, John (ed). *The Life and Speeches of Daniel O'Connell, M. P.,*
Volume II. Dublin: James Duffy, 1867, p. 16.

[35]   Editorial staff of the Catholic University of America. *New Catholic Encyclopedia*, Vol.
VIII. McGraw-Hill: New York, 1967, p. 408.

[36]   *Ibid.,* Vol. VII, p. 536.

Given this background, after the defection of Henry VIII from the Roman Catholic Church, subsequent British monarchs cast more than a wary eye at their Catholic subjects. Could they truly be loyal to them, or were they just bidding their time when by force and numbers they would, as good Catholics, have to rise up and overthrow their dissident rulers? Irish apologists argued that the Fourth Lateran Council happened at a time when there existed a *de facto* union of church and state. In that particular era the pope did function as a secular ruler and thus had every right to command civil obedience. But that time, now vanished, no longer shaped Catholic life. In the world of the 19th Century the pope did not have any civil authority or any right to interfere in purely secular affairs.

Our loyal yet patriotic priest based his firm and unwavering conviction concerning the separation of church and state on five arguments:

1. Civil government has as its origin the sovereignty of the people. It must provide for the temporal welfare of all its citizens, regardless of religious affiliation, because as citizens all are equal.

2. The church springs from the revelation of God's benevolence toward human kind. Its authority comes from God and has only one goal: the spiritual health, welfare, and salvation of its members. It has no authority in, nor duties regarding, secular and temporal matters.

3. Christ himself commanded this separation in his oft-quoted distinction between the affairs of Caesar deserving obedience on their own and not because of one's allegiance to God.

4. Contemporary Irishmen must uphold a proud tradition of Irish Catholics suffering poverty and even death in the age-old fight to keep their faith pure and undiluted by the politics of changing regimes.

5. Experience and history make clear that the state gives no favors without some expected reciprocation. To accept either Catholic Emancipation or Catholic Union would probably mean an intrusion of civil authority into the church's spiritual functions. Although our priestly apologist did not hold any necessity of religion being compromised where union of church and state existed, he counseled caution because of Irish Catholic experience under British subjugation.

Parliament, seeking to gain some control over Catholic ecclesial government, offered the lure of establishment. Any religion recognized officially by the state would deserve and receive financial assistance. Just as Irish Catholics had long been tithed to support the Anglican Church and its clergy in Ireland, so the acceptance of Catholic Union would mean the flowing of tax dollars into church coffers that could be used to pay clerical salaries and to underwrite church programs. For a poor church hitherto dependent upon an impoverished laity such an offer could scarcely be spurned.

But Father John rejected the notion. For the clergy to receive salaries from the state would create a vested interest. No longer could they solely look to the welfare of their people; they must also concern themselves with acting according to the needs and wishes of their employers. When others countered that the priests needed to rely only on their own integrity in the matter, he responded: "We will not put ourselves in the way of temptation."[37] Moreover, he saw clerical dependence on the free-will offerings of the laity as a powerful bond between them. It created an ever-present reminder of their mutual dependence in their endeavor to be a church living according to the teachings of Christ.

The veto question gave rise to heated discussions about the relationship between the universal and national churches. It became increasingly central as various elements in Rome began speaking in ways that could be interpreted as favoring exchanging veto power for religious freedom.

On February 16, 1814 the vice-prefect of *Propaganda Fide*, Monsignor John Baptist Quaranotti, issued a rescript that declared that Catholic doctrine di.! not of itself rule out the veto project. Subsequently, the secretary of state, Cardinal Ercole Consalvi, visited London prior to the Congress of Vienna. There he met with British ministers about Catholic Emancipation. This aroused fears that he, and Pius VII, would support the English Veto. These concerns were accentuated when Cardinal Lorenzo Litta, prefect of *Propaganda Fide*, on April 26th sent a letter from Genoa that allowed exclusive power to the British Crown in the selection of bishops. These actions set off such an uproar in Ireland that its bishops gathered in a national synod on August 23rd. This assembly soundly rejected any change in the selection of Irish bishops, and sent a deputation to Rome with a severe remonstrance about any attempt on the Holy See's part to do so.

Father John considered both the papacy and episcopacy to be granted by God through apostolic succession:

> The ordinary Apostolic power is lodged in the successors of the Apostles, upon whom our Lord bestowed it, and their successors are his Holiness, as successor to St. Peter, the Prince of the Apostles and Head of the Church, and the Bishops of the special place, as the successors to the

---

[37] *Op. cit.*, Carey, p. 64. Cf. *Cork Mercantile Chronicle*, June 6, 1814.

particular Apostles of that place, and who therefrom have ordinary jurisdiction therein.[38]

Both exercised a limited power. These limits came from scripture and tradition
and from the relationship of their separate authorities. In an open letter to the Irish
hierarchy on August 15, 1815, Father John stated his opinion on these limits:

> I have very little hesitation in saying, under correction, that any inter-
> ference of his Holiness in the local discipline, against the will of the
> Bishops, is an unjust aggression, and an usurpation of power which
> ought to be resisted, and in the present case [the veto question in
> Ireland] I am led to think it evidently beyond his competency.

The importance of this priest's position lies in his distinguishing between
papal primacy and church governance. He nowhere challenges the primacy,
though he correctly states that the Catholic faith did not [at that time] demand
assent to papal infallibility. However, such infallibility, as defined later at Vatican
I, addresses only the pope's teaching authority in questions of faith and morals. It
does not extend to the organization of the church or to the carrying out of its various functions.

Carey succinctly sums up England's view of the differing roles of pope and
bishops:

> The papacy was the center of Catholic unity; as such the pope had the
> duty to hold all the national churches in communion, support them and
> help them to maintain their local identity, call general councils when
> they were necessary, execute their decisions, and preserve the faith and
> general discipline of the church throughout the world (*Repertory*, I, 66).
> The local episcopacy, on the other hand, had the obligation to preserve
> the communion with the universal church, while accommodating the
> church as far as possible to the customs, traditions, feelings and political
> circumstances of the local surroundings.[39]

Episcopal defenders of the veto attempted to stifle dissent through identifying
the church in Ireland with themselves as bishops. Priests and laity, according to

---

[38]   *Ibid.*, p. 67. Cf. *Cork Mercantile Chronicle*, May 18, 1814.

[39]   *Op. cit.*, Guilday, p. 71. Cf. England, John. *The Religious Repertory for the Year of Our
Lord 1809*. Cork: J. Haley Publisher, 1810, p. 66.

them, had no place in these discussions as they concerned spiritual matters falling under episcopal authority.

Father John did not dispute the role of the bishops as judges and decision-makers. For example, they alone could decide to accept a change in the nomination process for bishops. And once determined they alone could reopen the matter. But prior to that final decision, both priests and laity had a duty to speak up and share their views: priests because their mission demanded both spiritual and material involvement, laity because as members of the body of the church they must prosecute its welfare, especially when issues touched upon their own political future and their place in the civic community.

On July 22, 1820 the *Congregatio de Propaganda Fide* notified Fr. John England of his appointment to the new bishopric of Charleston, South Carolina, United States of America. His ecclesiastical superior, Bishop Murphy of Cork, created him a bishop on September 21st. On Saturday, December 30th, he arrived in Charleston to begin his episcopal life in America.

Straightway, the new leader appointed Fenwick as his vicar-general, and granted full faculties to fathers Gallagher and Browne. He did so in order to put previous dissensions behind them all and so as to leave out any further involvement of an antagonistic Archbishop Marechal. Moreover, in the whole of his diocese he had the services of only six priests: Benedict Fenwick and James Wallace, both Jesuits, who would soon leave Charleston and return to Baltimore; Samuel Cooper in Augusta; a newly ordained Irish priest, Denis Corkery; and the two trouble-makers, Gallagher and Browne. The former, now older and ill, he allowed to be in the diocese without any specific assignment; the latter he took with him on his immediate visitation of the far-flung Catholic residents as he planned to install him as pastor in Savannah.

Regarding the dissident trustees of St. Mary's, he straightway preached in the church. He also distributed his initial pastoral letter. In it he stressed the passing down of religious authority, from Old Testament to New, from Christ to Peter, from pope to bishops. He left no doubt as to his own religious authority and his expectations of the Catholic people in following his teachings about the church and his governance of it in the Diocese of Charleston.

Problems, however, would still remain at St. Mary's. A group of rebellious trustees would insist upon rules that gave them certain pastoral authority. The Bishop would attempt to get them to rescind these offending rules. They would refuse. He then would take his rectory elsewhere, say mass in a temporary chapel, and place St. Mary's again under interdict. It was not until 1824 that the trustees would relent and the Charleston schism would finally dissolve.

Bishop John immediately set in motion the locating of another temporary church in Charleston that would be totally under his control. Moreover, plans were formulated for a cathedral. Soon he made it standard practice that no church would be incorporated except in the name of the bishop and for the diocese. Also, he abolished pew rents that gave pride of place and evidence of money to some parishioners. In these ways the new prelate sought to resolve the long-standing revolt against church authority in Charleston, and to lay the groundwork needed to waylay future lay insurrections against episcopal and pastoral authority.

These early actions, however, did not sit well with Archbishop Marechal. If he could have had his way, neither Gallagher nor Browne would be allowed faculties in the new diocese. He could only see episcopal reinstatement of them to good standing as a slap against him and a sign of their having trumped his episcopal authority. From the moment of the young bishop's arrival on the scene, Marechal treated him coldly and distantly. He tended to look upon this bishop with suspicion, as a kind of loose cannon who had insufficient regard for church authority and discipline.

Right off, the Bishop recognized the troubled state of the American church. He had the aftermaths of his own schism in Charleston to handle; he quickly got drawn into the schism in another St. Mary's, this one in Philadelphia, instigated by another Irish priest, William Hogan.[40] More than once he urged Marechal to gather the American bishops into a national synod that could address the issue of the havoc rained down upon parishes by the coalition of rogue priests and power-grabbing laymen. Marechal for his own reasons steadfastly refused. Bishop John, perforce, turned his attention to organizing his own diocese so as to forestall subsequent schisms from developing.

He began by writing a constitution for the diocese.[41] He clearly modeled it after the American document. In parallel with it, he meant to define the roles assigned to pope and bishop, priest and layman, to establish rules governing church behavior in his diocese, and to spell out the rights and duties of groups and individuals.

In the preface he distinguished between two modes of government in the Catholic Church. The first, of divine institution, dealt with apostolic succession: the primacy of Peter, the handing down of papal authority, and the sharing of the apostolic role through the episcopacy. The second, of human creation, flowed from the first and could not run counter to it. It concerned ecclesiastical discipline, the

---

[40]   Cf. *Ibid.*, pp. 380-425.

[41]   Cf. *Ibid.*, pp. 365-379. Cf. *The Constitution of the Roman Catholic Church of North Carolina, South Carolina, and Georgia, which are comprised in the Diocess* [sic] *of Charleston, and Province of Baltimore, U. S. A., as fully agreed to, and accepted; after repeated discussion, by the clergy and the several congregations, and regularly confirmed by the bishop, and subsequently amended to the form prescribed.*

regulating of church life, a prerogative of episcopal authority. However, it also dealt with the temporalities and material properties associated with the church and necessary for its ongoing support.

Title I in eight chapters defined the essence of the Catholic faith. To be Catholic one must assent to these articles as handed down through scripture and tradition and as defined by the teaching authority of the pope in union with the bishops of the world.

Title II addressed questions of church government. Concerning the relationship of church and state, it stated these fundamental principles:

> We do not believe,…that our Lord Jesus Christ gave to the civil or temporal governments of states, empires, kingdoms, or nations any authority in or over spiritual or ecclesiastical concerns. We do not believe that our Lord Jesus Christ gave to his Church, as such, any authority in or over the civil or temporal concerns of states, empires, kingdoms or nations.[42]
>
> We do not believe…that by virtue of this spiritual or ecclesiastical authority, the Pope hath any power or right to interfere with the allegiance that we owe to our State; nor to interfere in or with the concerns of the civil policy or the temporal government thereof, or of the United States of America.[43]

Certainly, one could be both a good Catholic and a loyal citizen.

Addressing directly the relationship between ecclesiastical discipline and lay involvement in parish life, the constitution firmly stated a principle meant to silence forever the claims of trustees concerning pastoral authority:

> We therefore disavow and disclaim any right or power, under any pretext, in the laity to subject the ministry of the church to their control, or to interfere in the regulation of the sacred duties, this being the exclusive province of those persons whom the Holy Ghost hath placed bishops to govern the Church of God.[44]

If this were fulfilled, no longer would a bishop need to struggle with lay trustees over claims of *jus patronatus*, the right to choose or to dismiss a pastor. No parish

---

[42]   *Ibid.*, pp. 366-367.

[43]   *Ibid.*, p. 367.

[44]   *Ibid.*, p. 367.

could receive a priest except one appointed by the bishop. No priest suspended by his bishop could function as a priest even during the period of appeal. No priest could be removed by any lay action; such could occur only through the exercise of episcopal authority.

Title III established regulations concerning congregational funds. They would be held in separate and independent accounts, designated for specific purposes. They could be raised as a levy or church tax only with the consent of the bishop. They were specifically regulated relative to clerical support. Finally, it created a *General Fund for the Church of Charleston*. Catholics must every quarter contribute fifty cents to that fund. It would be managed by a board of trustees for the diocese consisting of the bishop (*ex officio* president), the vicar-general (*ex officio* vice president), five clergy elected annually by their fellows, and five laymen elected annually by the lay delegates to the diocesan convention. These funds could be allocated for various purposes: erection and maintenance of a cathedral and seminary; aid to poor parishes and schools; assistance for widows, the aged and infirm, and orphans; support of missionaries and religious associations, especially in remote and neglected parts of the diocese.

Title IV answered the question of membership in the diocese and, by extension, the ability to be a parish trustee, a clergyman in good standing, and a member of the annual convention or one of its committees. Besides being a baptized male at least twenty-one years of age and living within the diocese, he must be free of all church censures and must subscribe to the diocesan constitution. Only those meeting the qualifications had active voice both locally and in convention.

Title V concerned the parish churches. The bishop alone erected new parishes. Each parish had its own vestry or lay board, elected by members of the parish in good standing. Vestry members had to subscribe publicly and in writing to the diocesan constitution. The vestry established its own by-laws according to local circumstances, but they required episcopal approval. It had the authority to elect its own officers as well as choosing minor church employees, such as the organist and sexton.

The most creative section of the constitution, and the part most in line with the U. S. Constitution, occurs in Title VI—The Convention. The bishop called together the annual convention at a time and place of his choosing. All clergy under his jurisdiction were expected to participate as the House of Clergy, whose president was the priest highest in dignity or first in ordination. Lay delegates came from various parishes or districts, representation apportioned relative to the size of the Catholic population there. They constituted a House of Lay Delegates with its own elected officers and own program of business. These two houses were to be considered—

...as a body of sage, prudent, and religious counselors to aid the proper ecclesiastical governor of the church in the discharge of his duty, by their advice and exertions in obtaining and applying the necessary pecuniary means to those purposes which will be most beneficial, and in superintending the several persons who have charge thereof; to see that the money be honestly and beneficially expended; wherefore the Convention has the following powers, viz.:

1. To dispose of the general fund of the Church in the way that it may deem most advantageous.

2. To examine into and to control the expenditures made by its own order or by that of a former Convention.

3. To examine into, regulate and control, with the exception of their spiritual concerns, all establishments of its own creation; or which being otherwise created may be regularly subjected to its control.

4. To appoint the lay officers and servants of such establishments.

5. The House of the Clergy has power to examine into the ecclesiastical concerns of such establishments and to make its private report thereon to the Bishop or Vicar, together with its opinion and advice, but such report or advice shall not be published in any other way, without the consent of the Bishop or Vicar first be had and obtained in writing under his hand and seal.[45]

In order to be valid a majority of both houses had to pass an act and the bishop had to accept it. Each parish or district needed formally to accept the constitution of the diocese in order to participate in the diocesan convention.

During his bishopric fifteen conventions were held in Charleston between 1823-1838, eight in Augusta from 1826-1835, and two in Fayetteville from 1829-1831. Bishop John convened three general conventions of the whole diocese at Charleston from 1839-1841. He summed up the results of these annual meetings in his address at the thirteenth convention in South Carolina in 1837:

My brethren, thirteen years have elapsed since this constitution has, by our solemn act, after repeated deliberations, become the rule of our proceedings. By its provisions the limits of our several powers and duties are accurately defined; it has prevented discord, it has banished jealousy, it has secured peace, it has produced efforts of co-operation,

---

45   *Ibid.,* pp. 375-376.

and established mutual confidence and affection between our several churches, as well as between the bishop and the churches, and by confirming the rights of all, it has insured the support of all. So long as its provisions are exactly and scrupulously observed, it is hoped that those blessings will also continue, but if a deviation be once made from its principles, I fear much that we should thereby be thrown into a chaos of uncertainty.[46]

One may reasonably inquire whether his peculiar organization of the diocese proved to be successful. In its goal to heal the schism brought about by the coalition of Gallagher and Browne and the Charleston trustees, most certainly his constitution and annual conventions contributed mightily to that end. In addition it constructed a solid foundation of prescribed roles that freed the Diocese of Charleston from like disturbances that roiled Catholic parishes throughout the former colonies.

The Bishop hoped to establish parishes throughout his vast diocese that could serve his scattered people. To do this he needed money for a seminary and sufficient funds to support pastors in communities unable to do so themselves. With these in place he could attract likely candidates for the priesthood from among his people and from his native Ireland. Indeed, he considered it to be vitally necessary that his future priests understand well the peculiar situation of America: a new republic, one struggling to build a civilization out of a virgin territory, one only lately granting religious freedom to Catholics, one in which Catholics lived among a Protestant majority. He emphasized this at the 7th South Carolina Convention on November 23, 1829:

I have frequently hitherto expressed an opinion that, however excellent clergymen coming from abroad might be, there were great additional benefits derivable from their education at home. I particularly alluded to the knowledge of American laws, intimacy with American people, the attachment to American institutions, the habit of American discipline, the zeal for American improvement, and the devotion to American rights, together with the adaptation of the great principles of Faith, of morality, and of science to American circumstances. I am not only confirmed in the opinion, but every day brings to my mind new evidence of its correctness;....[47]

---

[46] *Ibid.,* p. 377.

[47] *Ibid.,* p. 509.

He did begin a seminary; he secured seminarians from his diocesan family and from Ireland; he obtained funds from Rome, from *Propaganda Fide,* from other European religious societies. But he never generated enough funds from his own people. When he died, he left a sizeable debt (for that era) and barely sufficient churches and seminary. His diocesan organization gained good will, support, and gratitude from his people, but not the kind of loyalty that led to significant lay involvement in the material advancement of the diocese.

When one considers his influence on the American church outside his own diocese, he had little positive organizational impact. Archbishop Marechal did not trust this young Irish prelate. He considered him to be too liberal and to be negligent in protecting episcopal rights and authority. He also looked askance at his unique adaptations to American republicanism. Marechal ran his own diocese like a French aristocrat accustomed to obedience and control. For him the church functioned as a monarchy with the pope as supreme ruler and the bishops his supportive aristocracy. For him the South Carolina diocese's organization and lay participation smacked of a kind of Church of England episcopacy. He refused to gather the bishops in a national synod because he did not want this episcopal upstart's influence and intelligence to cut into his way of running his diocese or of directing his suffragan sees.

The Bishop's broad impact came rather through his writing. He began the first Catholic journal in America, the *United States Catholic Miscellany.* In its pages he addressed the controversies of the day, like trusteeism. He also confronted the widespread ignorance about the Catholic faith among Protestants and their bigotry against anything Catholic. He wrote and spoke constantly about the happy marriage of the Catholic religion and American republicanism. On May 18, 1841, for example, he preached on the "True Basis of Republicanism" at the Cathedral of the Holy Cross in Boston. In that sermon he declared emphatically that religion is, indeed, the solid bedrock of republican government. Moreover, the Catholic Church that preaches love for one's neighbor as a core value strongly supports this form of civil organization:

> In a large portion of the civilized world, charges are prevalent against the Catholic religion as being incompatible with civil and religious liberty.... The principle of republicanism is the equality of men. We teach that all Christians have a common Parent; that all are equally redeemed by the blood of the Saviour; that all must appear before a common God who knows no distinction of persons. Where, then, is the inconsistency? Look through the records of the world, and see where the principles of true republicanism are first to be found. They had their origin in Christianity, and their earliest instance is in the Church of

which we are members. Her institutions are eminently republican. Her rulers are chosen by the common consent; her officers are obliged to account strictly to those over whom they preside; her guide is a written constitution of higher force than the will of any individual. What call you this? Aristocracy? Monarchy? It is republicanism.[48]

His biographer, Peter Guilday, does not hesitate to proclaim this prelate's preeminent position as an "American bishop":

For undoubtedly John England became the most striking ecclesiastical personality of his day in the United States; and of all the prelates who graced the American episcopate during the score of years he ruled over the See of Charleston, none understood so thoroughly and with such mastery the genius of the American people and the ideals of their government.[49]

Bishop John died in Charleston on April 11, 1842. He was fifty-five. He had just returned from his fourth trip to Europe, once again seeking financial support and clergy for his poor diocese. Whatever the medical cause of death, he died prematurely because of exhaustion and worry. For twenty years he had struggled manfully and mostly alone to bring order, respectability, and service to his diocese. With controversy on all sides, within his church and throughout his chosen land, he preached and wrote, negotiated and prayed, begged and importuned with courage and consistency. Guilday calls him "one of the master builders of the House of God in the New World."[50] Ahlstrom, in his magisterial treatise on American religious history, denominates him as "one of the greatest prelates ever to grace the church in America...."[51]

Memorials written about him following his unexpected demise speak loudly of his impact upon the American people.

His vicar, Fr. Richard Baker, with these pain-filled words notified Fr. Thomas England of Passage, Cork, of his brother's death:

---

[48]   *Op. cit.*, McElrone, Vol. II. p 398.

[49]   *Op. cit.*, Guilday, Vol. I, p. 43.

[50]   *Ibid.*, p. 550

[51]   Ahlstrom, Sydney. *A Religious History of the American People.* New Haven: Yale University Press, 2004, p. 538.

I leave you to judge of the feeling under which I venture to apprise you (if you have not learned it before) of the death of your illustrious brother, our venerable and beloved Bishop who expired after a painful and protracted illness (inflammation of the intestines) on the morning of the 11th instant about 5 o'clock. 'Tis useless to expect details from me, I am unable to give them. Never was there such excitement in the city of Charleston, never will there be such again. The whole Union is this moment ringing with expressions of regret at what they term a national calamity. In the city on that morning all was uproar; the bells as day broke tolled out what all expected, the notes of his demise. Business was suspended, the shipping in the harbour hung their flags at half mast, the Judges of the several courts adjourned, the Governor of the State then in the city to hold a review as Commander-in-Chief of the forces, suspended and left the military at liberty, and at once the minute guns boomed in their awful tone the death of a great man. But what is all this to the death of the dying apostle? That was a scene which would win from any heart a tribute to *Religion*.[52]

The vestries of Charleston wrote a long tribute to their erstwhile leader. The initial sentences of their preface give a flavor of their pain at his parting:

As time rolls on its troubled stream into the peaceful waters of eternity it occasionally happens to bear as its burden some being more valued, more beloved and more useful than those whom every day life presents to our view, whose loss leaves a void in the community which cannot be filled up, casts a gloom over those prospects which were brightened by his labors, takes from a fond and devoted people the object of their admiration, their respect, and their love, and leaves behind but the memory of his virtues, his piety and his usefulness. Too well and truly have we experienced this during the last week in the demise of our pious, learned and much beloved bishop—an event as unexpected as it is mournful, bringing sorrow and sadness to all who knew him in public and private life, and making desolate the hearts of his own affectionate children, who from his lips were gladdened with the joyful tones of a Redeemer's promise, and by his hands were fed with that Bread which sustains man on his earthly journey. The child mourns the loss of a dearly beloved

---

[52]   Guilday, Peter. *The Life and Times of John England, Vol. II*. New York: The America Press, 1927, p. 542.

parent, and the burning tear of sorrow starts to his eye at affection's call as he beholds his father's dust restored to its parent clay.[53]

The Bishop had served as chaplain to the Washington Light Infantry of Charleston. The group passed a resolution on his passing that illustrates its collective judgment about him as a loyal and good American:

> *Resolved*, That it is with no ordinary feelings of sorrow that the company thus publicly recognizes the loss from among its members of the Right Reverend Bishop England. The eloquent tones that have stirred our hearts as with the sound of a trumpet shall no more command and arrest our attention. The lips ever devoted to the advancement of virtue and religion are forever mute, frozen into silence by the icy hand of death. The earnest vindicator of the liberty of his native land, the devoted admirer and constant advocate of the institutions of this, his adopted country; the man of unimpeached and unimpeachable character, of intellect and acquirements wide and far-reaching, of imagination fervid and poetic—the priest of self-denying and self-sacrificing virtues, whom all men of every sect and faith delight to honor—the careful and sleepless watcher over the flock committed to his care—has finished his earthly course. The good soldier of the Cross, he was ever girt with his armor, and ready to defend from assault the truths he conscientiously believed, and how widely soever we may differ from his doctrine, we all admit that he fought the good fight, and performed the task that was set before him.[54]

Nor were these deeply felt expressions confined to Charleston. As a final tribute, listen to these editorial words of the *Catholic Herald* of Philadelphia:

> No eulogy to which we could give utterance, could either add to the elevation of character of this truly eminent Divine, nor could the expression of our deepest regret and sympathy, do more than commingle in that one universal sorrowing so deeply felt for such a bereavement. In his death not only has Catholicity to mourn one of her purest and ablest champions, but Christianity one of its brilliant ornaments and justly proud boasts; for who, that ever listened to his defense of his faith, and

---

[53]   *Op. cit.*, McElrone, Vol. I, p. xviii.

[54]   *Ibid.*, p. xxi.

the explanation of her doctrines, but felt "That truth from his lips prevailed with double sway"? And even while those who differed from him in their mode of worship, either from education or prejudice, denied their acquiescence in the truth of his powerful reasoning, yet were those truths put forward in such accents of love, of charity and brotherly affection, that bigotry itself fell powerless before his mighty mind, and from the most strenuous of his political opponents he forced, if not their willing regard, their reluctant admiration.[55]

One hundred and sixty-three years after this Bishop's death, American Catholics despair of finding leaders who understand their needs. European popes, long schooled in the dictates of royalty, appointed these bishops to act as papal representatives. Our bishops think that shepherding the American church means enforcing the commands of a foreign regime, a distant pope and his Vatican congregations. They do not seek, as this loyal Bishop did, to understand the unique quality of America and wed it to a believing community. They do not see the God-given splendor of a nation built on equality and human rights as a gift to the Church. Instead of searching for ways of integrating the democratic American way into a monarchical and medieval one, they strive to keep democracy at bay so that a hierarchical, autocratic papacy may endure unchanged. Catholics today may not reasonably require that their bishops be as brilliant as Bishop John, as forceful a communicator, or as visionary a leader, but they should be able to expect them to be American rather than pseudo-Roman. Papal approbation proves nothing more than the ability to keep a boat from rocking too violently; it does not signify that a bishop is piloting his people on a faith-inspired journey to God. The church today is filled with episcopal patrolmen intent on preserving orthodoxy by stamping out the doubt and searching and questioning that flow from adult maturity and a hard-won independence. The people need new John Englands who will involve all according to their gifts in shaping their own American response to the message of Christ. Archbishop Marechal, a quintessential European prelate, distrusted this most American Bishop and his democratic ways. He excluded him from episcopal councils and tried to confine him to the sparse Catholic regions of the Carolinas and Georgia. This did not deter the Bishop. He led his people well. He earned their love and praise. Even more spectacularly, he garnered the affection and respect of their non-Catholic fellow citizens across the new nation. He lived with courage as an American Catholic. Is there no bishop in the United States today with the bravery to follow him?

---

[55] *Op. cit.*, Guilday, Vol. II, p. 547.

It took two full years before the pope appointed his successor, Ignatius Reynolds. Archbishop Purcell consecrated him at the cathedral in Cincinnati on March 19, 1844.

In his first clergy retreat Reynolds announced that he would no longer require the parishes to accept the diocesan constitution. Thus began a gradual dismantling, in the name of financial retrenchment, of his predecessor's many projects.

Although other American bishops would seek throughout the 19th Century for an accommodation between the Vatican and the United States, none would manifest the same knowledge of, and respect for, the unique situation of this new democracy as their two pioneering and eminent forebears.

What conclusions may we draw from the episcopacies of Carroll and England? For the first time in its history, the Catholic religion met with, and took root in, a democratic society. Its central administration in Rome, while remaining monarchical, adapted itself to the political requirements for acceptance within that people. Always maintaining its power and authority, it allowed some democratic processes to take place. The two bishops exercised their episcopal authority but remained mindful of the social and political facts of the emerging democratic people. Their parishioners played an energetic and active role in parochial and diocesan life, even to the extent of violating the boundaries traditionally held between clergy and laity. A different, a specifically American mode of ecclesial participation and governance was developing here until the influx of European priests and throngs of dependent immigrants turned back the tide. Gradually, the democratic initiatives receded as monarchical governance gained rarely disputed ascendancy. As history reveals, the American people, struggling to solidify a political democracy, were not yet ready for a democratic church. But the seeds had been planted. The time could someday come. We now ask: "When?"

Alexis de Tocqueville toured this land in 1830-1831, midway through the episcopate of Bishop John. After visiting New Orleans, he made his way to the southeastern states. Undoubtedly he visited with important citizens along our southeast coast. Perhaps he had the opportunity to speak with the renowned Catholic bishop about religion and democracy in America. Certainly he caught the flavor of the American Catholic church in the South Carolina diocese and throughout the former colonies.

Now that we have an overview of American Catholicism from its earliest days to the visit of this keen observer of American life, we may present, as he saw them, the essentials of its democratic system. Always we have before us this question: what may we learn from him and these two extraordinary bishops that may help us face bravely, imaginatively, and wisely the future of the church in America?

Chapter Two:
The Danger of Mixing Religion with Politics

I. Religious Immigration and the English Colonies

Harsh British laws precipitated a stream of religiously motivated immigrants during the 17th, 18th, and 19th centuries to America.

Since the revolt of Henry VIII against Roman supremacy, the faith of the English monarch determined the legally dominant religion. When Dissenters against the "popishness" of the Church of England saw slim hope of changing it, these Separtists fled to Calvinist Holland. There they attempted to worship God simply, as in the early church, and based their faith on private interpretation of the bible. As war drums rolled, warning all of an impending resumption of hostilities with Catholic Spain, and as the Separtists saw their families being absorbed into an alien religious and civil culture, these zealots set their sights on North America. Once there, they prayed they might worship in peace and according to their own lights.

On September 16, 1620 one hundred and one passengers—fifty-six adults, fourteen servants and hired artisans, and thirty-one children[1]—embarked on the *Mayflower* in Plymouth, England. A crew of forty-eight, non-Puritans, sailed the ship. Sixty-five days later it anchored off the New England coastline. There the company signed a solemn pact "for ye glorie of God, and advancemente of ye Christian faith."[2] Together these earnest Separtists would set up a civil community, ruled by law, promising each other to live according to commonly accepted rules and regulations. The people we know as the Pilgrims then disembarked at the spot revered as Plymouth Rock.

Ten years later, other Dissenters decided to leave England for the New World. Reformers, these Puritans were enduring mounting persecution during the reign of Charles I as the conflict between king and parliament become more and more

---

[1]   *Op. cit.*, Ahlstrom, pp. 137-138.

[2]   *Ibid.*, p. 136. Quote taken from the Mayflower Compact.

ominous. Despairing of reforming the Anglican Church in England, the trustees of the Massachusetts Bay Company voted to transfer their organization to New England. It elected John Winthrop governor of the colony, dissolved itself, and set about the task of emigration. On March 29, 1630 four ships with four hundred passengers, under Winthrop's command, sailed westward after religious freedom. On June 12th the weary travelers disembarked at previously settled Salem. Before the year ended eleven other ships arrived with six hundred additional emigrants. Winthrop shifted the colony's center to a "fine landlocked harbor at the mouth of the Charles River. Soon Boston, on its easily protected peninsula, became the seat of government."[3] Secured by a royal charter, the Massachusetts Bay Colony was established. By 1643, when the Puritan-dominated Long Parliament obtained control of England's government, "more than twenty thousand people had made their way to Massachusetts."[4]

Like the Pilgrims, these colonists wanted a simplified religion based on scripture. Moreover, they accepted the Calvinist doctrine of election and the necessity of manifesting one's chosen state through a life of religious observance and hard work. Unlike them, these Puritans dealt harshly with those who refused to be reformed and to live and worship according to their version of Puritan doctrine. When, for example, Roger Williams, a confirmed Separtist, maintained that nonconformists did not thereby merit and deserve punishment, the Puritan leadership determined to transport him back to England for trial. In January 1636 he fled the colony and founded the town of Providence, in present-day Rhode Island, a territory that drew Puritan extremists from across New England and became noteworthy for religious toleration.[5] Soon thereafter Anne Hutchinson, a housewife, was banished for publicly teaching that salvation came, not from works, but from faith alone. She, her husband and children, and sixty followers started the town of Portsmouth, Rhode Island. In the same period Thomas Hooker, disagreeing with the colony's leaders about voting rights, took one hundred followers, traveled southward, and established his community at the future Hartford, Connecticut. There in 1639 he penned his "Fundamental Orders," the first written constitution for an American colony.

Back in England, the Protestant king, Charles I, gave an erstwhile favorite, George Calvert, a recent convert to Catholicism, a grant of land carved out of the existing crown colony of Virginia but as yet un-colonized. This place, located between the Massachusetts and Virginia settlements, would be one where

---

3   *Ibid.*, p. 147.

4   *Ibid.*, p. 144.

5   *Ibid.*, p. 154.

Catholics and Protestants could live together fairly and peacefully. When the first Lord Baltimore died in 1632, "Charles I delivered the Maryland charter to his son, Cecilius Calvert."[6] The second Lord Baltimore, set in motion the formal founding of a place to be called "Mary Land." He named it after the wife of Charles I, Queen Henrietta Mary, on the king's request. Cecil, a Catholic, like his recently converted father, was determined to insure religious freedom in the new colony. He invited sons of prominent Catholic and Protestant families to immigrate; he appointed his brother, Leonard, its first governor; he himself remained in England in order to protect his colony from the religious vagaries of succeeding reigns. On April 2, 1649 he published "An Act Concerning Religion" that guaranteed freedom of worship to all Christians in Maryland just as long as they remained loyal to Lord Baltimore and obeyed the colonial government.

Somewhat later, during the rule of Charles II, George Fox and his followers, Dissenters derisively called "Quakers," endured various forms of persecution for their heterodoxy: Fox and thirteen thousand others were imprisoned, nearly two hundred were transported into slavery, over three hundred died during assaults on their meetings. Even with manifest royal antipathy toward them, the Quakers received a singular gift through one of their own. The father of William Penn held a note of large debt from Charles II. When Admiral Penn died, in order to cancel the financial burden, the king granted a vast tract of un-colonized land north of Virginia to son William. In August 1682 William departed from England on the ship *Welcome*, bound for the English colonies. Over half of his companions were Quakers. The ship docked at New Castle on October 27th. The group traveled inland to the area around today's Philadelphia. Penn, true to his Quaker faith, established a colony based on freedom of worship for all those professing faith in one, eternal God.

Religious motivation figured in the founding of Georgia. Colonel James Edward Oglethorpe was deputed to look into the conditions of debtors' prisons in England during the reign of George II. What he discovered horrified him. Moved by Christian charity, he determined to better the lives of these unfortunates, people in truly hopeless straits, and their families. In 1732 he presented his findings and a plan to king and parliament. Both approved his request to establish a new American colony, one to be located between the English Carolinas and Spanish Florida. It would become a buffer between the two antagonists, thus relieving the Carolina settlers, while offering renewed chance to debtors' families.

The ship *Anne* left London with thirty-five families, one hundred and twenty people, on November 6, 1732. Oglethorpe himself traveled with them as royally appointed governor of the colony. Their spiritual welfare rested in the hands of the

---

6   *Ibid.*, p. 331.

Reverend Mr. Shubert, a Church of England divine. They made land that January, journeyed through a welcoming and appreciative Carolina, and set up their community in a place later called Savannah.

James I, early in the 17th Century, brought Scotch Presbyterians to the region of Ulster in Ireland in an effort to transfer land titles out of Irish Catholic hands. This practice continued into the next century until the newcomers accounted for fully one third of the Ulster population.

Over the years, however, the English landowners in Ulster came to distrust and even fear the power of these Scottish transplants. In 1704 the English parliament passed a sacramental test act that discriminated against all not in communion with the Church of England. Among the act's noxious provisions, it delivered all religious lands and buildings to the state church and prohibited Presbyterians from worshipping in churches or teaching in schools. Their ministers could not perform valid marriages; their members were excluded from public office; they had to pay tithes for the support of the state religion. An added economic burden came in a tariff on all goods produced by Northern Ireland's competitive linen industry.

Given religious persecution, high rents, and economic restrictions, many Scots-Irish looked to the American colonies for a better life. During the middle years of the 18th Century, close to a quarter of a million of this population immigrated here. They settled primarily in Pennsylvania, Virginia, and the Carolinas. By the time of the American Rebellion, twenty-five American generals and nearly a third of the American army enlisted from this community long accustomed to struggling for their rights.[7]

At the same time, from the late 17th Century till 1829, Catholics suffered under Penal Laws meant to wipe popishness out of England's Catholic subjects, especially in Ireland. Various public oaths and declarations were required as proof of one's allegiance to the crown and abjuration of the Roman faith. Those refusing so to swear experienced a mounting deprivation of civil and religious rights. As far back as 1697 all Catholic clergy, of whatever status, became *personae non gratae* and were required to leave Ireland. Later they were jailed for twelve months prior to exile and, once transported, on daring to return they would be charged with high treason.

To prevent the spread of Catholicism, severe laws restricted inter-marriage. Any non-Catholic man daring to take a Catholic woman would lose his estate, could not be an heir, and could not be an executor or guardian of a Protestant child. Indeed, from that point on in the eyes of the state he became a Catholic. Any

---

[7]   For a discussion of the complex reasons for the immigration of the Scotch-Irish from Ulster, cf. Kenny, Kevin. *The American Irish: A History.* New York: Pearson Education, 2000, pp. 14-20.

priest presuming to marry two Protestants or to officiate over an inter-marriage faced death. In both cases the marriages themselves were declared null and void.

Irish Catholics could not teach publicly or in private homes nor could they educate their children as Catholics. Indeed, any parent sending a child out of Ireland to acquire a Catholic education thereby forfeited a host of civil rights: the parent or parents could not bring a suit in a court of law, could not be an executor or guardian, could not receive a legacy or bequest, could not hold public office, lost all titles to land and estates. In addition, these same penalties fell on anyone daring to support financially this prohibited endeavor.

Most troubling, of course, was the restriction against owning property. A papist could own neither land nor house. He could lease such but only for thirty-one years. He could not even possess a horse worth more than five pounds; indeed, an offending animal could be legally seized by anyone wishing it for the required five pounds.

During the 18th Century Irish Catholics who could manage the cost immigrated to the American colonies. Most sought the religious tolerance of Quaker Pennsylvania and Catholic Maryland. As we have seen, nearly 12,000 Catholics, a majority Irish, lived in these colonies in the period following directly upon the Revolutionary War.

As the Penal Laws failed to stamp out Catholicism in Ireland, as they attracted few Irish to the Anglican faith and the English crown, and since they justly earned international condemnation from Europe and America, beginning in the 1790's king and parliament began their retraction. The noxious restrictions finally imploded through the efforts of men like Daniel O'Connell in 1829.

When the potato famine devastated rural Ireland soon after, the Penal Laws had vanished, but the one hundred and fifty years of legal restrictions and prejudice could not be immediately erased. In Ireland's western regions the people lived as peasants on leased land. The rural farmer could hardly maintain daily sustenance for himself and his family even in the best of seasons. Living mainly on small plots of land, farming potatoes, and meeting the financial demands of their English landlords, these men had to produce a healthy crop to continue simply to survive. Thus when the dread disease struck their crops, the destitute either died, wasted away in county workhouses, or sailed off for America. Thus began the wave of peasant immigration from Ireland in the mid-1800's. These people came to live, to be free from English domination, and to taste religious freedom.

From this brief review of the influence of religion on the founding and early development of the United States, we may draw a number of conclusions. We can affirm that in its founding the American republic was determinedly religious, Christian, primarily Protestant of diverse sects, but with a small and growing Catholic population. Most immigrants sought this new land because of religious persecution in the Old World. With arrival here Protestant adherents found immediate relief; in contrast, the Catholic newcomers still experienced religious intolerance in the English colonies till some years after the ratification of the Federal constitution. Given this background, Americans then and now expect a diversity of faiths, the freedom to choose ones faith, and civil tolerance as one practices that faith. Americans from the outset regarded religious faith as personal, chosen, and neither dictated nor forced. When it comes to religion, they deeply distrust political intrusions by government agents, be they serving a monarchy or employed by a democracy.

II. The Practice of Religion in the New United States

When Alexis de Tocqueville visited this country in 1830, he opined that it contained close to a million Catholics. If correct, this number manifests a remarkable increase in membership since the late 1780's. He judged them to be zealous about their beliefs and practices of worship. Most surprisingly, he thought them to be the most democratic and republican class of citizen.[8]

He based this claim on the equality of conditions imposed on all Catholic believers. Although clergy by their position are separated from the body of the faithful, still all, including clergy, must hold to the same beliefs, participate in the same practices, endure the same austerities, and accept the same moral and intellectual standards.[9] The church compromises its positions with no one, be he pope or king, bishop or laity. All worship together the one God and share together Christ's saving gift of himself. He also considered that the position of Catholics in American society contributed to this: a minority, they needed the rights of all to be upheld and respected; poor, they needed all classes to govern if they were to be included. Finally, since the Catholic clergy turned resolutely away from political power and from involvement in the political process, they could embrace fully and champion equality for all.[10]

Of interest to today's reader, Tocqueville does not discuss how black Catholics, most of them living in Southern states and in slavery, could be said to participate in the democracy of the church. Certainly they shared the same obligations as their co-religionists, but they did not participate in church life to the same degree: they could not be taken up into the clerical order; they could not participate in diocesan and parish organizations and positions.

---

[8]   Tocqueville, Alexis de. *Democracy in America, Vols. I & II*. Harvey C. Mansfield & Delba Winthrop (eds.). Chicago: The University of Chicago Press, 2000, Vol. I, p. 275.

[9]   *Ibid.*, p. 276.

[10]   *Ibid.*, p. 276.

He does, however, dwell at length on woman's place in American society and her influence on religion. He recognizes that Americans have decided to give a woman a different and inferior position to a man in civil society. She cares for her husband and family, and maintains a reliable home; she does not enter into political and economic activities outside the home. Conjugal authority rests firmly in her husband.

However, American women, he says, are raised differently from their European sisters and earn a special attention from their male companions. In American homes daughters grow up with much the same freedom and advantages as their brothers. Instead of being protected from the world, they are introduced into it gradually so as to be ready to cope with adult society as free women:

> Long before the young American woman has attained the age of puberty, one begins to free her little by little from maternal tutelage; before she has entirely left childhood she already thinks for herself, speaks freely, and acts alone; the great picture of the world is constantly exposed before her; far from seeking to conceal the view of it from her, they uncover more and more of it to her regard every day and teach her to consider it with a firm and tranquil eye. Thus the vices and perils that society presents are not slow to be revealed to her; she sees them clearly, judges them without illusion, and faces them without fear; for she is full of confidence in her strength, and her confidence seems to be shared by all those who surround her.[11]

He draws this sharp distinction between her and her European counterpart:

> It is rare that the American woman, whatever her age, shows a puerile timidity and ignorance. Like the European girl, she wants to please, but she knows precisely at what price. If she does not indulge in evil she at least knows what it is; she has pure mores rather than a chaste mind.[12]

As a result, the young woman freely chooses to enter into matrimony and knows what it entails. She does not learn by default during marriage, after the fact, as European women do. Rather, she knows the freedom she is relinquishing in leaving the parental home, and she willingly accepts the obligations and restrictions she is assuming in joining her husband in the essential task of creating a stable, peaceful, and loving home.

---

[11]   *Ibid.,* vol. II, p. 563.

[12]   *Ibid.,* p. 564.

This did not mean that men in America look down upon women as inferior. Indeed, "Americans, who have allowed the inferiority of women to subsist in society, have therefore elevated her with all their power to the level of men in the intellectual and moral world."[13] In Europe women earn attention and flattery; "in the United States women are scarcely praised, but it is shown daily that they are esteemed."[14]

Given the moral and intellectual equivalence of American men and women, women play a major role in religious affairs. Religion touches human life through *mores*: habits of the heart, current notions and opinions about life, and ideas that form habits of the mind.[15] Women more so than men create, understand, and maintain *mores* in their home, with their husband, in raising their children. And religion speaks primarily, not through political power, but through influencing the *mores* of personal, familial, and societal life. If religion were to shape American life, it would do so primarily through its female members. Tocqueville states firmly: "the prosperity and growing force of America is due to the superiority of its women."[16] One may easily draw the inference that the impact of the Catholic religion on American life depends, most directly and essentially, on the respect that American women have for their church and vice versa.

Much has changed here in the one and three quarters centuries since Tocqueville examined this society. In the church black men now become priests and bishops; moreover, they participate in parish and diocesan committees. Lingering racial prejudice in America stems more from our history than it does from civil or religious policy. And women, Black and Caucasian, Hispanic and Oriental, may function in various liturgical and administrative church positions. This advancement parallels the important roles that women have assumed in American society: as heads of corporations, presidents of universities, members of congress, teachers and consultants and experts across the spectrum of current-day occupations. Although no woman has as yet served as her country's president, that position lies open to her and, undoubtedly, will be hers before long. The only position in Modern America still closed to her, and to her alone among her co-religionists, is the Catholic priesthood.

This exclusion rests on two social factors: John Paul II's, and the Vatican's, lack of knowledge of American society or a misguided belief that the American Catholic woman should and can resume the position of respected mother and wife

---

[13]   *Ibid.*, p. 576.

[14]   *Ibid.*, p. 575.

[15]   *Ibid.*, p. 575.

[16]   *Ibid.*, p. 276.

that Tocqueville eulogized in 1830. Let it be said directly: the American woman has long ago left the social confines she bowed under in 1830, and she will not and cannot return there with respect for herself or respect from her male companions. A non-American pope and the likes of American apologist Phyllis Schafley can urge that return and paint some idealized state in the most sentimental of pastels: it will not happen.

The pope also based his disciplinary exclusion of women from priestly ordination on this syllogism: the first followers of Jesus, only men, were called to be priests in order to carry on Christ's mission in the world; but women are not men; so women cannot be ordained as priests. Whatever one thinks of a syllogism that simply begs the question, we must consider its statement in theological terms. John Paul II maintained that the priest has become an *alter Christus*, is Christ continuing his salvific work for all ages. The priest takes on an iconic status, a holy representation of Christ that can only be recognized in a male.[17]

What should we make of this foundational theological argument: Christ is the bridegroom of the Church, his bride; since only men can be bridegrooms, only men can represent Christ the bridegroom? Not much, really. The metaphor echoes the Old Testament's characterization of the relationship of Yahweh to Israel. It meant to convey that the relationship was one of special closeness and divine steadfastness. It was not suggesting that Yahweh is male or Israel female. In an argumentative sleight-of-hand, the Vatican transforms a rhetorical truth (Christ is like a bridegroom) into a factual truth (Christ is a bridegroom) Transformation accomplished, it then argues that since only men can be bridegrooms, only men can represent Christ the bridegroom. Such lack of logic could lead to other absurdities. So, for example, one might argue that male Nazarene carpenters represent

---

17   Cf. *Ordinatio Sacerdotalis: Letter of Pope John Paul II to the Bishops of the Catholic Church*. In it the Pope says: "1) Priestly ordination, which hands on the office entrusted by Christ to his apostles...has...from the beginning always been reserved to men alone." He quotes the *Declaration Inter Insigniores* of Paul VI: "...and concludes that the Church 'does not consider herself authorized to admit women to priestly ordination.'" He ends the letter with the firm statement that "I declare that the Church has no authority whatsoever to confer priestly ordination on women..."Cf. also the *Commentary on the Declaration Inter Insigniores*, Sacred Congregation for the Doctrine of the Faith, January 27, 1977, paragraph #102: "Christ is the bridegroom of the church, whom he won for himself with his blood, and the salvation brought by him is the new covenant: by using this language revelation shows why the incarnation took place according to the male gender, and make it impossible to ignore this historical reality. For this reason, only a man can take the part of Christ, be a sign of his presence, in a word 'represent' him (that is, be an effective sign of his presence) in the essential acts of the covenant."

Christ more fully than male American priests do. Or again, since only women can be brides, only women can represent the Church fully to Christ and the world.

Let me respond personally: I lived as a Jesuit for nineteen years; I worked as a Jesuit priest for six years; as a religious psychologist I counseled, consulted with, trained, and had close friendships with diocesan and religious priests in the United States and around the world for thirty-five years. In all that time and across all these diverse situations, I have never considered myself an *alter Christus*, never listened to another priest identify himself as such, never heard a layperson extol his or her pastor as an *alter Christus*. Nor have I recognized any claim, exercised by me or from another, of some revelatory iconic status. Experience tells me this theological rationale, at its best, is abstract; at the worst, it is an illusory justification for male power.

Ever since the Second Council of Nicea's condemnation of iconoclasm,[18] for orthodox Catholics "iconic" cannot mean "sacrament" (a symbol that reveals presence and also creates it) but only "sacramental" (a sign that points outside of itself to a presence). A priest is not Christ but can only point to Christ. I have often myself thought, and I have heard other priests say, that we express Christ to the community of believers and represent him and his teachings to the world. We remind people of Christ's love, his promises, and make him present in and through the church's sacraments.

I have known many holy, strong, and capable women, whether religious or laywomen, who have consistently in their daily life performed these Christ-like functions, except those associated with the priest's exclusive sacramental role. To claim that a woman cannot witness to, represent, or be a sign of Christ's presence fails the test of reality. She can, and does.

Following the teachings of Vatican II, theologians write eloquently about "the church as the People of God"; since Pius XII's *Mysticii Corporis* in 1943 they routinely speak of Catholics as members of the body of Christ; some even agree with Dutch Dominican Edward Schillebeecx that the church is the sacrament of Christ in the world. I know of no theologian, no pope, who would dare to suggest that a woman by her nature could not be, or is not, included in the People of God, the Mystical Body, the Catholic Church as sacrament. Therefore, a Catholic woman participates by her baptism in the presence of Christ in this world. She is not simply "iconic" or pointing to Christ; she rather partakes in being the sacrament of his presence. In this order of things, she far surpasses being only a priest, an icon, a sign drawing attention to Christ. To be a priest would be an honor, would allow her to serve the community in ways she cannot now, but it would nowhere approach the worth and dignity she already has as the sacrament of Christ.

---

[18]   Cf. *Op. cit., New Catholic Encyclopedia*, Vol. VII, pp. 327-329.

One may argue that American Catholics would not accept women priests. It may be true that recently immigrated Catholics, ones from societies in which women have been traditionally relegated to inferior status, and ones who have had only minimal educational opportunities, may have difficultly adjusting to women in authoritative religious roles. But this would occur for social and educational reasons, not religious ones. The vast majority of Catholics in the United States, those with European roots and immigrant experience before the middle years of the last century, do not regard women as by nature excluded from the priesthood. If women can be religious sisters, parish administrators, eucharistic ministers, religious education teachers, and lectors at mass, then only a theological fiction and an unwillingness to share authority and power can explain an exclusion of women from the full ministry of Christ's sacraments.

Indeed, our bishops should think deeply and prayerfully about this. American women born since 1960 comprise the population that may furnish the church with priestly vocations. But these women—to the extent they have sound education, have integrated fully into American society, and have accepted the position of women as equal morally, intellectually, socially, and politically to that of men—can only regard the prohibiting of ordination to women as, at best, retrograde, and, at worst, prejudicial and nakedly greedy. Can anyone reasonably expect a mother to encourage a son whom she loves to enter into a clerical society she considers out of touch with reality and even immoral? In the latter years of the last century and the beginning years of this one, vocations to the priesthood have declined dramatically. No way can they be judged sufficient to the needs of the American church. Moreover, a majority of current vocations surfaces out of the latest waves of immigrant peoples from Asia and South America, from communities still living out of their former social prejudice about women in society, from families still struggling to find their place in this country.

In deference to recent Catholic immigrants and to a European society, including Roman, that still tends to consider women as morally, intellectually, and socially inferior to men, the bishops of America should institute immediately the role of lay deaconess in our church. This position has scriptural roots and a place in early church history; it does not tackle directly the theological obfuscations surrounding *alter Christus*; it opens up a position of dignity, respect, and authority for church women; and finally it offers some hope to more than half of our church that male exclusivity may someday disappear, like an outmoded dinosaur, as men garner further enlightenment and build up their moral courage.

III. Religion and Politics Then and Now

Tocqueville attributes democracy to Catholics because they draw a firm line between religious dogma and political truth. Revealed dogma, the fruit of scripture and tradition, once defined must be believed. No discussion except as regards interpretation of a dogma's meaning in light of current church experience is needed. Political creeds, the product of momentary rhetorical declarations, call for open inquiry and ongoing free discussion. As no Catholic dogma stands in opposition to democratic and republican institutions of government, Catholics may approach politics freely, independently, and with open and inquiring minds.

In other societies—notably in medieval, Catholic Europe—religion and politics united. Religion runs a serious risk joining itself to political power. It alone aims to give believers hope for immortality while political fortunes ebb and flow with fleeting experiences, fortuitous coalitions, and passing needs. However, if religion must seek a political partner, it does so more prudently with monarchies that tend to endure and remain immobile than with democracies that experience ongoing agitation and instability: the ruling party leads but also suffers a continuing challenge from its frustrated opposition. Unless religion desires to risk the fluctuations of democracy, it should scrupulously keep distinct from any and all political alliances. As Tocqueville wisely comments: "in allying itself with a political power, religion increases its power over some and loses the hope of reigning over all."[19]

Tocqueville's caution about close ties between religion and politics has special relevance in our time. Ever since the birth of the Moral Majority and the religiously inspired social conservatives, religion has flirted with political marriages of convenience. It offers a *quid pro quo* contract: if you will promise to pass laws in line with our moral values and institutional needs, we will line up denominational votes that you can bank on in your quest to remain in office. Politicians for their part may or may not buy into the religious agenda; they may or may not follow through with results surpassing lip service; they certainly will remain in this holy-appearing alliance only as long as the votes are delivered.

In the social landscape of this new century, many issues disturb religious certitudes. In a war against terrorism, do preemptive declarations of war against potential enemies fulfill the conditions of a just war? In a racially prejudiced society can capital punishment that falls disproportionately on black criminals actually be just? As we learn more about the biological and genetic contributions to a homosexual orientation, can we reasonably assert that all homosexual and lesbian behavior is unnatural and thus sinful? In the midst of a contentious and unresolved debate whether a human embryo is always and in all conditions

---

[19]   *Op. cit.,* Tocqueville, Vol. II., p. 284.

a human being, can we declare unequivocally that stem cell research into curing devastating human diseases, if it utilizes living human embryos, is intrinsically immoral?

The Republican Party has denominated itself as the home of socially conservative values. It trumpets raucous public stands on issues dear to many Catholics: a constitutional amendment banning gay marriage; judicial appointments aimed at overturning *Roe vs. Wade*; regulations against federal funding for stem cell research if scientists use living human embryos; federal laws against euthanasia; laws requiring juveniles to inform their parents before receiving birth control or abortion assistance from physicians; use of educational vouchers that needy students may use to attend religious schools; grants of federal monies to churches engaged in public charities. Many Catholics—laity, priests, and bishops—support this political party, privately and publicly, in the church's name, because of moral, "value" positions of these kinds.

The same Republican Party, however, glowingly supports a war in Iraq that John Paul II called unjustified. It continues to endorse training military, paramilitary, and police forces in Latin and South America that priests, religious, and laity have protested consistently and loudly over many years. It champions tax cuts that favor the richest among the population while giving scant relief to millions of struggling middle class families. It stands behind its prescription drug amendment to Medicare even though it promises a windfall to pharmaceutical companies and scarcely more than confusion to the elderly. The list could go on. The point stands starkly evident: if the Catholic Church marries itself to the Republican Party, it risks alienating large numbers of its members who judge, rightly or wrongly, that many of that party's positions are immoral. To echo Tocqueville: the church may gain power and allegiance from some because of this union; it certainly will lose moral authority over, and the membership of, many others. When the force of religion joins politics, religious allegiance slowly dissolves while the power of politics inflates.

As I write this chapter (in the presidential campaign year 2004), some American bishops have taken an astonishing stance involving the interface of politics and religion. They have threatened Catholic legislators who publicly support a Pro-Choice position with excommunication (the public denial of communion). Obviously, since the Democratic Party advocates a woman's right to choose without governmental interference, the targeted legislators are Democrats. The basis for this episcopal warning seems to be that a Pro-Choice legislator publicly flouts the bishops' stand against abortion. One can only speculate how an individual bishop determines that this disagreement merits such a severe ecclesiastical censure.

The kindest explanations center around two arguments. In the first one, the bishop might cite the third canon of the Fourth Lateran Council. As previously explained,[20] it cautions medieval monarchs that they must either assist the church in rooting out the Albigensian heresy or face forfeiting their civil power to rule. By stretching some, a Pro-Choice legislator could be considered an advocate of heresy who should lose both religious and civil support.

Secondly, a bishop might argue that one prominently holding this position causes grave scandal; namely, that some Catholic woman might choose to obtain an abortion because of the Catholic legislator's support of her freedom to make that choice. This argument lacks credence. No legislator is encouraging any woman to have an abortion. No woman has claimed that she actually procured an abortion because of a legislator's Pro-Choice stance. Indeed, it strains credibility to think that a woman would be induced to lose her freedom of choice, that she would meekly step into sin, by following a legislator who advocates her freedom to make her own unimpeded decision in the matter. Since a serious scandal involves a determination that one's sinful actions have led others into sin, without evidence of sin on the part of either legislator or woman a reasonable person strains to confirm that judgment.

Bishops by their office are required to teach, govern, and sanctify their people. Evidence abounds that current church authorities in America are failing. In particular, their teaching about sexual matters has negligible impact on increasing percentages of laity. Recurrent national polls reveal small differences between Catholic and Protestant respondents in their attitudes and practices concerning birth control, abortion, homosexuality, divorce and remarriage. The moral control the hierarchy used to exercise through the demands of Confession has all but vanished as the practice of that sacrament has substantially waned. One hates to think that these condemnatory bishops, faced with their own ineptness in persuading their people to follow their moral dictates, are resorting to civil authority to make Catholics obey them. If, indeed, they could force Catholic legislators, out of fear of being branded as evil and unworthy representatives, to vote for a federal law prohibiting abortion and that helped carry the legislative day, then Catholics, at least, would stop having legal abortions. Sadly, in this scenario their subsequent restraint and return to obedience would come, not from a sound and educated moral judgment, but rather from a servile fear of civil incarceration.

I suspect, however, that the real causes of these bishop's unprecedented threats lie in two ordinary human failings: ignorance and fear.

How could a bishop equate holding a Pro-Choice legislative position with supporting, encouraging, or suborning abortion? Our elected representatives live in a world of compromises and function in the realm of possibilities. They do not trade in absolutes; they rather strike as they can the best possible bargains. In an arena

---

[20]   Cf. discussion about the Veto controversy in Ireland, page 39.

of competitive and conflicting needs and desires and beliefs, they strive to obtain for their constituents and for our country the best law available here and now. And they do this always with an eye to future legislation, to bills they desperately desire to have pass or determinedly hope to derail. Pro-Choice legislators may be making a variety of statements by assuming that stance. They may want to block expanding governmental intrusion into the private life of our citizens and value highly the privacy of a citizen's relationship with her doctor. They may support the ongoing emancipation of women from male dominance or join others in fighting for women's rights, so that those others, in turn, may incline to line up with them in the struggle to expand the rights of other minorities. Or as sensible tacticians they may judge that the political and social environment at this moment is not supportive of legislation outlawing abortion and, indeed, that such action would create greater evils than we currently suffer under legalized abortion. Considering reasons such as these, who could condemn their authors as immoral or suborning immorality? One might disagree with these and similar positions, but how could one reasonably conclude that they merit excommunication?

If so-called Catholic legislators were championing abortion as a morally permissible act, as a private contraceptive method with no societal implications or repercussions, that might justly earn episcopal outcry. Or if they were publicly contradicting the church's teaching about the immorality of abortion, or challenging its right to instruct church members about that teaching, then bishops could condemn them as interfering with their legitimate authority. Or if they were taking public positions such as pressing for legislation for funding abortions with federal monies and for removing financial support from orphanages, they could rightly accuse them of suborning abortion and making the birth of an unwanted child more difficult.

If a bishop thought that one of his communicants was espousing such public positions, then his judgment to deny that person communion would stand on firmer ground. In the present instance, however, I know of no Catholic legislator who publicly urges any of the above.

American bishops have been losing control of, and moral authority over, their congregants since the revolt against *Humanae Vitae* in 1968. Moreover, responses to the Second Vatican Council left the American church split between advocates for change and advocates for the certainty and stability of the Tridentine, Pre-Vatican II church. In this divided community, Catholic strategists hit upon one issue that would unify the Catholic people, energize them to work together, and reinforce the bishops' role of moral leadership. Certainly, they opined, every Catholic would follow them in the drive to outlaw abortion.

Many Catholics, indeed, buy into the battle against legalized abortion. They faithfully troop to Washington every year on the anniversary of *Roe vs. Wade*. They stand outside abortion clinics in their community, trying to stop pregnant women from entering, attempting to convert them or to shame them into adhering to the official Catholic position. Some Catholics have, in their zeal, even bombed local abortion clinics and murdered hometown physicians daring to perform abortions.

Yet many other Catholics have not heeded the episcopal call to arms. Some would argue that neither scripture or tradition, the only spheres of episcopal authority, say anything about abortion.[21] An argument based on "Thou Shalt Not Kill" and "Right-to-Life" begs the question. The prohibition against the unjust taking of human life turns on a prior question: When does the fetus become a person? Neither scripture nor tradition responds definitively to that query. And modern scientific research has as yet given no compelling answer.

Others would maintain that "Pro-Choice" vs. "Right-to-Life" deals with public policy. It signals a scrimmage about whether a citizen consensus exists supportive of laws leaning one way or the other. The morality of abortion is neither the point nor the question.

In 2002 the American bishops became embroiled in the scandal of clerical sexual abuse of minors. It touched them all as abusive bishops offered up their resignations; and indirectly, as bishop after bishop stood nakedly embarrassed by their ineptness in handling this criminal situation and by their complicity of silence in protecting themselves, their priests, and the church to the detriment and harm of youthful victims.

This book addresses the erosion of episcopal moral authority. It seeks to show why it has plummeted to its present sad and weakened condition; it hopes also to point out solid ways of regaining that authority. In the present Pro-Choice furor it appears more than likely that an individual bishop, knowing that he must reassert his authority and frustrated that his efforts have borne meager fruit—in keeping Catholic women from getting abortions, in marshalling the laity to speak as one against the practice, in influencing legislation prohibiting it within the United States—in desperation pinned his hopes on excommunication as the sure way of forcing the issue and regaining moral standing among his people.

Tocqueville praised the Catholic Church in America of the 1830's because of its wisdom in separating the spheres of religion and politics. He congratulated the Catholic people of that time and place as being the most democratic of American citizens. He noted approvingly their religious faithfulness, on the one hand, and their free and independent entering into political discourse, on the other. Whatever else one may say in this 21st American Century, this much seems abundantly clear: by seeking to enhance episcopal authority and to enforce church

---

[21]   For an excellent, brief, theological statement, cf. Wills, Garry, "The Bishops Vs.The Bible," *The New York Times*, June 27, 2004, p. 13.

discipline through marrying religious and civil power, bishops diminish respect for themselves and their church. Moral authority does not grow by foisting their leadership tasks on to politicians' shoulders.

IV. Religious Signs and Symbols in a Democracy

Tocqueville offers this succinct description of the American way of approaching reality:

> To escape from the spirit of system, from the yoke of habits, from family maxims, from class opinions, and, up to a certain point, from national prejudices; to take tradition only as information, and current facts only as a useful study for doing otherwise and better; to seek the reason for things by themselves and in themselves alone, to strive for a result without letting themselves be chained to the means, and to see through the form to the foundation: these are the principal features that characterize what I shall call the philosophic method of the Americans.[22]

In other words, we tend to come to experience without a lot of preconceptions and strive to get to the core of situations without a lot of distractions. He goes on to emphasize that—

> ...nothing revolts the human mind more in times of equality than the idea of submitting to forms. Men who live in these times suffer [representational] figures with impatience; symbols appear to them to be puerile artifices that are used to veil or adorn for their eyes truths it would be more natural to show to them altogether naked and in broad daylight; the sight of ceremonies leaves them cold, and they are naturally brought to attach only a secondary importance to the details of worship.
>
> Those charged with regulating the external form of religions in democratic centuries ought indeed to pay attention to these natural instincts of human intelligence in order not to struggle unnecessarily against them.[23]

He realizes that religion, to take hold of a person's life, must engage, not only the intellect, but also the imagination. Religious people need various forms, different

---

[22]   *Op. cit.,* vol. II, p. 403.

[23]   *Ibid.,* p. 421.

practices, to internalize their beliefs. He urges, however, that these liturgical and devotional exercises be few and related specifically to the religion's dogmatic core. A multiplication of forms, especially those that sidetrack the believer in the task of "knowing, loving, and serving God in this world and preparing to be with him in the next" (as the Baltimore Catechism teaches) causes impatience and creates disdain. Religion "should be less burdened with external practices in democratic times than in all others."[24] If religious leaders insist on minute observances, they will generate a "flock of impassioned zealots in the midst of an incredulous multitude."[25]

In a monarchical system, the ruler, through his agents of control, seeks to enforce conformity to his desires throughout his kingdom. In a religious hierarchical system, control, indeed, may generate a similarity and continuity of behavior; it fails, however, to create belief or instill love. As long as the system stays in place, immobile, with fixed rewards and punishments, without the influence of competing exterior systems, external conformity of behavior will give an appearance of faith-filled adherence to internalized beliefs. But should the controls weaken or outside attractions gather strength, the expected behaviors become, at first, sporadic, and in the end, absent. Gradually, illusory faith just disappears.

Since the Protestant Reformation, the Catholic Church has constructed an ecclesiastical fortress. It has firmly separated itself from its heretical and schismatic foes, scrupulously condemned the least aberrant beliefs and behaviors, and demanded strict adherence to rules and regulations from its faithful. In this Tridentine church forms became necessary, even to the point of substituting for the core of beliefs that they were fashioned to reinforce.

With the Second Vatican Council, the church finally relaxed its defensive posture, reached out to embrace the world, and showed ways of joining others rather than condemning them. When Pope John XXIII's *aggiornamento* opened up windows to people and societies other than Catholic, it broke down the closed system that had contained, protected, and immobilized the Catholic faithful for at least four centuries. It also let in the exhilaration and instability of change. Many grasped the changes and signs of growth with relief and hope; many others recoiled with fear from a religious landscape suddenly made unclear and unstable. The former discarded forms that had manifested conformity but hindered core beliefs; the latter begged for, worked for, and demanded the return to the forms that had promised security here and certainty hereafter. To synthesize: some welcomed a church based on equality and communication; others yearned for the monarchical church in which leaders commanded and followers obeyed.

---

[24] *Ibid.,* p. 421.

[25] *Ibid.,* p. 422.

The Tridentine church had stressed the divinity of Christ. The Alpha and Omega, he has existed from all time and will come in glory to judge the living and the dead. He sits now at his Father's right hand in anticipation of our sharing forever with him the fruits of our constant belief in him here on earth. Our gothic churches soared heavenward, our priests celebrated mass in front of us and above us, and they offered Christ back to his Father with the sacred host elevated high over us all. Everywhere distance reigned: priests were raised up and out of the lay state; bishops and pope were chosen to rule over God's people; though one of us, Jesus, the Christ, has ascended to his Father and reigns victoriously over all of creation.

But as the distances increased between the divine and the human, reassurances were desperately needed. How, indeed, could we be sure that the divine really cared about us, truly listened to our heartfelt prayers, and actually intervened in our favor? Only intermediaries, people like us but holier, could calm our fears and offer the promise of divine assistance. In 1854 Pope Pius IX established Mary's unique holiness by declaring her Immaculate Conception. A century later Pius XII formally acknowledged her special place in heaven as having been assumed, body and soul there, to be now and forever with her divine son. At the Second Vatican Council the fathers spoke in the "Constitution on the Church" approvingly of her as "Mediatrix," and at its conclusion, Paul VI gave her the appellation of "Mother of the Church." This powerful woman now stands as our advocate in heaven. She forever bridges the gap between the human and the divine, one, we may say, that had already been closed through the life, death, and resurrection of her divine-human son.

From 1978 to 2005 John Paul II presided over the hierarchical church. He manifested a strong devotion to Mary; he also maintained firm control over the church. He did his utmost to preserve and strengthen its hierarchical structure. He, alone, ruled as pope. His chosen and entrenched aristocracy, the cardinals he created, surrounded him. He selected provincial governors, bishops faithful to his hierarchical concept of church, for dioceses around the globe. Over all, God, the Transcendent One, rules. In the world of John Paul II verticality, distance, and top-down authority carried the day.

As if to fill the ever-widening chasm between laity and priest, priest and bishop, bishop and cardinal, cardinal and pope, earth and heaven, John Paul led a concerted effort to seed the threatening space with a legion of saints. These men and women, human beings like us, lived out their human days in extraordinary holiness, faithful to their God and their church. In twenty-four years this pope canonized four hundred and sixty-eight people, more than the total number canonized by all previous popes since Sixtus V created the Congregation of Rites in

1588. We should pray to them, beseech them to represent us, before the divine, distant God.

In the Middle Ages, Catholics approached divinity through the adoration of relics, the performance of penitential acts, the participation in novenas and pilgrimages, and the public celebration of locally favored saints. All were methods of honoring God, or, at least, placating him. In the immigrant American church, many of the more absurd superstitions and idolatries gradually died out. But as late as the years of Vatican II American Catholics said the rosary, wore scapulars and miraculous medals, made novenas and attended retreats, went to benediction and walked the stations, faithfully made the seven first Fridays in honor of the Sacred Heart and the five first Saturdays out of devotion to the Blessed Mother, and crowned her as May Queen. For some, these rites brought a sense of closeness to, knowledge of, and love for an ever-present and immanent God; for others, they became the focus of the faith in lieu of an absent One. Some came to "know, love, and serve" God more; others, at least, served him by obeying his ordained ministers. Behind it all lurked the slippery question: Who is the good Catholic?—the one in a loving relationship with God; or the one who fulfills carefully the diversity of ritualistic requirements?

The church has long distinguished between act and intention. It recognizes that its sacramental ministers could in their official duties fulfill the requisite forms without having personal holiness or grace, while even being in a sinful state. If the forms were attended to exactly, the sacrament still becomes a font of Christ's saving grace *ex opere operato* (by the performance of the act). The sacrament's validity did not depend on the quality of the priest's intention *ex opere operantis* (by the performance of this particular actor).

Out of a lifetime of similar experiences, I recall one that seared the distinction, and its sacramental absurdity, into my soul.

Early one morning, as a grade school boy, I served mass for a visiting priest at a side altar. The middle-aged man appeared normal except that he seemed quite nervous. During the first part of the mass he recited the Latin prayers loudly and slowly, and his gestures were pronounced, even exaggerated. As the mass progressed, I found myself paying attention to him and to his actions; all inclination to pray or any sense of being in the presence of God faded away.

By the moment of consecration, the nervousness reached a shrill peak. As he bent over the host in his trembling hands, he struggled for minutes (that seemed like hours) to pronounce the formulaic words:

- *Hoc—hooc—hach—aoc—hoc-oc;*

- *Ess—iss—isss—est—eet—etat—tt;*

- *E-nim—e-nim—h-nim—n-im;*
- *Cor-pus—poos—posse—uss;*
- *Me-u-um—my-num—ay-num—may—may—maynum—num-um.*

At last, he sighed and genuflected for a whole minute. I too sighed—in sheer relief. And I felt afraid: what would happen if he had made a mistake? I really had no sense of Christ's presence; I only hoped that God was not angry. I know what theologians say about the requisite form and matter of the sacrament; I also know that on that day, there, for me, there was no sacrament.

In this dramatic instance the form, the sign required to point to God and to make Christ present, became its own reason for being. The form had no other foundation than itself. The stumbling exactness, an obscene idol, had taken the place of God.

A religious form as sign directs us toward God. It functions as a transmitter by which the desire for the divine is awakened and the way to the divine presence indicated. The sign, a sacramental, points outside of itself, humbly serving one greater than itself.

Tocqueville cautions that such signs should not be multiplied in a democratic society. Obviously, first to go should be ones that tend to become ends in themselves, ones that worshippers may readily fixate on as if they were God. A sign—be it a person or an action—can quickly become an idol.

Religious leaders should also eliminate actions that have slight worth or meaning other than as indications of obedience and as occasions of loyalty. One remembers in the Pre-Vatican II church, for example, the Friday abstinence from meat that had negligible dietary effect and functioned more as a minor irritation than as a penitential exercise. Or, again, recall the prohibition against swallowing water before taking communion as if its presence, or absence, affected the dignity of the reception. Or, finally, picture church visits and women, required at all times to wear something on their head while there, decked out with hankies that caused aesthetic shudders and contributed nothing to modesty.

Careful consideration should be paid to the signs that are constitutive of the rituals surrounding the sacraments. They are meant to direct the worshipper's attention to the sacrament; when, rather, they force a focus on the ritual itself, they should be eliminated. Music can awaken the imagination, elevate the mind, and open the heart when chosen well and performed expertly. Music that captures and holds one because of inferior quality and shoddy performance simply distracts from the sacred occasion. Prayers recited but not prayed; prayers using gender-biased words and phrases; prayers rushed through and mumbled unintelligibly all fail in their essential signing function. Sermons meant to complement and expand upon the sacrament of the word, if barely prepared and lamely delivered, are better off left unsaid than being allowed to generate feelings ranging from boredom to dismay to downright anger. Indeed, the overall ritual surrounding the sacramental moment calls for a presentation that introduces, highlights, and celebrates the mysterious glory of God's love made actual here, in this place, among us. The ritual, an interlocking series of words and actions meant to focus the worshipper's mind and heart on God, should be no more or less than the set within which the divine action occurs. As even a casual theatergoer knows, no play, even a superior one, can compete successfully with a wretched set. In that instance, the background grabs center stage and consumes the audience's emotions while the dramatic action retreats to the emotional margins of even the motivated and best-intentioned listener. As previously noted, the obsessive-compulsive explosion of the words of consecration simply cancelled out for me the accompanying miracle of transubstantiation.

A symbol differs from a sign, a sacrament from a sacramental. A sign transmits and occasions transferal; a symbol transforms in and through a relationship. A sign received leaves the same person in a different place and stance; a symbol experienced creates a different person in the same relationship and stance. In the context of this book the American hierarchy will find transformation, not by a multiplication of sacramentals, like John Paul's expansive roster of the holy, but by relating to the Catholic people openly and through love.

Somehow, over the course of the ages, Catholic orthodoxy has come to mean preserving Christ's revelation of his relationship to his Father rather than using his experience as a guide to our own relationship with our Father. And orthopraxis has become fulfilling correctly and wholeheartedly clerical laws, regulations, and rules, instead of striving ever more constantly to relate lovingly to God among us. The church, like a master jeweler, has been given a rare diamond necklace; it keeps it in a heavily guarded vault, seldom permitting any display of its gorgeousness. The church, like a master dance instructor, teaches the most elaborate steps to aspiring dancers, but few invitations go out for the royal ball. The soul, then, like a disappointed Cinderella, sits alone, ready but unadorned, with only her dreams.

Tocqueville wisely commented that democratic peoples become impatient with signs, especially those divorced from their foundation. Worth dwells, finally, in the foundation: in life, with love, in well-being. In religion, what essentially and ultimately matters is one's relationship to God. The church has only one task: to lead us to God and to support us as we relate to that Divinity.

The sacraments are symbolic moments, prepared for by sacramental signs, of divine-human relationship. In the sacrament we meet God and are transformed. Given our human nature, we need to approach the divine through our relationship to one another in community and through our faith-filled openness to our own life. As we draw close to the divine a great silence wells up within till we find ourselves, as Eliot graphically describes, "At the still point of the turning world...there the dance is."[26] In that instant we become transformed into the Living Spirit that embraces the fullness of divinity and the whole of our humanity. As the Apostle Paul states it: we are taken up into the God "in whom we live, and move, and have our being." God becomes our alpha and omega, not as transcendent, but as God-with-us, the God in whom we dwell.

V. Religion's Relationship to Public Opinion

Sprinkled among his observations about American life, Tocqueville gives us gems of practical wisdom. As if he could foresee the Catholic Church in America one hundred and seventy-five years in the future, he counsels our bishops as follows:

> As men become more alike and equal, it is important that religions, while carefully putting themselves out of the way of the daily movement of affairs, not collide unnecessarily with the generally accepted ideas and permanent interests that reign among the mass; for common opinion appears more and more as the first and most irresistible of powers; there is no support outside of it strong enough to permit long resistance to its blows.[27]

If one accepts the truth of this statement, then prudence should lead bishops to deliberate carefully between necessary and unnecessary collisions. Prudence would also dictate that the Vatican be informed of their conclusions.

Prior to 1964, the church held the position that artificial birth control was intrinsically immoral as being directly in opposition to the natural law. Being immoral *de facto* (by the very nature of things) nobody, including the church, could make such acts moral. Then Paul VI called together a papal commission to consider the possibility that the church's stance could change. By that very act the pope made clear that artificial birth control was immoral *de jure* (by church law) and not *de facto*. No theologian today questions that current ecclesiastical discipline prohibits artificial birth control; many, however, seriously doubt that the prohibition flows from natural law.

For Americans raised in a representative society, Paul VI made a fatal mistake when he summoned a lay commission of married Catholics, asked for their considered and prayerful decision about the morality of artificial birth control, and then

---

[26]   Eliot, T. S. *Four Quartets*. New York: Harcourt, Brace and World, 1943, p. 15.

[27]   *Op. cit.,* vol. II, pp. 421-422

summarily disregarded their decision. One does not in America gather experts together, seek their advice, and then dismiss it when the one dismissing it has no expertise in the field. As is obvious, neither the pope nor his celibate advisors have any noteworthy credentials when it comes to sexual intercourse in marriage. His rejection of the commission's advice can then be attributed to one or other of the following: he instituted the commission thinking that it would agree with the traditional position and thus lend the weight of combined expertise to it, or he had no intention, from the beginning, of listening to any advice that ran contrary to his already made-up mind. In either scenario he comes off poorly: he seriously miscalculated when he summoned these advisors, or he unconscionably played a game with them.

Since that political debacle, American Catholics have taken the matter into their own hands. They know their personal experience in marriage; they recognize that no one has the expertise about, and credentials in, their marriage more than the couple itself. In this situation they have, by a vast majority, agreed with their non-Catholic fellow citizens that immorality rests, not in artificial birth control, but rather in not using it when to forestall having children is judged to be necessary or reasonable. When the church plays hair-splitting, theological games about abstention and rhythm, the church, not they, sins.

American Catholics employ artificial birth control in family planning. Most do not consider it sinful; most do not confess their actions as if they were sinful; and most have concluded that the church is, on this issue, the sinner.

Following Tocqueville's advice, American bishops would be wise if they accepted that the prohibition against artificial birth control is a matter of church discipline, not dogma. The Catholic people in America know this, and attempts to convince them otherwise are doomed to fail and can only further weaken episcopal authority. That being said, our bishops need to impress on Rome that insistence on this prohibition simply discredits them and the church in the eyes of Americans, Catholics and non-Catholics alike.

By their decision American Catholics have concluded that marriage has two intrinsic and separable ends: procreation and conjugal love. They know, personally and emotionally, that sexual interaction in marriage adds to, and creates, a healthy relationship. Moreover, this activity sometimes includes a desire for, and a hope of having, children; most of the time, however, it does not. To restrict sexual intercourse to occasions when children are desired or when conception is physically improbable leaves married couples between the ages of 18-42 with long periods when their sexual interaction becomes artificially scheduled rather than flowing out of their marital love for, need for, and desire for each other. Our Catholic people have rejected this clerical position as unrealistic, destructive, and even immoral.

Moral theologians, however, rush to argue that the church cannot allow this separation of the dual ends of procreation and marital love. If love can actively be divorced from the possibility of pregnancy, they argue, then how can one logically hold that premarital sex and homosexual sex are immoral: the former employing birth control, the latter engaging in non-procreative sexual interaction. One can only respond: good question! Whatever the answer may be, that does not change the fact that most fertile couples in America know personally that marital love and the possibility of pregnancy are separable and require separate decisions.

We have already spoken about women priests. We may add here that Americans, at least educated ones and those fully integrated into our society, accept the equality of men and women as a given. For the church, therefore, to hold otherwise is to set up another unnecessary collision with public opinion. Scientific evidence, personal experience, social and political and economic data buttress this nearly universal judgment of gender equality. One cannot conceive how this perception ever could or ever would be changed; one only expects that it will grow firmer with the accumulation of ongoing and diverse evidence.

No matter the theological justifications floated by a European pope, American bishops would be prudent to follow these suggestions:

- Recognize that Benedict XVI, a devoted disciple of John Paul II, will never allow the ordination of women.

- Accept that both men thought they had a theological rationale for this rigid position, while most American Catholics recognize their prohibition as only a disciplinary one, as mandatory celibacy is, and subject to change.

- Communicate to Rome that any insistence on a dogmatic basis for excluding women from ordination will be both opposed and not accepted.

- Communicate to Rome that the sacramental system in America is weakening and may tragically disappear without the ordination of women.

- Communicate to their people that they disagree with this papal argumentation and decision while they recognize the papal authority to impose this disciplinary restriction.

- Recognize that a failure to implement these suggestions leaves them damned by association: the real reason why the Vatican and the current American hierarchy refuse to ordain women lies in a refusal to share power and authority, and in a self-centered determination to protect male prerogative.

In the first chapter we considered the struggle against religious intolerance that brought many Catholic immigrants to these shores in the 18th and 19th centuries. We also saw how they suffered that same intolerance in many of the English colonies and, indeed, in some states for years after the ratification of our federal Constitution. Given that history, the church in America and its people readily accept, in the abstract, at least, that government should not make any one religious faith an officially established one, nor should it allow discrimination against anyone because of a religious faith. Each and every person has the right to follow his or her own conscience in matters of faith and morals, as long as such does not disrupt public order. Therefore, churches and ecclesial communities have the right to organize themselves, to teach and govern their adherents without governmental interference. Indeed, Catholics join the bulk of their fellow citizens in standing firmly for religious tolerance and freedom.

At the Second Vatican Council, the assembled fathers issued a "Declaration on Religious Freedom."[28] In no uncertain terms it opens its first chapter with this ringing affirmation:

> This Vatican Synod declares that the human person has a right to religious freedom. This freedom means that all men are to be immune from coercion on the part of individuals or of social groups and of any human power, in such wise that in matters religious no one is to be forced to act in a manner contrary to his own beliefs.[29]

As an extension of that freedom, they further struck a solid posture against proselytism when it involves even subtle force:

> ...in spreading religious faith and introducing religious practices, everyone ought at all times to refrain from any manner of action which might seem to carry a hint of coercion or of a kind of persuasion that would be dishonorable or unworthy, especially when dealing with poor or uneducated people. Such a manner of action would have to be considered an abuse of one's own right and a violation of the right of others.

---

[28]   Abbott, Walter M. (ed), *The Documents of Vatican II*. New York: The America Press, 1966, pp. 675-696.

[29]   *Ibid.*, pp. 678-679.

The church, therefore, has officially come to a position contrary to much of its European history. One need only think of violent attacks against the followers of Islam as crusaders made repeated forays into the Middle East in a vain effort to drive them from the Holy Land. Moreover, both Muslims and Jews bore the fires of the Spanish Inquisition as Catholic monarchs joined Dominican inquisitors in forcing conversion or punishing resolute offenders with torture, banishment, and even death.

In our day the Jewish people still bore the stigma of being a race of Christ-killers. The perfidious Jew, the Shylockian merchant trading in diamonds and manipulating financial markets for personal greed, lives on in the Western imagination. Since September 11, 2001 shocked Americans with the lethal hatred of fundamentalist Islamic jihad, the adherents of Islam—innocent or guilty, American or not, patriotic or not, peaceful followers of Mohammed and Abraham or murderous disciples of Osama bin Laden—have become our emotional enemy.

Hear the Second Vatican Council's stern denunciation of discrimination in its "Decree on the Relationship of the Church to Non-Christian Religions"[30]: "...the Church rejects, as foreign to the mind of Christ, any discrimination against men or harassment of them because of their race, color, condition of life, or religion."[31]

If these words are to bear fruit, our religious leaders, our bishops, need to teach vigorously and constantly that no one may legitimately in the name of Christ label members of the Judaic religion as thereby perfidious, of the Islamic faith as thereby infidel, "without faith." Only knowledge of these two faiths and the firm affirmation of Catholicism's admiring stance toward them can begin to change the negative cultural stereotypes handed down to us through the Middle Ages, and reinforced by the politically motivated outrages of religious fundamentalists today.

A church teaching subtly fuels religious intolerance. In its "Decree on Ecumenism,"[32] a statement meant to embrace all Christian churches and ecclesial communities, the Vatican fathers had to include the following:

> For it is through Christ's Catholic Church alone, which is the all-embracing means of salvation, that the fullness of the means of salvation can be obtained. It was to the apostolic college alone, of which Peter is the head, that we believe our Lord entrusted all the blessings of the New Covenant, in order to establish on earth the one Body of Christ

---

[30]   *Ibid.,* pp. 660-668.

[31]   *Ibid.,* p. 668.

[32]   *Ibid.,* pp. 341-366.

into which all those should be fully incorporated who already belong in any way to God's People.[33]

They do concede that people born into other Christian faiths do not sin in that separation.[34] Moreover, they grant that these religious groups possess many aspects of Christian faith that build up Christ's body[35] and act in ways leading their congregants to salvation.[36] But still the referent remains the Catholic Church; separated, Christian brethren "properly baptized are brought into a certain, though imperfect, communion with the Catholic Church.[37]

I worked as a psychotherapist for thirty-two years. My patients were primarily adults, Catholics and Protestants and Jews. In our sessions we talked regularly about their religious faith and its place in their lives. In all that time I never heard any Catholic speaking of the Catholic religion as the only true religion, nor any Protestant or Jew desiring to come into union with the Catholic religion as being the fullness of God's revelation.

For thirteen of those years I offered psychotherapy as a religious psychologist in a pastoral counseling center in Connecticut. For nine years I directed that agency. As colleagues, I worked closely with Congregational ministers, a Baptist and a Methodist and a Presbyterian minister, a Lutheran pastor and a Quaker. My patients came primarily from Congregational and Catholic faiths with fewer representatives of other Christian denominations and a few Jews. However, most patients sought out our center specifically because they wanted a therapy in which their faith held a central and revered place. In this situation I never heard any Christian minister, pastor, or priest speak about Catholicism as the religion most faithful to Christ's desires, nor did anyone, minister or layperson, allude to any wish to become Catholic for that reason. On the contrary, I can firmly say that both colleagues and patients, over the span of my professional life, universally considered all religions to be equal in God's eyes and their own. They did not compare religions as being better or truer; they rather looked to the individual's faithfulness to a chosen religion.

As Tocqueville remarks repeatedly, the American democracy rejects any inequality that stems from heredity or group association. As citizens, each and every American stands as an equal to every fellow citizen. Difference comes from

---

[33] *Ibid.*, p. 346.

[34] *Ibid.*, p. 345.

[35] *Ibid.*, p. 345.

[36] *Ibid.*, p. 346.

[37] *Ibid.*, p. 345.

hard work, courage, and the pursuit of excellence. In terms of religion, how a person lives the religion matters far more than the religion one espouses. Americans care little about one's religious pedigree; they do, however, revere efforts flowing out of one's faith.

Our bishops may doctrinally hold that our religion is the one, true faith revealed by God through his son, Jesus the Christ. But to emphasize that point through preaching and teaching will generally fail to impress Catholic listeners and will generate animosity in non-Catholics. Catholics will not remain so because of Catholicism's claims, nor will non-Catholics be drawn into union because of them. Only lives lived as Christ did will accomplish either goal. Don't tell an American that you are number one unless you can demonstrate that in action. In that regard, most Americans come, emotionally, from Missouri, the "show me" state.

The framers of the U. S. Constitution resolutely turned their backs on historical precedents when they defined the relationship between government and religion. As far back as Ancient Rome, its emperor was proclaimed a god, worthy of worship, and many Christians died for refusing to pay him divine honors. Subsequently, when Christianity spread across the Roman Europe, the Holy Roman Empire employed "Two Swords" to maintain civil accord and combat heresy: one of church authority, the other of secular power loyal to the church. When the Protestant Reformation shattered the marriage of church and state, the situation became, aphoristically stated, *cujus regio, illius religio* (the king's religious faith determined the state religion). Early immigrants to this country came from Catholic Spain, Calvinist Holland, Catholic France, and Anglican England. In the First Amendment, Madison and his companions broke the golden chains linking church and state. They courageously declared: "Congress shall make no law respecting an establishment of religion, or prohibiting the expression thereof." In America, no religion—Christian or non-Christian, Protestant or Catholic—could rely on federal assistance in furthering its faith. Moreover, in this new country religious communities need not fear that the practice of their faith would bring negative attention, create legal obstacles, or stimulate persecution from federal authorities.

The First Amendment did not prohibit the states from entertaining officially and legally a given faith. As we have seen, some states kept their religious preferences for many years after 1783. Today, however, throughout our union no legal traces of religious establishment remain.

Americans unanimously agree that government has no place in supporting one religion over another, or in preferring any denomination at the expense of another.

At the Second Vatican Council, the participants did not reject universally the establishment of state religion. They did, however, demand that any such identification must respect the religious freedoms of all citizens. In the "Declaration on Religious Freedom" they wrote:

> If, in view of peculiar circumstances obtaining among certain peoples, special legal recognition is given in the constitutional order of society to one religious body, it is at the same time imperative that the right of all citizens and religious bodies to religious freedom should be recognized and made effective in practice.[38]

In our era scant possibility exists either that the state will infringe on the free exercise of religious faith or that the Catholic Church in America, through its hierarchy, would seek preferential treatment detrimental to other religious bodies. However, the vagueness of the First Amendment phrase "respecting the establishment of" and its common translation into "separation of church and state" does open realms of contention, debate, and danger for religious freedom. It all revolves around one's understanding of "separation." Does it mean that the government "pays no attention to religion," "does not acknowledge religion," "does nothing to encourage religious faith," "does not support religious activities," "does not legally allow public expressions of faith that are unacceptable to some of its citizens," "does nothing to show preference for one religion over another"? It makes a difference. Depending upon one's interpretation, we may or may not include the phrase "under God" in the Pledge of Allegiance or keep "in God we trust" on government currency; allow a period of prayer in public schools or make available public vouchers valid in religious schools, dedicate some public monies for non-religious activities in church-run schools or faith-based public charities.

To date, the United States Supreme Court has interpreted the First Amendment to mean that federal and state governments may not legally prefer one religion to another, may make no law that supports one religion and not all, and have no direct function in aiding the practice of religion in civil society. Contention roils primarily around this last rendering. It makes "separation" mean "not encouraging religious faith." Many religious advocates would maintain that it rather should be understood "does nothing to show preference for one religion over another."

When Tocqueville praised our democracy for separating the practice of religion from public policy, he underlined the injuries that could visit both government and religion should politics and religion mix. Leaders in each area should heed his warning. What happens to democratic government when executive orders

---

[38]   *Op. cit.*, p. 685.

are given, laws are passed, and legal decisions are made that support a religious agenda and result in encouragement, money, and votes for the political party or administration distributing the favors? In appearance, if not in fact, the government is supporting one segment of the population and is not acting on behalf of all the people. It champions one group over another: conservative over liberal, religious over non-religious, large denomination over small, wealthy denominations over ones of modest means. Such a government may not be choosing explicitly Catholicism over Protestantism or adding its weight to an evangelical agenda over a mainline one, but, in fact, that does occur. The perception of this *quid pro quo* deal leads to a distrust of representative democracy, especially among those whose agenda cannot buy equivalent assistance. Politicians who invite religion to bed seeking political advantage risk the serious charge of an unconstitutional "establishment infidelity."

Religious leaders may woo politicians with offers of congregational support if the political powers of the moment issue favorable executive orders, pass legislation in accordance with religious social issues, and appoint judges with records favoring that agenda. The danger for religion lies, not with the agenda, but the reality of, or the perception of, getting in bed with a particular political party.

During his travels in America, Tocqueville inquired about the factors contributing to religion here. He noted: "...all attributed the peaceful dominion that religion exercises in their country principally to the complete separation of church and state."[39] He goes on to warn against religion seeking political power:

> I know that there are times when religion can add to the influence that is proper to it the artificial power of the laws and the support of the material powers that direct society. One has seen religions intimately united with earthly governments, dominating souls by terror and by faith at the same time; but when a religion contracts an alliance like this, I do not fear to say that it acts as a man would: it sacrifices the future with a view to the present, and in obtaining a power that is not due to it, it risks its legitimate power.[40]

Finally, he explains the risk this way:

> But when religion wishes to be supported by the interests of this world, it becomes almost as fragile as all the powers on earth. Alone, it can

---

[39] *Op. cit.,* p 283.

[40] *Ibid.,* p. 284.

hope for immortality; bound to ephemeral powers, it follows their for-tune and often falls with the passions of the day that sustain them.

In uniting with different political powers, religion can therefore con-tract only an onerous alliance. It does not need their assistance to live, and in serving them it can die.

The danger that I have just pointed out exists in all times, but it is not always so visible.[41]

How might our bishops endanger us through unwise flirtation with politicians and political leaders? Consider the following example.

As mentioned previously, in the last decades of the 20th Century, after the 1963 *Roe vs. Wade* decision legalizing abortion, the bishops launched an ambitious cam-paign to get that decision reversed. They preached continually about the evils of abortion; they encouraged the laity to demonstrate publicly against pro-abortion legislation and for abortion limitation; some threatened Pro-Choice legislators with excommunication; many have left no doubt that Catholics would act as loyal citizens and moral Catholics should they vote to remove such legislators from office. Since the Republican Party professes a Pro-Life stand and the Democratic Party a Pro-Choice one, this, in effect, supports the former and attacks the latter. The bishops base this crusade on their judgment that abortion involves the unjust taking of human life. Where, indeed, do they stand on modern warfare and the killing of untold numbers of already born human beings?

Since the dawn of the nuclear age, many moralists have wondered if the condi-tions for a "just war" can any longer be satisfied. Doubts turn on the following questions:

- If legitimate authority alone can declare war, in an interrelated world where the effects of war register worldwide, can any one state legiti-mately declare war or must a body like the United Nations do so?

- If the post-war state must be preferable to the pre-war one, in hostilities using devastating weapons of massive proportions, can the evil of the pre-war state anywhere equal the evil of the post-war disintegration?

- If the war's violence must be proportionate to the pre-war injury and the force used aimed only at addressing that injury, in all-out, technological, modern warfare is proportionality even possible?

- If weapons must discriminate between combatants and non-combatants, if civilians can only be killed as unavoidable victims when a military

---

[41]   *Ibid.,* p. 285.

target is deliberately attacked, in wars open to using weapons of mass destruction is such discrimination possible?

- If a declaration of war must follow an injury suffered, and if it can only be prosecuted against the political entity causing the injury, in a modern world where injuries come primarily from shadowy, loosely linked, terrorist organizations that *may* attack us, can pre-emptive war against them ever be just?

In March 2002 the United States government declared war against the nation of Iraq. It did so without the explicit authorization of the United Nations, yet only the United Nations could claim any actual hostilities against it as its member states patrolled a U.N. designated "no-fly" zone in that country. The U.S. president justified this aggression because the government of Saddam Hussein hated the United States and would like to attack it. And Hussein could, out of that mad animosity, distribute weapons of mass destruction to worldwide terrorist groups to use against the United States, its interests, and its allies. The United States instituted a pre-emptive war because of Hussein's madness, hatred, and possible complicity with terrorists. It unleashed a technological nightmare employing devastating aerial bombardments that could not discriminate between military and civilian targets; it used massive force that unraveled the civil society, leaving it in the hands of competing religious factions, and in danger of civil war between various ethnic and religious groups.

John Paul II branded this war as unjustified; the American bishops, after an initial concern before the invasion, were subsequently subdued about its morality or immorality. If, indeed, the conflict was unjust, then Iraqi people were being unjustly killed. The bishops sound off vociferously and with firm indignation against the unjust killing of unborn fetuses; how could they remain quiet when our forces were murdering thousands of Iraqi men, women, and children? Why were these bishops not threatening Catholic legislators who publicly endorse this war with excommunication? The bishops run the risk of appearing to stand with the Republican Administration no matter what because it takes various social positions in line with their desires. If their lack of purposeful confrontation flows from the hope of garnering necessary political power, they have sacrificed their moral authority. As a result, reflective Catholics must wonder if abortion is really morally wrong, or have the bishops strategically chosen this emotional issue as a unitive one calculated to restore their moral authority. Does episcopal neutrality about the war in Iraq mean that modern war is possibly just, or does the silence point more to the desire to keep the Republican Party and Republican Administration on the church's side? How can our righteous Pro-Life leaders condone capital punishment in modern America; is their acquiescence just another example of episcopal blindness for political gain?

Cardinal Joseph Bernadin of Chicago spoke prudently when he counseled his fellow bishops to stand resolutely for the "seamless web of life"; that is, against abortion, war, and capital punishment. Only this way can bishops, already distrusted by many scandalized Catholics, escape the suspicion that their mobilization against abortion and acceptance of modern warfare are crass examples of politically-motivated morality.

Our bishops have every right to take moral positions on issues confronting American society. But the stances they assume better be consistent; they must not appear to be casting their lot for power with some political entity; they should take firm and reasoned moral stances, not because others would favor them, but because they stem faithfully from the revelation of Christ. Even the question of backroom deals and secret handshakes with political operatives easily becomes a twofold sin: establishment and moral infidelity. Both church and state, ultimately, will condemn them.

Tocqueville came to America in another era. He gazed at us as a Catholic from France, a European and Catholic nation. He had personal experience of the disasters attendant upon the unhappy marriage of politics and religion. He saw clearly the temptations leading to that union and the subsequent loss for the church of its own special authority. Across the ages he counsels today's American hierarchy: if you wish to restore your authority as churchmen, you must abandon the slight-of-hand maneuvers of politicians and regain the simple directness of Christ. Stand openly and without hesitance for religion, not power.

Chapter Three:
The Sovereignty of the People of God

I. Democracy and The People's Government

On March 19, 1863 Abraham Lincoln concluded his brief remarks at the Gettysburg battlefield with the declaration that "government of the people, by the people, and for the people, shall not perish from the earth." The familiar ring of those phrases, memorized by generations of schoolchildren, make almost prosaic the political revolution those words underscored.

The American colonists escaped a European society long-schooled in aristocratic modes of governing. No matter its ancient beginnings in the narrow democracy of the Greek city-states, and in the oligarchic republic of Imperial Rome, government in the Middle Ages in Europe gradually transformed into a political landscape of hereditary kings. Through right of birth, God chose those who would rule his people. These privileged ones did not spring from the nation's citizenry but rather from a bloodline divinely appointed. Once christened, the king primarily represented God, secondarily his family, and finally his country. He assumed the burden of governing in a manner true to this triad that had conspired in his royal birth.

Louis XVI of France, Charles IV of Spain, George III of England: neither they nor their ilk would have smiled at Lincoln's firm declaration. For them he should have resolved: "government blessed by God, acting through a king's commands, and for the perpetuation of his rule, shall not perish from this earth."

Early on in *Democracy in America* Tocqueville highlights "the dogma of the sovereignty of the people [where] one must begin." Whereas in most institutions this idea lies buried in their foundations, occasionally brought forth but then plunged back into darkness, "In America, the principle of the sovereignty of the people is not hidden or sterile as in certain nations; it is recognized by mores, proclaimed by the laws; it spreads with freedom and reaches its final consequence without obstacle."[1] If one should inquire of him how Americans govern in accord with Lincoln's outline, he would respond:

---

[1]   *Op. cit.,* Tocqueville, vol. I, p. 53.

There are countries where a power in a way external to the social body acts on it and forces it to march on a certain track.

There are others where force is divided, placed at once in society and outside it. Nothing like this is seen in the United States; there society acts by itself and on itself. Power exists only within its bosom; almost no one is encountered who dares to conceive and above all to express the idea of seeking it elsewhere. The people participate in the drafting of the laws by the choice of the legislators, in their application, by the election of the agents of the executive power; one can say that they govern themselves, so weak and restricted is the part left to the administration, so much does the latter feel its popular origin and obey the power from which it emanates. The people reign over the American political world as does God over the universe. They are the cause and the end of all things; everything comes out of them and everything is absorbed into them.[2]

But how, one may reasonably inquire, does such a government avoid chaos? Do we not find here a recipe for disaster, the creating of a soup concocted, not by one, but by millions? In a kingdom one declares the law, the rest obey: assemblies make laws in accord with the king's will, administrators reach down and through the strata of society to insure their fulfillment, and judges deal sternly with anyone who, daring to cast aside the will of the sovereign, seeks to enshrine his own. Obedience by all to one, governing under God and by God's will, promises a single recipe, not only fit for, but, indeed, written by, the king.

Neither Lincoln nor Tocqueville described a government conducted by a concert of individuals. Just as the king rules alone, so only the people govern. Tocqueville explains:

In nations where the dogma of the sovereignty of the people reigns, each individual forms an equal portion of the sovereign and participates equally in the government of the state.

Each individual is therefore supposed to be as enlightened, as virtuous, as strong as any other of those like him.

Why therefore does he obey society, and what are the natural limits of this obedience?

He obeys society not because he is inferior to those who direct it or less capable than another man of governing himself; he obeys society because he knows that this union cannot exist without a regulating power.[3]

---

[2]   *Ibid.*, p. 55.

[3]   *Ibid.*, p. 61.

A democracy encompasses one governor, the people. It depends for its wisdom upon the intelligence, goodness, and moral strength of its citizenry. It rules well if the individuals that compose it make it virtuous and wise, and obey it as the political representation of what they hold dear about their shared life.

Which brings us to the core of the matter: what makes one country gravitate toward an aristocratic form of government while another chooses a democratic one?

From the dawn of civilization groups have sought experienced and capable leaders to keep them safe, secure, and economically viable. These requirements realized, societies search for those who may enhance the quality of communal existence through their wisdom and knowledge, integrity and steadfastness, values and vision. In dangerous and insecure moments, with questions of security paramount, the experienced and courageous commander comes to the fore, chosen because of previous exploits or that of his family.

Confronted by thousands of seasoned British redcoats, the threatened colonists turned to an experienced officer of their own, one who had fought bravely and successfully beside these same troops during the French and Indian War. They asked General Washington to lead them into battle against their former motherland, to save them from her punishments for their treason, and to free them, finally, from her tyranny. During that period, joined in a loose confederation, they united in a Continental Congress to oversee the war and to enlist assistance from the separate colonies.

When Washington defeated the British forces, when the colonies had secured their independence, many wanted to proclaim him king. In this way they would assure an aristocratic hereditary line that could guide and protect them, at once, and into the future. Washington declined, accepting instead the office of elected president, one chosen out of, appointed by, and serving at the pleasure of the people.

He did this, most immediately, because the military crisis no longer obtained, and the colonies, by their physical isolation from the kingdoms of Europe and because of their primitive conditions, faced no significant external threats for the foreseeable future. But, most importantly, he and other colonial leaders realized that their new nation consisted in its core of a middle-class society. From the beginning, shopkeepers and artisans, farmers and merchants had fled across the ocean from imperial and religious tyrannies. Educated and hardworking men, self confident and brave, they were willing to endure extreme hardships in order to be free to live and worship according to their own faith and virtues. Their leaders recognized a people sick to death of the inequalities and injustices of hereditary kingdoms, and one desiring nothing more than to be masters of their own destiny. By its very existence this people demanded a democratic form of government.

Where might men find others of proven virtue, steady courage, a dedication to values, and a willingness to sacrifice for oneself and for others?—well, indeed, right next door. Who might one trust as they walked together into a common destiny?—for sure, one's neighbor. Kings and lords had failed them miserably; now the people would have its chance to govern.

Catholics fleeing from religious persecution in the British Isles numbered, as we have seen, among the early colonists. Because the American colonies founded by English immigrants maintained the strictures of English law until after the Revolution, Catholics received an unvarnished welcome, at first, only in Maryland and Pennsylvania. The laws of the latter forbade religious discrimination among Christians; those of the former, though still in force, claimed little public support and less governmental attention. Except for their Catholic faith, these colonists should not be distinguished from their Protestant compatriots. Indeed, during the Revolutionary War, Catholics fought loyally and with distinction in support of the American cause. Afterwards they contributed their share in the birth of the American Union.

An examination of the European monarchies born out of the Middle Ages reveals the source of the grievances that led emigrants to flee from their domains. In them the king identified himself with the nation, its land, and its people. When "England" negotiated on and off with "France," we must understand that the two rulers not only represented their countries and people; indeed, they *were* the incarnation of both. Moreover, the king chose his administration, shaped his government, determined its directions and goals, and finally embodied them all. He not only owned the government; he *was* the government. One who worked for the administration served the king; one who obeyed the law showed allegiance to him; one who resisted the commands of the least powerful of his ministers insulted the king. All power came from God who appointed this, his royal representative. Thus by divine right the monarch ruled, answering to no one but the Almighty that created him.

In *The Republic* Plato singles out the philosopher-king as the ideal ruler. Fine qualities would distinguish this person: knowledge of the eternal and unchanging nature of things; a lover of all true being; disposition both truthful and temperate, not cowardly or unjust or mean; a lifelong student who rejoices in learning and possesses a sound memory; an interior man absorbed in the pleasures of the soul. A person of mature years, overflowing with intelligence and wisdom from a solid education—

> "The philosophers must become kings in our cities," I said, "or those
> who are now called kings and potentates must learn to seek wisdom like
> true and genuine philosophers, and so political power and intellectual

wisdom will be joined in one; and the crowds of natures who now pursue one or the other must be excluded. Until that happens, my dear Glaucon, there can be no rest from troubles for the cities, and I think for the whole human race. Until then, this constitution which we have now evolved in words will never grow into being, as something possible; it will never see the light of the sun, but it will live only in our description."[4]

One might argue, with Plato, that such a sovereign would descend as a blessing on his kingdom. Regretfully, however, such men seldom wear gold crowns; indeed, their opposites ordinarily ascend the throne. Fierce warriors stand out in times of war; greedy tyrants plunder in eras of scarcity; lascivious weaklings surround themselves with riches and tokens of beauty to hide their personal poverty; and crafty politicians forever shift and sway with the more favorable winds. The immigrants to the American colonies were not fleeing the likes of St. Louis of France who founded hospitals, visited the sick, and invited the poor to dine with him daily. They rather escaped rulers who persecuted those espousing religions not their own, who deprived heretics of ordinary civil rights, and who demanded total obedience even at the expense of violating one's conscience.

Our founding fathers resolutely turned their backs on European monarchies in which the government acted as the king's personal possession. Here government, a capacity "of the people," belonged only to them. Moreover, they rejected the notion that a king appointed by God should rule them. Here the people, out of their own resources, would direct themselves through a government formed "by the people." Finally, instead of a kingdom bringing fame and fortune, power and honor to a king and his minions, they would construct a government "for the people," one that would bring all the blessings of the new nation to its citizens.

Consider the monarchical system that preserves the sovereignty of a king. The success of his reign depends in part on the ruler's personal strength and the people's perceptions of his ability to embody their values and meet their needs. In addition, he surrounds himself with a court made up of his extended family, of flatterers and those seeking royal favors, as well as minor lords who rely on his firm hand to undergird their local power. From among this cadre he appoints regional leaders whose loyalty he commands and expects. They must support his national goals, uphold and mimic his governing style, and determine that his laws will be carried out in their jurisdiction. They, in turn, select agents who will fan out through towns and neighborhoods to enforce obedience and punish the

---

[4]   *Great Dialogues of Plato.* W. H. D. Rouse (trans). "The Republic," Book V (472c-474A). New York: New American Library, 1956, p. 273.

disobedient. Through this royal chain of command the king's desires touch everyone and make immediate his presence and power. Finally, he controls the assembly that enacts laws in conformity with his will, and he appoints and removes judges based on their strength and cleverness in enforcing those laws.

Such monarchs bank on the dependency of subjects. In the first place, they must need him to insure safety for citizens and their families. Through his police and military forces he must maintain security, protecting the people from foreign invaders and domestic criminals. Also, he must see to it that everyone enjoys the basic necessities of life as regards food, clothing, and shelter as well as the possibility of partaking in the good life of the kingdom on a par with one's peers.

Stability reinforces this dependency. People need to visit their families and neighbors; they forswear extensive contact with peoples living under another ruler or ruled under a different governmental system. Foreign travel tends to broaden horizons and to open up new vistas for exploration. It awakens both delight and dissatisfaction. Education too must be limited to that necessary for the life allotted within the kingdom. At most, it offers only modest advancement for the energetic, determined, and loyal citizen. Strict boundaries limit expressions of independence and potential for leadership: citizens must always need the king; they must fear both royal abandonment and displeasure.

American democracy preserves the people's sovereignty much differently. It directs citizens to choose from among their own a person who can execute federal tasks necessary to maintain the common good. This leader acts in accordance with the powers granted by a founding constitution and laws subsequently passed in compliance with it. He or she serves at the people's pleasure and for a discreet period of time. Continuance in the position depends upon the people's perception of their representative's faithfulness in office, effectiveness in meeting its demands, and suitableness in furthering the principal agenda, both domestic and foreign, of the era.

To safeguard its sovereignty from possible executive tyranny, the citizenry elects legislators who may introduce legislation required to sustain, protect, and develop the nation and its people. Once enacted, these laws become embedded in the nation's life through executive action. The legislature maintains oversight of the executive branch to make certain that its activities conform to the letter and the intent of the legislation. It, in turn, stays within constitutional limits through citizen oversight in frequent elections and ongoing judicial review of laws in light of the original constitution.

Unlike a monarch, our democratic president does not appoint regional governors loyal to this administration and its political agenda. Instead, the people, independent of federal direction, except as demanded by the constitution and federal law, selects its own governors. It chooses among candidates giving promise of satisfying the needs and desires of individual states and its citizenry. As in the federal system, these local governors may act only in line with the state constitution and its laws; and their power is checked both by periodic elections and by legislative and judicial oversight.

Our government employs the principle of subsidiarity to further governmental effectiveness. People personally confronting a public question introduce legislation. Moreover, their neighbors discuss the proposed law, argue about its provisions, and shape its intent and demands, rewards and punishments, according to the local situation. Finally, administrators actualize legislation, from federal to state, from county to town, at the appropriate level, and enforce it by local judicial review and police power. Citizens interview and elect, legislate and review. They protect their sovereignty through consistent and intelligent participation in public affairs. The government belongs to them, they engage in its activities in every strata of public discourse, and their actions have only one goal: the safety, well-being, and persistent development of the American people.

To succeed with a people's government, citizens must be capable of self-rule and be willing to join together in intelligent, prudent, and wise community-rule. Monarchy, depending upon need and obedience, restricts its people to fit governmental parameters; democracy, depending upon enlightened engagement, challenges its people to their farthest boundaries so as to profit by the fruits of individual and corporate experience. We encourage travel to other countries, encounters with diverse systems of government, and engagement in a range of personal and public enterprises. Although we consider each citizen the equal of each other, we reward the excellence of the one who through personal effort excels. We expect followers; we delight in leaders; we urge followers to become leaders. Finally, we need citizens who will choose wisely their representatives, actively keep track of their success in governing, and constantly communicate encouragement, as deserved, and displeasure, as earned. In a monarchical system, the king's will looms over all and must be communicated to all; in a democratic one, the government must inform the people of its activities, and the people must communicate its assessment of the worth and quality of these actions taken in its name.

II. The Catholic Church and its Administrative Monarchy

The Catholic Church operates through a hierarchical system much like a monarchy. The two systems differ primarily in the mode of obtaining their leader. A king takes the throne through the uncontested ascendancy of his ruling family; a man, usually a cleric, most often a bishop or cardinal, receives the papal tiara through the secret vote of the church's aristocracy, its cardinals. They who have climbed through the layers of ecclesiastical governance and have demonstrated a steady faithfulness to orthodoxy pick one at least their peer in qualities deemed, at the moment, essential. Both king and pope rule as selected, finally, by the will of God.

In most other respects the church in structure and function operates as a monarchy. The College of Cardinals serves as the pope's royal court, faithful to him and his administration, governing in his stead the church bureaucracy as he would have them do so. They give shape to the organization according to the inspiration and in the style of this supreme pontiff.

Through their advice and that of papal ambassadors posted in countries around the globe, the pope identifies clerical candidates to become governors over local dioceses and archbishops to oversee ecclesiastical regions. The reigning pope normally selects those in sympathy with his administration's directions, goals, and specific decisions. Once consecrated, "Bishops govern the particular churches entrusted to them as the vicars and ambassadors of Christ."[5] Theologically, each bishop realizes the fullness of Christ's priesthood. He enjoys both the right and duty to teach, govern, and sanctify the people of his diocese. In this way bishops become more like governors over states in a democratic system than minor lords in a monarchical one. Practically, however, bishops tend to see themselves as, and act as if they were, delegates of the pope. They know full well that the auxiliary bishop who demonstrates sustained loyalty to the pope will obtain someday his own diocese. They have no doubt that appointments to the large dioceses, archbishoprics, and cardinalates reward the loyal, the orthodox, and the successful. They certainly possess their own authority; they clearly must exercise it with an eye to advancement within the patronage ranks. Ambitious prelates serve to please the pope and his administration according to the current measures of success and orthodoxy; the non-ambitious may earn reputations for holiness or compassion for the poor or as advocates for peace, but they seldom taste any choice hierarchical plums.

Bishops appoint pastors to administer parishes and monsignors to look after the various deaneries within the diocese. Once again, the principal positions, those of prestige or wealth, go to priests who have modeled their ministry along the lines favored by the bishop and, ultimately, Rome. Thus does the hierarchical system, an interlocking cascade of clerical orders, speak as one, teaching and governing according to the papal will.

In order for this system to work successfully, the laity must be dependent upon the church and its hierarchy. They must require assistance to obtain necessities, here and hereafter. It reigns supreme in societies where the laity cannot care for themselves and their families because of insufficient education, poverty, minority status, inability to protect their belongings, and a dearth of resources to advance

---

[5]   *Op. cit.*, "*Dogmatic Constitution on the Church*," chapter III, p. 51.

within their political and social group. In such situations, the clergyman functions as the wise and experienced father who knows the local political system and uses contacts to move it in favorable directions. He can loosen the purse-strings of the rich, direct the resources of religious charities, move employers to offer choice jobs, furnish temporary housing, obtain church-sponsored educational opportunities, and occasion salutary contacts with the powerful. One need only think of the role the church played in 19th Century America as successive waves of immigrants arrived here with few material resources. Unlike their more self-sufficient colonial predecessors, they relied upon the church to integrate newcomers into American society and to lift them, eventually, into its middle class.

The laity must, moreover, agree that salvation depends upon their belief in church dogma, acceptance of its moral positions in public situations and in personal issues, and steady adherence to its disciplinary rules and regulations. The effective communication of these requirements for salvation depends upon a constant, stable contact between the hierarchy and its people. In Pre-Vatican II America, this came primarily through the local community. Every Catholic lived in a geographically outlined parish. Every Catholic above the age of reason attended mass at the parish church every Sunday, received communion, and made confession regularly. Every Catholic learned about the church and its requirements, as adults through Sunday sermons, as children in parochial schools or Confraternity of Christian Doctrine programs. The pastor and his assistants, the teaching sisters, and occasionally the bishop, defined the faith and described the life of the "good Catholic." Salvation awaited those who accepted and lived their teachings.

The Catholic Church in the United States continues to rely on a hierarchical model of organization and function. From pope to pastor the all-male clerical order governs the institutional, communitarian, and spiritual life of the People of God. Because of the ongoing and worsening scarcity of priests, church administration in many parishes is, of necessity, delegated to lay deacons, religious, and selected laypeople. But all appointments to church positions issue from the institutional hierarchy.

The duty of teaching the Catholic community about its religion resides primarily in diocesan ordinaries. In the past, they delegated this duty and authority to their priests and sisters. Education happened for the most part in parishes and through Catholic schools. With fewer priests and sisters available, with regular Sunday mass attendance falling to as low as 25%, and with numbers of Catholic schools, both diocesan and religious, decreasing, bishops rely more heavily upon laypeople to teach Catholic youth. Religious education for the average adult occurs less regularly than previously: now through a Sunday sermon, now through participating in a parish program, now through assuming some teaching role in the parish. In addition, the college-educated Catholic may take courses in theology, attend church-sponsored seminars, read Catholic journals and newspapers, or participate in study groups focusing on Catholic faith and life.

The sacramental and liturgical life of diocese and parish stay in the jurisdiction of the bishop and his priests. Confirmation and Holy Orders remain exclusively in episcopal hands; priests routinely perform the sacraments of Confession and Holy Eucharist, Matrimony and the Sacrament of the Sick; lay deacons at times baptize, deliver sermons, assist at mass, perform weddings and conduct burial services; laypeople serve as eucharistic ministers and lectors at mass. In practice, therefore, male clergy possess church authority; the laity, however, increasingly facilitate the daily life of the church.

Some observers of the American Catholic Church, in trying to explain the exodus of priests from dioceses, religious from their orders and congregations, the decrease in mass attendance and the de-utilization of confession, blame the changes instituted by Vatican II. Others attribute this breakdown of moral authority to Paul VI's traditionalist stand about artificial birth control in his encyclical *Humanae Vitae*. Still others point to the sexual revolution of the 1960's that opened the floodgates of sexual activity outside of marriage between unmarried persons, homosexuals or lesbians, including affairs between male clergy and lay or religious women. Since 2002 we must include sexual relationships indulged in by priests, religious, and even bishops with children and young people. This criminal behavior, aided and abetted by scandal-wary bishops, certainly raises feelings of anger, disgust, and shame among average Catholics regarding widespread clerical betrayal. Undoubtedly, all of these purported reasons exacerbate the wearing down of the hierarchy's previously unquestioned moral authority.

In the context of the present discussion, another contributing factor surfaces. While the hierarchical church structure has remained stubbornly unchanged in the United States since late in the 19th Century, the personal profile of the laity has altered dramatically.

III. The Maturing of the American Laity

As we have already seen, the original immigrants to the American colonies worked as tradesmen and merchants, had a sound education for the era, and cherished independent lives. After the American Revolution and the establishing of the American Union, with the assurance of religious and civil freedom as well as the myriad possibilities of the new nation expanding across our vast continent, waves of immigrants flowed over our shores during the 19th and early 20th centuries. Many had scant education, worked as common laborers, and settled into the blue-collar class. They generally knew little about this country except what they had gleaned from reports from family or townsmen who preceded them. They arrived with few material resources; many could not even speak or understand English; they brought hope, courage, and a willingness to work as their main resources. Catholics such as these relied on their pastors to direct them in their adjustment to an alien culture and to share the burden of integration into its social structure.

These immigrant peoples fit well into, and made up an essential part of, the hierarchical church in the United States. They needed father and sister and brother, not only to grow as faithful Catholics, but also to become contributing members of American society. Their needs and limitations supported the paternal teaching, governing, and sanctifying roles of the hierarchy.

By the 1960's the immigrant peoples, at least those from Western and Central Europe, had attained the acceptance of, and integration into, American society. Where their ancestors had arrived barely educated and lacking resources, descendents now lived indistinguishably among their neighbors. Many of these young men had fought through the Second World War. After returning from worldwide battlefields, they attended college on the G. I. Bill. With this education came advancement into the middle and upper middle classes. They claimed positions as managers, professionals, and highly skilled technicians. Now their children have moved from aging cities to wealthy suburbs, many have a college education and even graduate training, and have taken over prestigious positions in business, academics, and the professions. In the ultimate show of arrival, a Catholic man, John F. Kennedy, became president of the country. With advanced education, expanding wealth, and a revolution in the communication and travel industries, Catholic men and women traveled widely, met varieties of peoples and encountered exotic situations around the world, and grew personally through absorbing the cultural heritage of western and eastern civilizations.

From its earliest beginnings in the ministry of Jesus and his followers, the Catholic Church has dedicated itself to helping the poor and the needy. In this country the missionary mandate took on an added sociological form: the transforming of immigrant outsiders into full-fledged, successful citizens. The church did them and the country a tremendous service through its selfless charities and superb educational system, and by funneling people through its parishes into all the ranks and strata of political, social, and economic endeavors. Unwittingly, its success may well have initiated a hierarchical unraveling.

Educated, cultured, independent Catholics do not need the church's continuing assistance to become Americans. Moreover, as their life experiences expand beyond the limits of the clerical world, they often show themselves to be brighter, better educated, and more experienced as modern people than their religious pastors. Even in the realms of theology and philosophy, special clerical domains, thousands of former priests and religious possess at least equivalent education. And increasing numbers of college students major in one or other discipline; many go on for graduate degrees, exiting with a higher quality and more current education than the one possessed by their pastors back home. American clergy know well the following: Catholic orthodoxy as currently understood and interpreted by church professionals; the requirements for advancement in, and the means of working successfully in, the hierarchical system. For the most part, the laity care little about hierarchy; as for orthodoxy, they listen to their religious teachers but weigh the application to one's life in light of personal education, training, and experience.

In a dependent religious world, the laypeople believed that they could earn heaven by obeying the Ten Commandments, fulfilling their religious obligations, and living in accordance with the directions of church professionals. Indeed, they accepted this equation: being good equaled being Catholic equaled being saved. Strict attention to orthodoxy, in practice, often substituted for drawing close to God. But, sadly, a gnawing spiritual hunger, for many, remained. If God truly loves us, if Jesus is actually "Immanuel, God-with-us," if Christ is the God "in whom we live, and move, and have our being," if Christ has really sent his Holy Spirit to dwell in us to enliven and direct us, then should we not experience a divine presence in the depths of our being? No substitutes, like obedience to father, or faithfulness to church regulations, or submitting to the least jot and tittle of the law did the job or slaked the need. When the church puts its primary concern and effort into preserving Christian orthodoxy, it must make substantive efforts to lead its people into a closer relationship with God or lose those Catholics with a deep, spiritual craving for his presence.

With each passing year fewer American Catholics look to their clergy for political influence, or material assistance, or for introductions into civil society. They no longer need them to preserve a piece of the Old World or to make a place for them in the new one. They can get educated without church aid, obtain fine jobs without its influence, buy a nice home and raise a loving family without its advice. Finally, they reject the notion that "father knows best" when it comes to making prudent and just decisions affecting their own lives and those of their family.

A monarchical government needs a dependent, personally limited populace, literally, to "lord over." The hierarchical church, to the extent it utilizes this mode of functioning, requires the same. Over the last forty years the American laity have achieved significant personal and social independence. They have grown out of the restrictive limits essential for a smoothly functioning monarchy. This creates an irresolvable conflict if the organization demands a dependency that violates a hard-earned self-possession.

No one expects the Catholic Church, universally or in the United States, to dissolve its hierarchical structure. Too many reasons—some theological, many historical, and most political—solidly oppose such a decision. Nor would a reasonable person expect that independent adults should forfeit their growth and resume a childish dependency on religious leaders. What, then, can be done? In order to regain its moral authority in the church community, the American clergy must recognize and accept the reality of their people. They would show that concretely to the extent that they act as if the church's government functioned "of, by, and for the people." To the extent the clergy understands how the people exercise a true sovereignty and treat them with deserved respect, to that extent they may regain the authority they have nearly lost. For the remainder of this chapter consider how this might be done.

IV. A Sovereignty of Importance Inherent in Being the People of God

The Pope Is Not A King

The delegates at Vatican II, concerned with concluding the work of their predecessors, reaffirmed Vatican I's understanding of the papacy. It upheld unequivocally the doctrine of papal primacy:

> In order that the episcopate itself might be one and undivided, He placed blessed Peter over the other apostles, and instituted in him a permanent and visible source and foundation of unity of faith and fellowship. And all this teaching about the institution, the perpetuity, the force and reason for the sacred primacy of the Roman Pontiff and of his infallible teaching authority, this sacred Synod again proposes to be firmly believed by all the faithful.[6]

Whatever other Christian denominations think about the primacy of the Roman Pontiff, Catholics must accept it as an article of faith. That being said, the question remains whether, and in what sense, the pope can be called "sovereign."

In the first chapter of the *"Dogmatic Constitution on the Church,"* these same fathers with equal certainty asserted that Christ alone might claim sovereignty over the church. Building on the image of the church as Christ's mystical body they teach:

> The head of this body is Christ. He is the image of the invisible God and in Him all things came into being. He has priority over everyone and in Him all things hold together. He is the Head of that body which is the Church. He is the beginning, the firstborn from the dead, so that in all things He might have the first place (cf. Col. 1:15-18). By the great-

---

[6]   *Op. cit., "Dogmatic Constitution on the Church,"* p. 38.

ness of His power He rules the things of heaven and things of earth, and with His all-surpassing perfection and activity he fills the whole body with the riches of His glory (cf. Eph. 1:18-23).[7]

The pope, therefore, may not claim what belongs exclusively to Christ: the church and its one supreme authority. The pope represents Christ to the world and to the People of God, but he can no more assume an identity with Christ or Christ's church than can any other church member. Kings speak of themselves as embodying their nation, their people, their government; popes have no rights to such titles. No pope *is* the Catholic Church, the People of God, or the papacy; he, rather, belongs to the church as a member, has become through baptism part of the People of God, and exercises the Primacy of Peter during his elected reign. Moreover, kings in the past placed themselves above the law, even identifying themselves with it. Popes, however, stand subject to, and limited by, divine revelation and the tradition of the church. Even when exercising his supreme teaching power, the pope must be faithful to these certain guides:

> But when either the Roman Pontiff or the body of bishops together with him defines a judgment, they pronounce it in accord with revelation itself. All are obliged to maintain and be ruled by this revelation, which, as written or preserved by tradition, is transmitted in its entirety through the legitimate succession of bishops and especially through the care of the Roman Pontiff himself.[8]

The pope assumes both the right and duty of teaching, governing, and sanctifying Christ's church: "For in virtue of his office, that is, as Vicar of Christ and pastor of the whole Church, the Roman Pontiff has full, supreme, and universal power over the Church. And he can always exercise this power freely." In that sense alone may the pope claim the right of sovereignty. He possesses during his papacy the authority and power over the worldwide church to shepherd it in light of scripture and tradition.

In many aspects, papal sovereignty resembles that of a democratic president more than of a king. Consider the following chart:

---

[7]   *Ibid.*, p. 21.

[8]   *Ibid.*, p. 49.

		King	President	Pope
1.	Source of Power	by divine right	by people's right	by right of the People of God
2.	Mode of Election	by heredity	by the people	by cardinal representatives
3.	Term of Office	unlimited	limited	unlimited
4.	Extent of Power	absolute	representative	representative
5.	Position	over the people	serves the people	serves the People of God
6.	Exercise of Power	absolute	limited by constitution	limited by revelation
7.	Shares Authority	by delegation	with governors	with bishops
8.	Relationship To Law	identity	obedient to	obedient to
9.	Legislates	by self	by power of veto	by self

Upon examination, we see that kings possess an absolute and unlimited sovereignty while popes and presidents exercise a limited one. A significant identity between a king and a pope appears to be regarding the making of laws. Both do so. However, the pope may legislate validly only as consistent with, and in accordance with, scripture and tradition. Like a king, a pope reigns until he abdicates power, by his will or through death. Regarding tenure, popes and kings know the same right.

One may argue that the pope exercises absolute legislative authority because of the doctrine of papal infallibility decreed at Vatican I. Consider, however, the doctrinal limits imposed upon the exercise of that power.

As indicated above, any doctrine proclaimed by the pope can indicate the infallible direction of the Holy Spirit only to the extent that it conforms to, and is consistent with, divine revelation as expressed through scripture and tradition. God could not contradict himself. Therefore, no matter the solemnity of a papal declaration, should it be, in fact, in contradiction to divine revelation, it would not be infallible; it would, rather, simply be wrong. The doctrine of infallibility does not by itself confer wisdom, intelligence, or uprightness upon a ruling pontiff. He, like everyone else, may make assertions that can claim nothing of God's omniscience, but only an excess of his own limitations.

A pope exercises his charism of infallibility when he formally defines Catholic faith or morals *ex cathedra Petri*. Infallibility does not pertain to church discipline as demanded by a given pope or in line with his private theological opinions. Moreover, although he may exercise his judicial power without the formal involvement of the world's bishops, "The pope's juridic autonomy does not entail discommunity or isolation; his juridic independence is never a solitary independence."[9] Infallibility is bestowed by Christ on his church; the pope must declare only articles of faith that flow demonstrably out of scripture and tradition, and that have ordinary acceptance in the faith of the Catholic people and their bishops:

> This symbiosis of faith is a great datum of church life about which the Roman Pontiff, while remaining juridically independent in his plenary act of definition, cannot be incurious as an irrelevancy, but which he must acknowledge and honor as capable under the Spirit of significantly enriching the religious worth of his act of definition.[10]

A king may make a law regardless; a pope may also, but he cannot claim its infallibility without a relationship to scripture, tradition, and the ongoing faith of the church.

In his encyclical *Humanae vitae*, Pope Paul VI reaffirmed the hierarchy's ban on artificial birth control. He did this against the advice of his own commission of lay experts, in opposition to the opinions of many moral theologians, and without the concurrence of significant conferences of bishops. Most notably, his judgment did not take into account the actual practice of married Catholics. In his declaration did Paul VI define *ex cathedra* an infallible teaching of the church? The very fact of needing to ask the question indicates that he did not. An infallible definition must be formally done in such a manner that no doubt remains as to its essential nature as church dogma. That, plus the widespread non-acceptance of his position, both before and after his encyclical, brands his opposition as a private theological opinion or, at most, a matter of church discipline.

John Paul II staunchly objected to all discussion about the possibility of women priests. As previously noted, he based his objection on theological grounds: Christ chose only men as apostles; throughout the church's history bishops have ordained only men; only men can symbolically represent Christ's presence today in our world.[11] He maintained his position even though church history contradicts him, many theologians dispute his argumentation, and significant numbers of the faithful disagree with him. Did he teach *ex cathedra* that Catholics must believe that

---

[9]   *Op. cit.*, *New Catholic Encyclopedia*, vol. VII, p. 497.

[10]   *Ibid.*

[11]   Cf. page 63, footnote #17.

only men can be ordained?—no. He certainly made his private theological position clear, and as long as his loyal successor, Benedict XVI, occupies the chair of Peter no woman need apply for ordination.

The same pope refused to consider lifting the requirement of mandatory celibacy for priests. He based his position, primarily, on the witness that this discipline gives to the church and, indeed, to the modern world. Through it men declare Christ's presence and the priest's living faith. It underlines the sacrifice of a fundamental human need and right for his sake alone. The pope maintained this discipline in the face of an avalanche of information that contradicts the supposed witness value in the United States. Over the last forty years significant numbers of priests have left the active priesthood, creating a troubling shortage that gives promise of getting worse. Parishes are closing and the availability of the sacraments is decreasing in many others. Of the priests who remain in active ministry many are old, burdened, and ill. Among them alcoholism, extramarital affairs, and sexual encounters with children and youth are widespread enough to tarnish any glowing claims about celibacy as a positive witness to Christ. A solution exists: A married priesthood has long been active in Uniate Catholic churches; married Episcopal priests who convert to Catholicism are allowed to become married Catholic priests; in opinion polls Catholic laity decidedly support a married priesthood.

The American bishops undermine their own authority and that of the pope when they support papal positions, non-infallible or personal or disciplinary, simply because the pope holds them. Outside of infallibly declared doctrines of faith a pope is blessed with no greater wisdom or intelligence, prudence or flexibility, openness or imagination than anyone else. Moreover, he lives as a product of his own life, his peculiar experiences, and his specific culture—just as we all do. He makes decisions out of his base of knowledge; these may or may not be appropriate for other peoples in other cultures. To support him uncritically makes our bishops appear to be foolish, or unreflecting, or neglectful of the American church in favor of political capital within a Rome-centered hierarchy. Our bishops, out of such misplaced loyalty, give up their own voice; instead, they seem to others to act as robots, programmed to perform as directed by Rome, or as puppets mouthing Vatican-inspired words. How can they expect to be respected by their people when they manifest such glaring disrespect for themselves and for the diocesan community they are supposed to lead?

To American eyes the royal trappings and ceremonies of the Vatican look medieval, concoctions served up by a Hollywood movie mogul. Meant to honor the papal office and to show unusual respect for the reigning pontiff, they instead generate feelings ranging from disgust to dismay to shame. How may a Catholic striving to follow Christ who was "meek and humble of heart" find him modeled in an excess of pomp and circumstance? How may American Catholics raised in a government "of, by, and for the people" appreciate this pretentious throwback to the lavish courts of kings?

A professor of English at Boston University, William L. Vance, has written a fascinating book detailing how Americans view Catholic and contemporary Rome. In one illuminating section he describes how Catholic observers from America reacted to the ceremonies of three successive popes. His accounts, taken together, illustrate how popes pretending to be sovereigns disturb their co-religionists. At the same time they vividly offer a glimpse of a people's pope who earned, not only respect and honor, but also love.

Pope John XXIII, by most accounts a genial and humble person, opened the Second Vatican Council as the main character in a Vatican extravaganza. He endured it, performed as directed, but at times his humanity shrugged off the rites designed for a medieval monarch. Vance explains:

> If most American writers—including Catholics—are made uneasy by the ceremonial trappings of the Vatican that John still consented on special occasions to use, their sarcasm about the props are not made to be commentaries on the pope, as in former days. To Xavier Rynne the opening ceremony was a "dazzling spectacle," a vision of Eternity. But Robert Blair Kaiser, a Catholic reporter for *Time* who at the end of the first session published a full account, described the same ceremony as "just a bit ridiculous," "something that Cecil B. DeMille could have staged." Pope John was "carried undulantly along on the *sedia gestatoria* by nobles in outrageous red knickers and capes, surrounded by half a hundred young men in blue and orange bloomers, iron breastplates and lace ruffles, and a score of other cartoon characters out of O[tto] Soglow." The flabella, ostrich feather fans flanking the sedia, were "a sobering symbol of the ties binding even a pope with a new vision to the traditions and ancient usages of the past." But John, the pope of aggiornamento, was to be separated from these anachronisms: on entering St. Peter's, he dismounted and walked; he glanced "painfully" at the venerated statue of St. Peter, which wore a jeweled crown and pontifical cloak for the occasion; he had refused to have his throne placed five feet in the air, and he left his tiara untouched upon the altar.[12]

---

[12]   William L. Vance, *America's Rome*, vol. II. New Haven: Yale University Press, 1989, pp. 55-56.

Through this summation we already cherish a simple man so pained by the efforts to exalt him above his brother bishops. He clearly wanted to be with them, not over them, and to walk among them and the People of God.

One of the bishops present, Robert E. Tracy of Baton Rouge, described the opening ceremonies for his people back home. Vance records his observations:

> [He] felt obliged to justify to his readers (who were in the first instance his own parishioners) the fact that the beloved pastor-pope was carried into St. Peter's in the sedia gestatoria. This was the only practical way to make him visible to everyone, "like a notable visitor sitting on the back of a convertible." Yet it did "project the image of an oriental prince," thanks especially to the huge flabella. Tracy is certain that not only was John "embarrassed" by these props that distinguished him from his "brother bishops," but that other bishops too thought they should be sent "back to the Cleopatra movie set."[13]

How conflicted he sounds! He clearly wanted to enjoy, even to celebrate, this portentous moment in the modern church. But the theatrics kept getting in the way. In the end, as he gazed through field glasses at the pope's face, he discovered a man he could follow and proudly present to the world:

> "I could look at those kindly features and immediately sense, somehow, that here was a man of God. Pope John's very presence breathed the supernatural. It is my view that if canonization by acclamations were in order today, as they once were, Pope John would be acclaimed a saint just as readily as was St. Francis of Assisi."[14]

Tragically, this good man, beloved by Catholics and non-Catholics alike the world over, died the following June.

His successor, Paul VI, had labored for years in the Vatican during the pontificate of Pius XII. For many his papacy had more in common with that of his former boss than with the *aggiornamento* of John XXIII.

Frederick Franck, an American artist of Dutch origin, reverenced the late pope. When John XXIII died, Franck settled in Rome for a period of time. He attended the ceremonies elevating the next successor of St. Peter. Again, we have Vance's summary:

---

[13]   *Ibid.*

[14]   *Ibid.*

At Paul's coronation all the "imperial, royal, and feudal props" of the church's history were brought out once more for a triumphal show, which was staged in the piazza to accommodate the crowds. Franck tried to rationalize it: "It is far too easy to scoff at all this pomp, this cinematographic panoply of past triumphs, whose only real deficiency is that its symbolism is too exclusively Western—and specifically Roman—for a Church that claims to be universal. Roman robes, "medieval habits, Renaissance armor, Napoleonic tunics" are now joined by "television booths on the Colonnade,"...[15]

His most damning conclusion that "it is in ludicrous contradiction to the simplicity of the Gospels"[16] draws sharply the distinction between the populist John and the royal Paul. Catholics in America loved the former; they generally judged the latter cold and untouchable.

The manner in which a pope acts in the midst of ceremony portrays not only the man, but also the shape of his pontificate. In this instance, Catholics wondered if Paul VI would further the efforts of John XXIII, or, instead, retreat back to the insular papacy of Pius XII. Vance reports how others saw Paul in later gatherings:

On October 28, 1963, during a ceremony commemorating the election of Pope John, Paul VI "had entered on foot and lifted up his arms in greeting to his brother bishops." Five weeks later there was a ceremony commemorating—of all things—the Council of Trent, and Paul was back in his sedia gestatoria, "in full Roman and triumphalist splendor," blessing the bishops "from aloft." There were other signs. At the ceremony marking the end of the second session the next day, everything from the Swiss Guards to the Roman aristocracy was back in full prominence, and Pope Paul's throne in St. Peter's stood on a platform higher than the altar. His cautious speech—coming as it did a few days after a shocking procedural maneuver "from above" had prevented votes from being taken on religious liberty and on the Church's relation to the Jews—made some begin to think not only of Pius XII but even of Pius IX.[17]

---

[15] *Ibid.*, p. 58.

[16] *Ibid.*

[17] *Ibid.*, p. 58.

This comparison of the new pope to *Pio Nono*, the author of the anathematizing "Syllabus of Errors," warned Catholics and the world that the open window of John would soon be slammed resolutely shut. With him would begin the determined retreat toward a Pre-Vatican II church.

Paul VI reigned in papal splendor and aloofness for twelve years. He died in August 1978. When the ensuing papal consistory finally chose Cardinal Albino Luciani, Patriarch of Venice, a surprising choice to many, a ray of hope brightened the hearts of those who had endured the pontificate of Paul and remembered with joy the too-brief years of John. In his book *The Making of the Popes 1978*, Andrew Greeley shared his reactions to the even briefer weeks of John Paul I's pontificate. Vance describes Greeley's view this way:

> After years of enduring the always sorrowful and usually pained expression of Pope Paul on world television, Catholics again had a pope who smiled, as Pope John had smiled, and who exuded a similar natural goodness, little "bambino pope" (as he called himself) that he was. He provided a new "model of what the papacy might be" if it "shed its outmoded monarchic trappings." Pope John Paul I began with a "coronation" at which he refused to be crowned, to sit on a throne, or to ride in the sedia gestatoria. He eliminated the absurdly anachronistic references to temporal power in his titles, along with the word *pontificate* and the use of the royal *we*.... But Greeley's hope is that the popularity of his thirty-three day reign in this new style was enough to make any return to the "Renaissance papacy" impossible. According to Greeley, the "enormous power" the pope might exercise as "the most influential" religious leader in the world depends upon his avoiding the "trappings of papal power" and being instead a smiling, humble, holy man in the style of John Paul I.[18]

If a pope, or a bishop, wishes to impress American Catholics, he would do well to stop posturing as if he were a Renaissance lord. For us pomp and pomposity most often flourish together. We will readily follow, serve, and honor the leader who treats us as one of his own. Jesus, the charismatic leader whom the hierarchy professes to represent knew this:

> The next day John was there again with two of his disciples. As he watched Jesus walk by he said, "Look! There is the lamb of God!" The

---

[18]   *Ibid.,* pp. 64-65.

two disciples heard what he said and followed Jesus. When Jesus turned around and noticed them following him, he asked them, "What are you looking for?" They said to him, "Rabbi (which means Teacher), where do you stay?" "Come and see," he answered. So they went to see where he was lodged, and stayed with him that day (Jn. 1:35-39).[19]

The Bishop is not a Delegate

Significant confusion exists in the United States about the nature of the Catholic Church. Non-Catholics generally identify it with its hierarchical structure. The pope runs the church from Rome. For some, this means governing it as a king does his kingdom. He reigns supreme; he makes and approves all laws; he uses his curia to regulate church operations around the world; he appoints local bishops to manage the daily life of the faithful and to make certain that churches function in accordance with his will.

For others, the pope acts more like a modern CEO directing a multinational corporation. He oversees the task of converting the world to Christ by baptizing all nations into the Catholic faith. He has local managers, the bishops, situated strategically to realize that goal. Vatican offices and papal legates posted to various countries assist them and keep them in line. The pope sets the directions, the standards, the five-year goals; he expects his managers to enforce them and demonstrate ongoing progress. He removes the unproductive and wayward; he appoints only those showing loyalty and giving promise of success.

In either scenario, bishops serve at the pleasure of the pope. They have no independent authority, and they may exercise power only as directed. Whether one views them as minor lords in a kingdom or mid-level managers in an international organization, bishops end up as papal delegates.

American Catholics tend to think of the pope as head of the church. Through the power of the Holy Spirit he keeps the church faithful to the revelation of Christ as embodied in scripture and tradition. He tells Catholics what they must believe, gives directions how they should worship and receive the sacraments, and instructs them on appropriate behavior that will earn heaven. His Roman Curia channels laws and regulations to dioceses around the world; it also keeps a keen eye pealed for bishops, priests, and theologians failing to follow church teachings or to conform to ecclesiastical discipline. Through the recommendations of curial officials, papal nuncios, and a country's senior hierarchy, he appoints to the episcopate priests who have previously given proof of loyalty to Rome and who stand

---

[19] *The New American Bible*. New York: P. J. Kenedy & Sons, 1970. All subsequent scriptural quotations are taken from this edition.

squarely behind his brand of orthodoxy. These bishops serve as his extension into dioceses and their parishes. They teach, govern, and sanctify the people according to papal directives. They function as the pope's alter ego: he cannot be everywhere; they serve as his surrogates wherever church organization exists. They represent him in local communities.

For the most part, Catholics have only vague notions about what bishops actually do. Most know that only bishops, not priests, confer the sacraments of Confirmation and Holy Orders. They also understand that they appoint pastors to churches, move priests from parish to parish, and have a say in opening a new parish or closing down an old one. Otherwise, bishops work at the diocesan chancery in some kind of oversight capacity. How they teach, govern, and sanctify, if considered at all, remains at best a question. They grab the spotlight when special sacraments are needed, when problems enflame between pastors and parishioners, or when a priest falls into scandalous trouble. In the final analysis, they somehow make the diocese work smoothly and as dictated from Rome.

In the life of most Catholics the pastor has daily, ongoing importance. Whenever they attend mass, go to confession, work on parish committees, frequent church bazaars and bingo nights, participate in special devotions, father is present with answers and definitive decisions. He runs the parish, teaches the faith, performs the sacraments, says mass, preaches how Catholics should live, and exhorts them to lives of prayer and sacrifice.

The pope leads as first in authority and power, but he comes in a distant follower in daily importance. He functions as the source of unity for the worldwide church. He makes certain that Catholics know their duties, live their faith, and remain true to the revelation of Christ. Without him there would be no Catholic Church; without him Catholics would simply be Protestants. Although he dwells far away in Rome, although most Catholics never see him in person, he exists always in their imagination as "The Holy Father."

As for their bishop, most Catholics do not spend any effort thinking about him. He serves as the pope's mouthpiece, communicating from Rome to parishes. In that regard, anyway, he seems useful. Perhaps he has offered mass on a special occasion at their parish; if he celebrated a pontifical high mass, all the ceremony would impress the parishioners in attendance. Otherwise, he functions like a combination county sheriff and superior court judge. He steps into local disputes, separates the conflicting parties, hears both sides of the argument, and makes a decision. Whatever he concludes ends the matter. Usually he stands with his pastor and selects solutions that will reflect favorably on the church. Whether he serves justice may be open to question.

If a Catholic happens to work on some diocesan committee, he or she probably has met the bishop. For the most part, however, the engagement ends there.

Few, if any, enjoy an ongoing relationship with him. In the name of dignity and authority, the bishop dwells in an episcopal mansion, operates from his office at the chancery, consorts primarily with other clergy, flits in and out of parish functions, and graces civic ceremonies as the representative of the Catholic diocese. Although he lives in the cathedral city, for many Catholics he might as well be established in Rome, so seldom do they see him or interact with him. They don't know him; he doesn't know them. In general, they understand some bishop runs their diocese, but they would only miss him if he, or a successor, vanished. He may call them his people; he may claim to be their father. In actuality, most Catholics simply recognize that he directs regional religious activities and oversees their parish. How can "his people" and "their father" be more than empty metaphors when little or no relationship exists?

The bishop-delegates to Vatican II sketched a starkly different picture of themselves. Although the pope approves the individual candidate for elevation to the episcopate, the Holy Spirit appoints the new bishop.[20] He and his fellow bishops receive the fullness of the priesthood[21] in a permanent office flowing from the apostles[22] that realizes its continuance from the early church up to the present.[23] Bishops "exercise their own authority for the good of their own faithful"[24] and "automatically enjoy in the diocese entrusted to them all the ordinary, proper, and immediate authority required for the exercise of their pastoral office."[25] The power and authority comes with consecration from Christ and through his chosen apostles. In their dioceses bishops act as "vicars and ambassadors of Christ." Neither their power nor authority comes to them through the pope or as a delegation of power properly his. The council fathers firmly declared: "Nor are they to be regarded as vicars of the Roman Pontiff, for they exercise an authority which is proper to them, and are quite correctly called "prelates," heads of the people whom they govern."[26]

Bishops, primarily "placed in charge of particular churches,"[27] do not have the authority to govern in other dioceses. However, "as a member of the episcopal

---

[20]   Op. cit., "Decree on the Bishops' Pastoral Office in the Church," p. 397.

[21]   Op cit., "Dogmatic Constitution on the Church," p. 41.

[22]   Ibid., p. 40.

[23]   Op. cit., "Decree on the Bishops' Pastoral Office in the Church," p. 399.

[24]   Op. cit., "Dogmatic Constitution on the Church," p. 44.

[25]   Op. cit., "Decree on the Bishops' Pastoral Office in the Church," p. 401.

[26]   Op. cit., "Dogmatic Constitution on the Church," p. 52.

[27]   Ibid., p. 44.

college and a legitimate successor of the apostles, [he] is obliged by Christ's decree and command to be solicitous for the whole Church."[28] Indeed, in concert with the pope this episcopal college, whether gathered together in ecumenical council, or dispersed around the world, may proclaim church doctrine infallibly.[29] They and the Roman Pontiff may only "pronounce it in accord with revelation itself."[30]

In their own diocese bishops exercise the authority to teach, govern, and sanctify their people. They teach primarily through preaching the gospel, expounding "the whole mystery of Christ."[31] It is expected that they "present Christian doctrine adapted to the needs of the time."[32] In doing so they "should manifest the Church's material solicitude for all men, believers or not."[33] They need to seek out contacts and foster dialogue with all; their speech must be noteworthy for charity, humility and gentleness, truth and clarity and prudence.[34]

In 1969 I spent a portion of my summer at Ivan Illich's missionary center (CIDOC) in Cuernavaca, Morelos, Mexico. A staff member encouraged me to celebrate Sunday mass at least once at the cathedral. I decided to inquire if I could concelebrate a mass presided over by the bishop, Sergio Mendez Arceo. I had only to ask.

On that day, I was standing behind the altar with five other priests, all Mexican, waiting for the bishop to appear. He entered through the main door to the church and walked slowly down the aisle. As he proceeded, I was impressed with three things: a tall man, he was wearing a cassock made of rough homespun and was carrying a shepherd's staff for a crozier; he wore no miter; and he was smiling and exchanging greetings with parishioners as he approached the altar. The upbeat, catchy, alive rhythms of a mariachi band enveloped us in sound. This would be the people's mass.

After vesting in the sanctuary in ordinary garments appropriate to the liturgical season, he greeted us and motioned me to stand next to him at the altar. He offered the mass prayers in the vernacular in a strong but soothing voice. When the church exploded in native hymns backed by the mariachi players, he joined in lustily. When it came time for the sermon, he himself preached, positioning himself next to the congregation, near the front row of pews. His contact with

---

28   *Ibid.,* p. 45.

29   *Ibid.,* p. 48.

30   *Ibid.,* p. 49.

31   *Op. cit.,* "*Decree on the Bishops' Pastoral Office in the Church,*" p. 404.

32   *Ibid.,* p. 405.

33   *Ibid.*

34   *Ibid.*

the people and their happy response to him warmed me. Indeed, although I spoke only rudimentary Spanish, I found myself caught up in a vibrant experience of a community singing and praying together because they loved being with one another and their bishop. At some point I realized that the altar truly held the center and high place in the cathedral: the bishop had previously removed all side altars and stripped the cathedral of its ornate gold plating. Nothing distracted from the central drama of the mass.

I left impressed and deeply moved. I heard subsequently about the extraordinary life of Bishop Mendez. Before Vatican II he had promoted small bible reading groups among his people; in time they would become the celebrated "base communities" espoused by liberation theology. He also had for years reached out to his Protestant brothers and sisters, all believers in the revelation of Christ. I saw the beginnings in his poverty, in his closeness to his people, and in his simplicity of the bishop who would become a world-recognized force for social justice. Some would in mocking tones call him the "Red Bishop of Cuernavaca"; I remember him as a leader who preached in word and action the presence of Christ to all and especially the least. As I think about the episcopal self-portrait laid out in the Vatican II documents, I once again join the Bishop of Cuernavaca—deep inside my own spirit.

Bishops do not govern in pride, lording it over their charges as would a king or his appointed delegates. They preside as ones who serve[35] and they minister rather than seek for others to minister to them.[36] As a father and pastor—

> ...a bishop should stand in the midst of his people as one who serves. Let him be a good shepherd who knows his sheep and whose sheep know him. Let him be a true father who excels in the spirit of love and solicitude for all and to whose divinely conferred authority all gratefully submit themselves. Let him so gather and mold the whole family of his flock that everyone, conscious of his own duties, may live and work in the communion of love.[37]

As they govern they must listen to their subjects[38] and become knowledgeable of their lives, the circumstances in which they live, and their needs. They

---

[35]   Op. cit., "Dogmatic Constitution on the Church," p. 40.

[36]   Ibid., p. 52.

[37]   Op. cit., "Decree on the Bishops' Pastoral Office in the Church," pp. 407-408.

[38]   Op. cit., "Dogmatic Constitution on the Church," p. 52.

should show honest concern for all and invite them "to collaborate actively in the building up of the Mystical Body of Christ."[39]

"In fulfilling the duty to sanctify, bishops...offer gifts and sacrifices for sins."[40] They "are the governors, promoters, and guardians of the entire liturgical life in the church committed to them."[41] Through celebrating the Eucharist, through dispensing the other sacraments, and through exhorting all to prayer, they foster the faith and holiness of their people. As for themselves, "They should also be mindful of their obligation to give an example of holiness through charity, humility, and simplicity of life."[42]

In this regard Walter Abbott, editor of *The Documents of Vatican II*, in a footnote shares the following story:

> During the Council, there was much criticism of the signs of pomp and wealth seen in the lives of bishops. The subject was as delicate as the proper age for episcopal retirement. But as the fourth session closed, Paul VI made an adroit gesture, full of his own generosity, but pointedly symbolic of "this simplicity and humility of life." He gave each bishop a ring, simple in form and tasteful in design, bearing no jewel nor declaration except a small engraved miter. The ring spoke more eloquently than a hundred decrees.[43]

I know one council participant who wholeheartedly embraced the pope's message. Bernard Joseph Topel became the bishop of the Spokane, Washington, diocese in 1955 at the age of fifty-two. I lived in Spokane from 1957-1960; I met him through his nephew and my good friend, John Topel. Bishop Topel had previously been teaching mathematics at Carroll College in Helena, Montana, after finishing his doctoral studies at Harvard. He struck me as a pleasant person, more than usually intelligent, and an efficient and capable administrator. Aside from that, nothing else seemed particularly noteworthy about him.

At age fifty-nine Bishop Topel accompanied his brother bishops from around the world to Rome. He participated in Vatican II, voted on decrees about the church and the bishops' role in it, and came home a changed person. He moved out of the episcopal residence and—

---

[39]   *Op. cit.,* "*Decree on the Bishops' Pastoral Office in the Church,*" p. 409.

[40]   *Ibid.,* p. 406.

[41]   *Ibid*

[42]   *Ibid.,* p. 407.

[43]   *Ibid.*

...will always be remembered as a sort of St. Francis of Assisi of American prelates. He lived in a rather ramshackle old house with no heat, no phone, and little or no food in the icebox. He lived more than the spirit of poverty, he lived it literally, in spirit and in reality. His labors and lifestyle took a heavy toll on his health.[44]

At age seventy-five he retired. He lived eight more years, in the same weathered house, growing his own vegetables in a backyard garden. People speak, at times deridingly, of the celebrated "spirit of Vatican II." I take it they did not attend themselves; I also would bet that they never met a bishop who came home living it. When he voted to call the bishops to humility and simplicity, Bishop Topel truly meant it.

As if to emphasize their own authority, the council fathers desired a clear distinction between themselves and the pope's actual delegates: his cabinet (the Roman Curia) and his ambassadors (papal legates or nuncios). As regards the former, they called for its reorganization, with special attention to its internationalization and adaptation to the realities of the modern world. As for the latter, they directly petitioned the pope to differentiate the authority of legates from their own in order that the two powers with interacting duties might not conflict.[45]

By way of summarizing the essentials aspects of these two descriptions of the episcopate, consider the following chart:

	Characteristic	Differing Views of Bishops By Bishops	By Laity
1.	Appointment	by the Holy Spirit	by the pope
2.	Authority	from the apostles	from the pope
3.	Delegate	of Christ	of the pope
4.	Position	one's own	delegated
5.	Duty	to teach, govern, sanctify	to orthodoxy
6.	Teaching duty	bishops with pastors	pastors
7.	Governing duty	in light of revelation	as willed by pope
8.	Sanctifying duty	through liturgy, sacraments and example	through reserved sacraments
9.	Responsibility	for the whole church	for his diocese
10.	Infallibility	bishops with the pope	pope
11.	Relation to people	shepherding	ruling
12.	Peoples' relation	collaboration	obedience

---

[44]   Catholic Diocese of Spokane website, "A Short History of the Diocese."

[45]   *Op. cit., "Decree on the Bishops' Pastoral Office in the Church,"* p. 402.

Clearly, the bishops see themselves as exercising authority primarily and essentially within their diocese, and secondarily and importantly as members of the college of bishops in behalf of the whole church. The laity, however, understands the bishops' position as primarily and essentially maintaining Catholic orthodoxy according to the pope's directions, and secondarily as leading their dioceses. How may we explain the gap between the two views? As regards the bishops themselves, this disparity would exist either if they no longer accepted the viewpoint of Vatican II, or if they were not living it. As for the laity, the explanation could be ignorance about the episcopate; it could come from prejudice over any authority; it might be attributed to their informed perception about the reality of episcopal behavior. Whichever explanation or grouping of explanations fit, the bishops have a problem. They need either to communicate better their ecclesiastical role or they must live more transparently the vision of Vatican II. To do neither simply contributes to an ongoing diminishment of moral authority.

The Sovereignty of the People of God

In the year 867 A. D., a long-evolving process of dissolution took visible form. Christendom split into two jurisdictions. The pope, patriarch of Rome, ruled the West. The four patriarchs of the East—Constantinople and Antioch, Alexandria and Jerusalem—placed themselves, their bishops and people, under the authority of the patriarch of Constantinople. When the Eastern Church finally rejected the decrees of the Council of Florence (1427), the process was completed. A once-united Christendom no longer existed.

On October 31, 1517, a thirty-four-year-old cleric, Father Martin Luther, nailed his ninety-five oppositional theses to the weighty door of the Wittenberg Cathedral. He thereby initiated a massive exodus from Roman authority, both schismatic and heretical, out of which issued the splintering of western Catholicism into a multiplicity of independent Christian churches.

The Great Eastern Schism and the Protestant Reformation attacked at its core the primacy of Peter. Multitudes withdrew from Rome's ecclesiastical jurisdiction, bestowing it, at first, on their own bishops and, finally, distributing it across a spectrum of authorities from bishops to congregations to individual Christians.

In desperate defense of Catholic orthodoxy, the council fathers at Trent stood resolutely behind the papacy. Over succeeding centuries "to be Catholic" assumed the meaning "to follow the pope." The hierarchical structure of ecclesiastical authority, from pope to bishop to pastor, claimed utmost importance in standing for, and defending, the Catholic faith. In the view of many, both within and outside the church, Catholicism equaled obedience to the hierarchy and loyalty to the Roman Pontiff.

Because of this history of painful defections and the church's rallying in defense of papal authority, many Catholics identify the church with the papacy. The reigning pope not only exercises supreme authority over the church; he, indeed, also becomes its touchstone of orthodoxy: who obeys him, obeys Christ; who rejects him, rejects Christ and his church. In effect, the pope and the church meld into one being. In the order of importance, the pope stands aloft as the Vicar of Christ. After him rule the bishops, the successors of the apostles. Pastors and their assistants, to whom bishops delegate power to teach, govern, and sanctify the faithful, play crucial ecclesiastical roles that lift them out of, and place them over, the Catholic people. An outsider could quite understandably decide that the Catholic Church is primarily the pope, secondarily the bishops, followed by priests and religious, and lastly the laity.

This suggested order of importance does not conform to the view sketched by the early church. In recounting the ministry of Jesus, the New Testament authors portray him as teaching in the temple as a twelve-year-old boy who amazed his elders (Lk. 2:46-47). At the start of his public life, "Jesus began to proclaim this theme, 'Reform your lives! The kingdom of heaven is at hand'" (Mt. 4:17). His words began to attract others: "The great crowds that followed him came from Galilee, the Ten Cities, Jerusalem and Judea, and from across the Jordan" (Mt. 4:25). He expanded his ministry to include healing, both spiritual and physical: "As evening drew on, they brought to him many who were possessed. He expelled the spirits by a simple command and cured all who were afflicted..." (Mt. 8:16). As the crowds increased, out of compassion for them he even fed them, turning two fishes and five loaves of bread into a meal for a great number: "Those who ate were about five thousand, not counting women and children" (Mt. 14:21). On behalf of individuals who believed in him, he overcame possessions, diseases, and even the disintegrating forces of death (cf. Mt. 6:5-13).

As believers multiplied, as many openly wondered whether he was the promised Son of David (Mt. 12:23) when he cured the blind and mute, when he preached with such power and wisdom, his heart went out to them. They were becoming his people, his community, even his family. "At the sight of the crowds, his heart was moved with pity. They were lying prostrate with exhaustion, like sheep without a shepherd." They needed more help than he alone could give them to orient them to a new religious faith. "The harvest is good but laborers are scarce. Beg the harvest master to send out laborers to gather his harvest" (Mt. 9:36). He must choose suitable apostles to share in his ministry to his people.

Consider for a moment: if Jesus had preached and nobody listened, if he had performed miracles and nobody believed, if he had offered a different way of life and nobody followed, would he still have selected twelve apostles to assist him or sent out seventy-two disciples to carry on his ministry? If no crowds of excited countrymen and women had flocked around him, Jesus probably would have gone back to Nazareth; he certainly would not have distributed unnecessary power and authority, duties and responsibilities for a nascent church that did not exist. The apostles came into being because of the church. Because the crowds manifested a real need, he designated men who could lead them. The church, the body of Christian believers, generates the offices of bishop and pope; without the Christian people neither papacy nor episcopacy would have reason to exist.

Jesus makes this clear in his instructions to his apostles. In the first place, "Whoever does the will of my heavenly father is brother and sister and mother to me" (Mt. 12:50). Union with him comes through faith, not with position or through power. When "The seventy-two returned in jubilation saying 'Master, even the demons are subject to us in your name,'" Jesus counseled them, "Nevertheless, do not rejoice so much in the fact that the devils are subject to you as that your names are inscribed in heaven" (Lk. 10:17-20). Faith creates the true Christian, not miraculous abilities. When his apostles began jousting for position, Jesus confronted them: "Many who are first shall come last, and the last shall come first" (Mk. 10:31). He realized that this teaching had to seem strange to his close followers. They had no examples of power and authority, both civil and religious, except as exercised *over* people:

> Jesus called them together and said to them, "You know how among the Gentiles those who seem to exercise authority lord it over them; their great ones make their importance felt. It cannot be like that with you. Anyone among you who aspires to greatness must serve the rest; whoever wants to rank first among you must serve the needs of all. The Son of Man has not come to be served but to serve, to give his life in ransom for the many" (Mk. 10: 42-45).

Even Peter, the first pope, will shepherd the church, not for his own glory, but as one who serves. Jesus called him with these words: "I for my part declare to you, you are 'Rock,' and on this rock I will build my church" (Mt. 16:18). Peter becomes the church's foundation, the firm base for its growth. The church does not serve Peter, but rather as pope he exists for its sake.

After his resurrection Christ appeared to the apostles, Peter among them. As if to confirm his choice of him to care in his stead for his little community,

> Jesus said to Simon Peter, "Simon, son of John, do you love me more than these?" "Yes, Lord," he said, "you know that I love you." At which Jesus said, "Feed my lambs." A second time he put his question, "Simon,

son of John, do you love me?" "Yes, Lord," Peter said, "you know that I love you." Jesus replied, "Tend my sheep."

A third time Jesus asked him, "Simon, son of John, do you love me?" Peter was hurt because he had asked a third time, "Do you love me?" So he said to him, "Lord, you know everything. You know well that I love you." Jesus said to him, "Feed my sheep.... When Jesus had finished speaking, he said to him, "Follow me" (Jn. 21: 15-19).

Christ emphasizes that Peter's relationship to him, one of faith and love, must be central. Only on this basis may he be summoned to ecclesiastical leadership. Moreover, he must use his office solely on behalf of Christ's people, not for himself. He and the apostles, their papal and episcopal successors, receive authority only as Christians, believers in Christ. First and foremost, Christ founded his church. He could have done so without denominating one supreme leader, Peter, a pope. Thus do Orthodox Christianity and Protestantism believe. He could also have dispensed with any episcopal rank, with apostles, with bishops. Most Protestant churches and ecclesial communities maintain that he did so. He could even have left all exercise of good works of faith and love to the people themselves, without designating any particular positions with peculiar authority. Some denominations, like the Quakers, espouse that belief. But no group, East or West, claims to follow Christ without a Christian community. However one may believe that Christ structured his church, all recognize that he created a body of believers who together would, according to his teachings about life and death, about God and humankind, about faith and love, confess their unity. Without the church, Christianity ceases to exist; without a clerical hierarchy, it can and does. Catholicism requires a hierarchically organized society presided over by a pope; Christianity does not.

Theologians regularly speak of Catholicism as "the hierarchical Catholic Church" as if that describes its essential feature. It does not. Members of the hierarchy must be Catholics before they can become clerics. Each pope, each bishop, each priest receives through baptism his essential dignity as a Christian. This remains the necessary requirement for entering the hierarchical cadre. The hierarchy is not the church; rather, it points to the church's way of organizing itself based on its interpretation of the faith of Christ's early followers. This hierarchical organization does, in fact, differentiate Catholicism from all other Christian denominations; no other group has its leadership centralized through a pope, extended around the world through bishops, and actualized in local communities through priests. But to understand the church, in itself, we must look elsewhere.

In its *Dogmatic Constitution on the Church*, the fathers at Vatican II devoted a whole chapter to the image of the church as the People of God. The editor of the *Documents of Vatican II* comments on the reason for this special emphasis:

This title, solidly founded in Scripture, met a profound desire of the Council to put greater emphasis on the human and communal side of the Church, rather than on the institutional and hierarchical aspects which have sometimes been overstressed in the past for polemical reasons. While everything said about the People of God as a whole is applicable to the laity, it should not be forgotten that the term "People of God" refers to the total community of the church, including the pastors as well as the other faithful.[46]

The authors of scripture, popes and councils and theologians, have utilized a variety of images to illustrate "The Mystery of the Church."[47] It "is a sheepfold whose one and necessary door is Christ"(Jn. 10:1-10), "a tract of land to be cultivated, the field of God," and the edifice of God (1 Cor. 3:9). In more personal terms it is "our Mother" (Gal. 4:26), the spouse of the Lamb (Apoc. 19:7), and even the mystical body of Christ (1 Cor. 12:13). But after centuries spent defending the church's hierarchical structure, the council fathers definitely decided to shift the emphasis on to the community of the church:

This was to be the new people of God. For, those who believe in Christ, who are reborn not from a perishable but from an imperishable seed through the Word of the living God (cf. 1 Pet. 1:23), not from the flesh but from water and the Holy Spirit (cf. Jn. 3:5-6), are finally established as "a chosen race, a royal priesthood, a holy nation, a purchased people.... You who in times past were not a people, but now are the people of God" (1 Pet. 2:9-10).[48]

They further underlined that Christ, not the pope, heads this messianic people.[49] The church community lives through his life in the Spirit. The pope may lead the church but he does not infuse it with life: that activity belongs to God alone.

Because of this unity with Christ, its head, the People of God makes visible in our world the resurrected Lord. Indeed, as his church, this People becomes the very sacrament of his presence:

---

46   *Op. cit.,* chapter II, footnote 27, pp. 25-26.

47   *Ibid.,* cf. chapter I.

48   *Ibid.,* chapter II, p. 25.

49   *Ibid.*

God has gathered together as one all those who in faith look upon Jesus as the author of salvation and the source of unity and peace, and has established them as the church, that for each and all she may be the visible sacrament of this saving unity.[50]

The sacraments depend ordinarily for their administration upon the ministerial priesthood. But they and their clerical ministers only have efficacy as they are imbedded in the sacrament of the Christian community, as expressions of those gathered as one in their belief in Christ's saving presence.

We, the People of God, embody Christ today, here and around the world. We are the sacrament of his presence. As members of this People, the pope and bishops and clergy share this essential dignity and mission; their ministerial offices function only as expressions of that People and in the service of its life. The church's ministers receive from it sacred orders, but they do not, thereby, identify with, exhaust, or become the sacrament. Only the People of God, Christ as its head, filled with the Spirit, *is* the sacrament of Christ. Baptism, the doorway into the Temple of God, transforms its recipient into a member of God's People. Holy Orders and episcopal consecration confer the fullness of the ministerial priesthood; baptism creates the fullness of the life of Christ on earth. Both come as awesome gifts of the Spirit, but the latter, as a foundation, allows the former to occur.

In a church shaped by the Council of Trent and reinforced by Vatican I, we have grown accustomed to think of members of the hierarchy as being "higher than," "better than," "holier than" the rest of the community. Even the honorific titles—his holiness, the pope; your eminence, the cardinal; your grace, the bishop; reverend father, the priest—bespeak a worth and dignity attached to "a higher state of life." Being higher, however, carries a grave risk. As Jesus himself warned, "Everyone who exalts himself shall be humbled..." (Lk. 14:11). The present state of widespread clerical scandal vividly demonstrates the danger of pretending to be what one is not: he who causes others to believe in his holiness had better be holy. The prudent man climbs only a tree with strong, deep roots. Sometimes the ground proves to be both safer and more honest.

Vatican II adjusts our sights and brings our focus back to earth. As members of the People of God, no pope outranks the smallest child, no bishop deserves greater respect than the poorest communicant, no reverend father can demand more honor than my father or yours, the ones who raised their children to take vital places in the community of believers. After all, does not the pope himself claim to be "the servant of the servants of God"?

---

[50]   *Ibid.,* p. 26.

We all have experience—in our own lives, through books, in movies—of the faithful servant who spends her life, her energy, and her love for some good family. In American history these figures in antebellum Virginia and Victorian New England have attained almost iconic status. Bishops, servants of the American Catholic family, should take her image and historic story to heart. She serves her master and mistress; she becomes an honored member of their family. Christ's church summons every bishop to serve his master and mistress, the People of God. Herein lies the needed transformation that may yet rescue the American episcopacy from degradation, disuse, and, worst of all, irrelevance: "...and he who humbles himself shall be exalted" (Lk. 14:11). Consider the actions of this selfless servant who calls forth the highest of praise and deepest of love.

A fruitful relationship requires above all else an atmosphere of mutual respect. All parties must recognize the essential dignity of human life. Every person, no matter the age or status in life has needs and desires, hopes and goals, worries and triumphs that shape a uniquely valuable existence. No one person's life and qualities deserve more respect than any other's do. Certainly, one's job merits neither greater nor lesser dignity. A family situation demands different functions and diverse abilities, but each adds to the peace, harmony, and growth of the home. The father who works to feed his family, the wife who cooks the food, and the servant who serves and cleans up afterwards, each contributes through time and effort a necessary portion of the meal's success. Each basks in the ensuing round of thanks.

Bishops should realize that all of us share an equal dignity as children of God and merit equal respect as members of his people on earth. No one questions whether some in the church perform tasks of greater importance for the community. But all members, from the woman who presses linen for the altar, to the deacon who assists at marriages, to the bishop who shepherds his flock, further the diocesan life. All perform necessary jobs and earn our gratitude. The extrinsic value of the job neither adds to, nor detracts from, the respect due each and every member of the diocese.

An attentive servant learns to listen. This means putting aside for a nonce one's own agenda. What does the master want or need or require? In the layers of messages coming at this moment, which one holds decided importance, demands an immediate reaction? If every interaction encodes a request, what must be the first response?

Careless listeners either do not understand the request or they respond inappropriately. How often do we hear someone bemoaning an inability "to say the right thing" to a person coping with a family death? The untested assumption here that the friend is requesting that one say something, especially when sitting quietly and with compassion would probably mean much more, leads the listener astray.

The fumbling words, moreover, most likely mask the erstwhile comforter's lack of comfort over the demise, and anxiety in struggling with the other's troubled emotional state.

People in authority, including bishops, often think that a subordinate's request is meant to elicit a wise solution. The other has a problem that must be addressed, and he or she does not possess the intelligence or experience to figure out a sufficient response. Some requests, indeed, seek answers; many others, however, ask simply for support or permission.

I recall a period when I felt disturbingly overstressed. I was pursuing a master's degree in theology during the day and a certificate in family therapy in the evenings and on weekends. Recognizing I needed a respite, some relief from the unrelenting demands, I asked our rector for permission to go visit friends for a week. He replied that I should just go to bed. I told him that I did not require additional sleep as I was not tired. I repeated that I was seeking a change of venue, a chance to get out of the intense milieu of my studies. He repeated, "Go to bed." He had not heard my request. I was not asking for his advice nor did I need his years of experience to figure out a suitable solution. His permission, only that, I sought; that I never received. I left, frustrated. After a week staying with a nearby family, I felt myself again and resumed work. The clueless rector never inquired, subsequently, how I was doing or whether I had garnered enough sleep.

Bishops exercise a teaching role in the church. Sermons, public lectures, pastoral letters give them opportunities to fulfill this duty. The wise bishop, however, does not presume that his adult audience is uneducated, without theological knowledge or Christian sophistication, or is incapable of making prudent moral choices. Wisdom dictates that unchecked assumptions should be set aside. Only after listening, after understanding the people's request, should the teaching begin.

In a wealthy Victorian household, each person donated time, effort, and abilities to the task at hand. Separately, less would have been accomplished and not as well. Master and servant, mistress and children—all contributed toward making the home a loving, happy, growing place. Together they could outstrip any one person's solitary endeavors. As in any healthy system, the leadership of tasks rotates according to the specific situation, experience required, and the momentary capabilities—physical and emotional, spiritual and social—of all involved. A mother may oversee the raising of her children; a trusted servant may, on occasion, have functioned more successfully in a mothering role with a teenage daughter struggling for independence. Or a growing boy may have confided his fears about girls to a loving outsider who could listen objectively without getting tied up in parental knots. As the day of the important dinner party approached, the experienced cook would take over necessary arrangements, would supervise purchases, and direct kitchen activities while the mistress followed her directions. In cases like these roles reverse, the mistress serves and the servant commands, the first actually becomes last and the last becomes first, for the good of the family.

In a closed system this cannot happen. Roles there define persons, and the power of roles measures the worth of those exercising them. The master command, but never obeys; the mistress directs but never follows; teenagers move out but never help out; children take but never give; hirelings do as ordered but never initiate. Everyone works out of self-interest, functions to earn praise or increase power or to strengthen position. Contributions may accidentally further the common good; essentially they must enhance each one's ego. "*I*" and "*my*" stand ready to overrule and even sabotage, if need be, any "*we*" or "*ours*" that challenges individual territory and control.

During the Second Vatican Council the bishops spent considerable time defining roles. They gave us a *Decree on the Ministry and Life of Priests*, another *Decree on the Apostolate of the Laity*, and they addressed their own role in the *Decree on the Bishops' Pastoral Office in the Church*. Given the aborted discussions of Vatican I that managed to address only the role of the papacy, these documents serve as extensions of the prior council.

In discussing various roles, the bishops instructed themselves to listen carefully to the views of others. They specifically stated:

> It is highly desirable that in each diocese a pastoral council be established over which the diocesan bishop himself will preside and in which specifically chosen clergy, religious, and lay people will participate. The function of this council will be to investigate and to weigh matters which bear on pastoral activity, and to formulate practical conclusions regarding them.[51]

Besides these pastoral councils, they also directed themselves to listen carefully to a variety of people:

> Hence, for the sake of greater service to souls, let the bishop engage in discussion with his priests, even collectively, especially about pastoral matters. This he should do not only occasionally but, as far as possible, at fixed intervals.[52]

---

[51]   *Op. cit., "Decree on the Bishops' Pastoral Office in the Church,"* p. 416.

[52]   *Ibid.,* p. 417.

> In order to foster harmonious and fruitful relations between bishops and religious, at stated times and as often as it is deemed opportune, bishops and religious superiors should be willing to meet for discussion of those affairs which pertain generally to the apostolate in their territory.[53]

> An individual layman, by reason of his knowledge, competence, or outstanding ability which he may enjoy, is permitted and sometimes even obliged to express his opinion on things which concern the good of the Church.... Let sacred pastors recognize and promote the dignity as well as the responsibility of the layman in the Church. Let them willingly make use of his prudent advice.[54]

They are even encouraged to enter into dialogue with the world in which they live. This constitutes a necessary condition for bringing the message of Christ to modern men:

> Since it is the mission of the Church to converse with the human society in which she lives, bishops especially are called upon to approach men, seeking and fostering dialogue with them. These conversations on salvation ought to be distinguished for clarity of speech as well as for humility and gentleness so truth may always be joined with charity, and understanding with love.[55]

Besides listening to various church constituencies, bishops should actively support each group in its role. It falls to others to accept the teachings of their bishop, to obey his directions, and to pursue the pathway to Christ laid out for them.

The council documents urge collaboration between all groups within the church. For the bishops this means listening and supporting; for priests and religious this requires sharing information and taking to heart episcopal directions; for the laity this requires sharing of their expertise and advice for the good of the church in the secular world, and in their apostolate "union with those whom the Holy Spirit has assigned to rule God's Church...."[56] Throughout their texts, collaboration, "working with," means to fulfill one's role. Other groups support and interact as required. Thus pastors are to—

---

[53] *Ibid.*, p. 423.

[54] *Op. cit.*, "*Dogmatic Constitution on the Church*," p. 64.

[55] *Op. cit.*, "*Decree on the Bishops' Pastoral Office in the Church*," p. 405.

[56] *Op. cit.*, "*Decree on the Apostolate of the Laity*," p. 512.

Recognize and promote the dignity as well as the responsibility of the layman in the Church.... Let them confidently assign duties to him in the service of the Church, allowing him freedom and room for action. Further, let them encourage the layman so that he may undertake tasks on his own initiative. Attentively in Christ, let them consider with fatherly love the projects, suggestions, and desires proposed by the laity.[57]

Nowhere do the bishops suggest that "collaboration" could also be understood as "filling up what is lacking in another's knowledge or ability for the good of the church." Such an expanded definition would entail sharing power through delegation, stepping aside and allowing another to act for the common good, and relying temporarily on another's expertise in meeting of one's responsibilities.

The bishops tend to think in categories, to divide the church into discreet groupings with specific tasks. Although all relate as members of the same church, they do not share together the same action. Each one does his or her job with the outside support and encouragement of others. To employ a common metaphor from the world of sports: for the bishops collaboration is likened to a track team in which each person independently sets a time or achieves a distance, winning or losing in individual events; the overall victory is achieved by the addition of individual points. They do not understand collaboration such as that seen on a basketball court where individuals freely switch roles: picking or setting picks, driving for the basket or opening a lane, blocking an opponent under the boards or gathering in a rebound, jumping to interrupt an opponent's shot or taking one's own. In basketball no one individual wins; only the team does. Teamwork, collaboration, rules the game.

As noted above, in a closed system roles, positions, activities, and responsibilities stay frozen. They do not change with the demands of diverse situations, even when another may be demonstrably more capable in this instance of accomplishing a mutually desired goal. Power and authority, like personal possessions, belong to the one occupying a position; to share them even for a limited time diminishes the status, the ego, the very sense of self of the owner. The mother alone mothers her child; the hostess alone oversees and directs preparations for the feast; parents alone guide their children's lives. In the diocese the bishop alone teaches while delegating a share of his responsibility to priests, religious, and laypeople as needed. But who teaches him? The bishop alone governs his flock, delegating some responsibility to pastors. But who governs him or steps in for him when he is unable to handle particular circumstances beyond his expertise? The ordinary of

---

[57] *Op. cit., "Dogmatic Constitution on the Church,"* pp. 64-65.

the diocese strives to fulfill his obligation to lead his people to God through regulating church rituals, overseeing the administration of the sacraments, exhorting all to live prayerful lives of sacrifice, and offering to them his example of a humble, simple, Christ-centered life. But what happens when increasing numbers of his people stay away from mass, do not utilize the sacraments, never hear his exhortations, and have little if any contact with him? Add to that widespread knowledge of clerical corruption with episcopal mismanagement and even collusion in crimes and shame. If his people do not trust the holiness and Christ-like dedication of his life, how can the bishop hope to be a sanctifying force in his diocese?

The answers lie here: in certain circumstances and for a discreet period of time, delegate power and share authority with others to attain specific goals. The bishop retains a negative check over his surrogate's actions. If he judges the decisions taken are failing to achieve their intended results, he may draw back all power and authority to himself. In this manner roles exist for the common good and do not become personal emoluments of status or power.

What might this kind of collaboration look like in practice? Consider how a bishop might share his teaching, governing, and sanctifying roles.

1. Teaching by Listening

I cannot predict if the bishops, or how many of them, might read what I write. Even less can I guess if any might learn from my reflections. They do, however, give every indication that the cruel stresses in the American church would be resolved, they think, if the following occurred:

- The Catholic people blindly obeyed them.

- Catholics returned to faithful attendance of Sunday mass and to the regular reception of the sacraments.

- Married laity once more urged their sons and daughters to study for the priesthood or enter religious life.

- The Catholic community put behind it the scandal of clerical sexual abuse as being aberrations of a few bad priests and bishops, and not indications of a morbidity in the clerical culture.

- The Catholic faithful accepted their bishops' judgments about the morality of a host of modern issues: artificial birth control, abortion, stem-cell research, divorce and remarriage, premarital sex, homosexuality, capital punishment, and modern warfare; lived accordingly; and exerted pressure on American society to shape our culture in line with their teaching.

I know that the American Catholic people will never accept these conditions. Their bishops must regain their trust, prove to be disciples of Christ instead of clones of a self-perpetuating cadre of church professionals, and convince their flock of their Christ-like leadership. The problem, I'm bold to say, does not stem from the Catholic people; it flows, tragically, from the failed role of their bishops.

Bishops have been ordained to teach. So far, their teaching over the last quarter century has only exacerbated the troubled state of the American church. Unless they have some new wisdom forthcoming, it seems time for them to let others teach them about the church, its troubles, and necessary solutions. They need to sift through novel ideas, gain fresh perspectives, and discover different strategies for transformation into new life. The church today requires their humility, not their pride.

2. Governing through Delegation

The Vatican II documents leave no doubt that bishops "who are placed in charge of particular churches, exercise their pastoral government over the portion of the People of God committed to their care...."[58] What happens when conflicts arise which bishops find distressingly outside of their expertise and experience? As noted above, they may consult with a variety of people in pastoral councils, with priest federations, or with lay experts. Others' advice may or may not help them to address serious problems. The bishops, however, remain firmly in charge. But what about situations in which the bishops themselves become part of the uproar, when a perception exists that they have participated in behavior destructive of the church community? They may be removed by Rome and replaced by a credible successor (as Cardinal Bernard Law was kicked upstairs to oversee the Patriarchal Basilica of St. Mary Major, and Archbishop Sean O'Malley was sent in to sooth a rebellious local church). They may also temporarily delegate their governing power over the disturbance to someone able to handle it effectively.

In 2002 the American Catholic community woke up to a clerical scandal that involved priests and bishops across the country. Going back as far as the 1960's, some priests and bishops had been sexually abusing Catholic youth. This behavior, both heterosexual and homosexual, obviously violated any promises of celibacy and vows of chastity. In many states it constituted, in addition, statutory rape, a criminal felony.

For upwards of forty years, the American hierarchy dealt with this outrageous behavior as momentary failures of clerics overstressed, inebriated, or lonely. In order to shield these errant brothers from legal prosecution and public denunciation

---

[58]   *Ibid.,* p. 44.

that could seriously compromise their ministerial effectiveness, the hierarchy routinely removed the offenders from the criminal scene. Superiors either sent them to psychiatric treatment centers like the Institute of Living in Hartford, Connecticut, or to a distant position where a resolute, contrite beginning was promised. They negotiated financial settlements with victims and extracted legal promises of silence lest public scandal awaken that could seriously injure the church. Remarkably, bishops often moved offending priests to other parishes without informing pastors of the past sexual offenses, or allowed them to go to another diocese, armed with a positive letter of reference from them. Thus did the abuse live on as supposedly cured priests returned to ministry with unsuspecting young charges, and the uncured ones simply took up their former lives in other locales.

The bishops revealed themselves as sorely incapable of managing this tragic problem in their dioceses. Most states have mandatory reporting laws that require all counselors, including ministers, to inform civil authorities of sexual abuse of children, both in the past and ongoing. These laws do not allow bishops to hide behind any so-called "paternal relationship" that might absolve them of legal obligations. Only statutes of limitation have operated to protect offenders and their episcopal collaborators from criminal prosecution.

As personnel managers the bishops failed miserably. "Cures by transfer" rarely occur. A fresh start when the person remains the same, with continuing needs and addictions and pathologies, simply distributes the abusive behavior to another parish, another community, and another group of youngsters. Even when some mental health practitioner declared the offender cured, prudence would dictate that that person should never again be placed in any environment in which he or she has authority over youth.

Even though they live in the richly psychologized society of modern America, the involved bishops seem clueless of the realities of addiction. Abundant evidence exists that addictions never get cured; at best, they simply shift to another object. And most often, addictions exist in tandem with other psychological problems: a personality disorder, a neurotic condition, or emotional and social immaturity. They require extensive treatment, often long-term psychotherapy, and lifetime attention. Repeat sexual offenders evidence addiction; they should be treated as addicts. Even one-time abusers of youth, acting in a manner seriously offensive to religious and non-religious people alike, reveal themselves to be at least emotionally immature, if not emotionally disturbed. It passes the bounds of credibility to accept that any bishop could reasonably or prudently or honestly think that shifting offenders from here to there could help them, their victims, or the church.

In the immediate aftermath of the breaking scandal, it appeared that the bishops might, finally, be taking the issue in hand. At their annual meeting they passed an acclaimed "zero tolerance" policy. On the face of it this seemed a decisive action. But, instead, it has become a legal quagmire and a public relations disaster. It did not sufficiently distinguish between clerics accused of sexual abuse of minors and ones proven to have done so. It lumped together one-time abusers with chronic offenders. It treated the seventy-year-old pastor who, on a solitary occasion, abused a youth thirty years ago identically with a forty-year-old serial offender acting criminally up to the present time. It ran afoul of due process assured in canon law as well as the American legal code that presumes innocence until proven guilty. Subsequently, Rome modified the decision of the bishops' conference in order to conform to church law, priests' federations rose up in arms about the transgression of a priest's rights, and the public stood by aghast at the bishop's continued imprudence.

They also gathered together a commission of lay experts to advise them, to oversee compliance with their own sexual abuse policy, and to remove any appearance that they were still going to protect the church, the clerical order, and their reputations instead of repairing the damage done to victims, their families, and the Catholic community.

From the beginning this commission was doomed to failure. The bishops treated it as if it were an advisory body instead of one with independent authority. It was supposed to gather data about the extent of the sexual abuse, and to monitor each diocese's actions to deal with offenders and to institute procedures to forestall future abuse. The bishops agreed to set up the commission, settled upon its mandate, but then refused to be governed by it. After all, bishops alone "govern the particular churches entrusted to them as the vicars and ambassadors of Christ.... This power, which they personally exercise in Christ's name, is proper, ordinary, and immediate...."[59] What right does anyone, including this commission, have to tell them how to run their own dioceses? Is this not a bald usurpation of their governing authority? Complaining and obstructing bishops conveniently forget the remainder of the sentence quoted above: "...This power...is proper, ordinary, and immediate, although its exercise is ultimately regulated by the supreme authorities of the Church, and can be circumscribed by certain limits, for the advantage of the Church or of the faithful."[60] If ever "the advantage...of the faithful" would apply, it should do so in this case.

The bishops, standing before the whole world as tragically inept in dealing with clerical sexual abuse, should have delegated their governing power to address it to

---

[59]   *Ibid.,* p. 51.

[60]   *Ibid.*

their lay commission. As long as that group acted in accord with relevant ecclesiastical and civil law, it should have had the authority to force everyone, bishops included, to accept decisions and directives taken in support of its mandate. No bishop should have been allowed to complain, obstruct, refuse to comply, or claim executive privilege. But the bishops rather chose jealously to hug all authority to themselves, as if any delegation would somehow diminish them. This refusal to share their authority fits perfectly with a closed and unhealthy system that protects itself first, instead of responsibly caring for the Catholic people whom bishops are ordained to serve.

The bishops kept piling one public relations fiasco on to another. When questioned, they evaded responsibility for their part in allowing clerical predators to continue harming young people. They have used church funds secretly to buy silence from victims so as to protect the offenders and themselves. They have alienated their priests by restricting their due process when accused. They have consolidated parishes, depriving long-time parishioners of their religious home, to pay damages and legal fees. Some dioceses have declared bankruptcy in order to avoid legal claims, doing so in the name of not having enough monies to pay all victims equally, or being unwilling to disburse funds needed for diocesan charities. They have emasculated their own oversight commission to preserve their authority. They have shamed the Catholic community before its non-Catholic neighbors. They have destroyed the trust of the People of God that its leaders will act prudently, responsibly, and straightforwardly for it and in its name.

If ever bishops had a reason to collaborate to resolve this scandal and reestablish their credibility in the Catholic community, now is the time. To cooperate successfully will require a true sharing of their authority to govern. For the sake of the people, for the sake of that precious authority of theirs, they must be willing to delegate to experts who have the will, authority, and ability to conclude this most painful chapter in American church history. And they must also be prepared to obey.

3. Sanctifying in a Community

Children and many adults establish worth, meaning, even their sense of self through identification with something outside the self. A small child may gain respect through the boasting assertion that "my dad is bigger than your dad"; a young man may claim fame as "a Harvard man"; a young executive may garner personal status by trumpeting her managerial position in "a Fortune 500 Company." To be "a good Catholic" one must fulfill a variety of duties laid out by religious authorities: believe in the articles of the Apostles' Creed; participate as required in church rituals; learn prayers and faithfully address God through them; and obey the Ten

Commandments. If one acts accordingly, he or she will live as a loyal Catholic and may expect, someday, to be given an eternal reward for doing so. At the very least, bishops preach these duties, exhort their regular fulfillment, and furnish structured liturgies for prescribed participation. In this sense, "drawing close to God" equals "being a good Catholic," and "sanctifying" means "acting faithfully."

Young people, and adults who stay psychologically immature, find themselves through group membership. A teenager may "die if he doesn't call," "be nobody if I don't make the team," "be ruined if I don't get a date to the prom." Though sounding exaggerated the emotional reality may cause exquisite pain. The same dynamic forces neighbors "to live up with the Joneses," upward climbers to go through cycles of divorce and remarriage, and would-be politicians to pay exorbitant sums to play golf at a particular exclusive club. Being "a good Catholic" for such as these means obeying the dictates of religious authorities, making socially approved moral choices, and participating enthusiastically in parish affairs. The will of God is identical with the commands of the pope, directions of the bishops, desires of the pastor, and the behavior of the accepted and acceptable parishioners. Bishops stress Catholic morality, acting in conformity to the teaching magisterium, and putting aside one's will in order to be a faithful member of the church and companion of Christ. They sanctify their followers by creating a receptive community in which they may feel safe, secure, and at home. These parishioners need only to "follow the crowd" all the way to heaven. They will "draw close to God" within the church group that gives them meaning.

As people mature they become emotionally independent. They no longer need group acceptance to reinforce a sense of self. In fact, they actively resist any attempts by authorities to make them obey without sufficient and compelling reasons. A young woman, hoping for a financially fruitful job, will go to a promising college over her own fears and the weak objections of her parents; a young man, convinced about his patriotic duty, will dare himself to join the armed forces engaged in war, even when his family and friends do not support the present conflict. Both have to trust themselves as they truly cannot rely on the steady and selfless love of others. People like these practice their Catholic faith because they have been raised up as Catholics and can think of themselves only as such. They consider it to be the best means for them to live a disciplined and self-sustaining religious life. They want to draw closer to God and the church seems to furnish some suitable ways of doing so. They will listen carefully to religious leaders, think about their instructions, and make their own decisions. If experience proves that acting as directed seems right and productive, then they will continue to do so, but always with calculating reservation.

Bishops and pastors should get to know these church members personally. They need to listen to them, get to understand their hopes and hesitations, and strive to put the requirements for a "good Catholic life" into their frame of reference. Sensitivity to them, reasonable and easily understandable explanations, and specific and personal guidance are essential in helping them to "draw close to God." "To sanctify" means here "to offer appropriate guidance."

In each of the preceding stages, bishops act as authorities. They teach, govern, and sanctify others according to their subjects' psychological capacity for, and openness to, authoritative interventions. As experts they judge, demand, or guide the behavior of these people. In doing so they stand in for a transcendent God: God the Father, lawgiver and judge; Jesus the Son, companion and friend; and Christ the Redeemer, the soul's guide to heaven through the free grace of the Holy Spirit. The hierarchical church works effectively for the spiritual journey so far described, just as long as the bishops' moral authority is sustained and is respected by the ones journeying.

With successful personal experience and solidifying emotional strength, adults may pass a threshold where faith in one's own life replaces previously required external certainties. They now dare to open themselves up to the world, revealing their lives, and offering their personal energy to others by way of gift. When others in gratitude receive their gift and reciprocate, "we" is created. In that union new life grows: individual lives deepen and flourish, and the relationship itself, springing into existence, becomes an ongoing fountain of life. We call this life-producing gift: love. In earlier psychological growth stages, feelings of love surface but always with admixtures of need, hesitation, and fear. Here, as these hindrances fade, love joins with faith, growth generates hope, and life becomes greater than itself.

This growth stage requires three elements: faith in the worth of one's self, a willingness to present oneself to another, and the transcending of self-boundaries in the resulting relationship.[61] Before, Catholics strove through duties performed, authorities obeyed, and discipline applied to approach a transcendent God; now they dare to transcend themselves in relationship. In that action they discover life, love, and the presence of the imminent, indwelling Spirit of God. Where once they looked for God in heaven, now they find him sustaining life here on earth, for "In him we live and move and have our being" (Acts 17:28).

"To sanctify" now translates as "to transcend in relationship." This happens in a community of believers. Jesus promised: "Where two or three are gathered in my name, there am I in their midst" (Mt. 18:20). At the Last Supper, he further promised that, although he was leaving his disciples, he would send them the

---

[61]   For a fuller explanation of these psychological and spiritual growth stages, cf. Willis, Robert. *Transcendence in Relationship: Existentialism and Psychotherapy.* Norwood, New Jersey: Ablex Publishing Corporation, 1994.

Paraclete, His own Spirit, to be with them. That tingling energy, that burning fire, that flowing life makes itself known and recognized in love.

Love grows through presence, equality, and mutuality. By its very nature a hierarchical church sustains itself through distance, inequality, and authority. Structured vertically, it serves well when "higher" and "lower" are necessary, but it fails when a horizontal presence is required.

The People of God may be defined as "the sacrament of horizontal presence." Through baptism all become equal in Christ. As members of his mystical body all exist as one with him and one another. In his Spirit all live, transcend themselves, and share the life of God with one another. In this manner they become the sacrament of God on earth, at once witnessing to and recognizing his presence, while entering into the eternal generating of his life on earth through their love absorbed into his Love.

Bishops exercise their authority in regulating and making available the seven sacraments of the Catholic faith. They do so as possessing power within the hierarchical church. But these sacraments scarcely help people in this stage of personal, interpersonal, and spiritual growth unless they are means, in the present, of experiencing the enlivening Spirit animating the People of God. The sacraments must function as symbolic doorways through which one enters into, and get taken up by, that Living People.

We have all experienced losing track of the passage of time. As our attention becomes concentrated on a task, a person, a conversation or a recreation, "time flies." During that fleeting period we may even become unaware of the place where we are located, the body we inhabit, and the very processes of thinking and feeling and imagining. This may occur, unwittingly, when we fall asleep, sink into a coma, become intoxicated or anesthetized. In such conditions we simply have given up the means of staying aware.

At other times we may choose to become absorbed into something or someone other than ourselves. The other catches our attention; our focus narrows into a deepening concentration that excludes all else; our being, our life, our imagination, our self opens up and flows out toward the alluring object; and in a cascade of energy we become connected to, and alive with, another existence. We may experience this as we become absorbed into, and become alive in, a vibrating sunrise. As the powerful tones of a symphony surround us, we may pass from listening to it into a state of being the flow and rush and swelling of the music itself. In the peak of sexual crescendo we may drop all recognition of separateness, making love to, or being in love with, another. Nothing exists, neither he nor she, except the throbbing energy that is the relationship. In such magical moments we, myself and the other, change from being two separate entities "who are." We two fade into a meaningless distance, capture nothing of awareness, as the living relationship becomes all. Indeed, ungrammatical as it sounds, "we is becoming" the relationship.

We know this process comes through the unifying capabilities of the imagination. We could think forever about oneness and never experience it; we could will being one with all our heart and never achieve it. In fact, unity happens to us; we cannot make it occur. All we can do is open ourselves, place ourselves in a state of active reception, and in an act of hospitality make ourselves eager to be taken up into the arrival of a special guest. The guest, the other, arrives as invited, but at his or her own moment.

The hierarchical church exists through the powers of the intellect and will. The intellect distinguishes roles, defines them, and separates authorities, one from another. By the force of will, each official strives independently to meet peculiar responsibilities, alone or with assistance. Each formulates possible goals and selects from among them; each generates a range of strategies for achieving them and prioritizes them; each initiates specific actions to set into motion a process aimed at eventual completion. Intellect and will predominate; imagination may support the intellect in supplying possible alternatives; emotions may contribute energy that reinforces the will; neither initiate action nor carry it into completion.

We call the church the People of God. In doing so we are likening it to members of a family, participants on a team, citizens of a country, or a body of close friends. We may intellectually define it, we may willingly support it, but we do not really know it except in and through lived experience. In the relationship itself we draw close, feel a range of emotions, and see ourselves in various degrees of intimacy. Each experience generates its own images and feelings; these become the gateways for entrance into subsequent moments of oneness. It may be truly asserted: if we cannot imagine being one in the Spirit with the People of God, for us it will not happen, at least not in this lifetime.

The People of God is a sacred space of potential, felt unity. It lives in, and by, the Life of God, the Holy Spirit. As a body of baptized believers, we participate in that life. Though we are, in truth, one in the Spirit, we only grasp it experientially in special mystical moments when, as Paul humbly reported, "...the life I live now is not my own; Christ is living in me" (Gal. 2:19). When they are gathered together at one time and place, liturgical worship may become the imaginative and emotional vehicle of a unitive experience. The sights and smells, the sounds and movements, may so capture attention and deepen concentration that one or more worshippers may enter through them into the living presence of the Spirit.

For Catholics like these, then, "to sanctify" becomes "to prepare sacred space." Bishops and their pastors, through baptism, create the People of God on earth. They need to form it into a community of believers, individuals aware of each other and of the life they share. They do so as they shepherd them through various stages of spiritual growth. And they construct a physical, emotional, and imaginative environment that may function as an entranceway into the experience of the living God. Bishops may build churches, but they must become the emotional and imaginative homes of their people. Bishops may shape sacramental liturgies, but they must capture worshippers' attention and compel concentration. Bishops may count scores of believers, but they must form them into a community. Finally, bishops may preach about God, but they must "prepare a sacred space" in which it may happen that God's presence becomes, at least for an eternal moment in time, all.

As we conclude this chapter, we may ask directly a question critical to the thesis of this book; namely, "Is the Catholic Church a democracy?" I would reply as follows:

- Since in a democracy, the people most certainly are sovereign;
- since the People of God is the incarnate presence of Christ;
- since Christ, the head of the church, is sovereign over his church;
- since, therefore, the People of God exercise true sovereignty;
- then, most clearly, the Catholic church is a democracy.

It is, in truth and in essence, the democracy of God. Politically, it still remains shackled to the historical trappings and actions of a monarchy. But through their deliberations at Vatican II, the church fathers from around the world have laid open the possibility that ecclesial democracy may be accepted. In the American democracy, now three centuries old, as the result of the episcopal and ecclesial crisis here, it may, at last, happen.

Chapter Four:
Uniformity: The Hidden Virus That Destroys Unity

Early in *Democracy in America* Tocqueville makes a useful distinction. In his words—

> Centralization is a word that is constantly repeated in our day and whose sense no one, in general, seeks to clarify.
>
> Nevertheless, two very distinct kinds of centralization exist, which it is important to know well.
>
> Certain interests are common to all parts of the nation, such as the formation of general laws and the relations of the people with foreigners.
>
> Other issues are special to certain parts of the nation, such as, for example, the undertakings of the township.
>
> To concentrate the power to direct the first in the same place or in the same hand is to found what I shall call governmental centralization.
>
> To concentrate the power to direct the second in the same manner is to found what I shall name administrative centralization.[1]

In this context, "government" means the making of laws, while "administration" points to the overseeing of their application. By "centralization" Tocqueville refers to the exclusive power to govern or to administer.

I. Governmental Power to Make Laws for the People

Tocqueville speaks initially about the nation as a whole. In both monarchies and democracies, an ultimate lawmaking authority exists, king or legislature, that directs the general affairs of the people and relationships to foreign powers. No other persons or entities possess this authority. As Tocqueville notes, such

---
[1]   *Op. cit.,* p. 82.

centralization appears to be essential for the ultimate good of the nation: "For my part, I cannot conceive that a nation can live or above all prosper without strong governmental centralization."[2]

The similarity between monarchy and democracy stops there. A king makes laws at his sole discretion. Every strata of society feels their impact. Other laws, rules, or regulations fashioned by minor officials throughout the realm serve as local extensions and interpretations of the royal will. No jurisdiction exits to pass laws independent of the decrees of the king.

Lawmaking in a democracy occurs separately at various levels of governmental organization. The national legislature votes on bills, then signed by the chief executive, which apply to the whole country and become laws of the land. In America, each state has a parallel system to legislate its own affairs without contravening federal law. This same process extends downward to counties, municipalities, and even townships. As regards these last and most local of legislative authorities, Tocqueville notes:

> In the township as everywhere, the people are the source of social powers, but nowhere do they exercise their power more immediately. The people in America are a master who has to be pleased up to the farthest limits of the possible.
>
> In New England, the majority acts through representatives when it must treat general affairs of the state. It was necessary that it be so; but in the township, where legislative and governmental action is brought closer to the governed, the law of representation is not accepted. There is no municipal council; the body of electors, after having named its magistrates, directs them itself in everything that is not pure and simple execution of the laws of the state.[3]

Democracies govern using the principle of subsidiarity. As much as possible, the body of citizens who must obey given laws enacts them. Just as the nation's citizens elect representatives to Congress to legislate on their behalf, so a state's citizens elect its legislature and so on down to the most local unit. At each level the legislative body has specific and independent jurisdiction concerning matters exclusive to its own citizenry. As Tocqueville indicates, this principle is carried to its ultimate in township government where the people legislate for themselves, without designating any representative intermediary.

---

[2]   *Ibid.*, p. 83.

[3]   *Ibid.*, p. 59.

In the Catholic Church, universal legislative authority resides with the pope. He functions as a constitutional monarch, one who reigns supreme but is always restricted by scripture, tradition, and the faith of the people. He alone, or in conjunction with his bishops, makes laws applicable to the whole church. They are expressed formally in papal encyclicals, through the decrees of ecumenical councils, and in the *Code of Canon Law*. Papal speeches and the formal decisions of various Vatican congregations give further indications of the will of the current pontiff.

As discussed in the previous chapter, bishops have their own proper authority to govern their dioceses. This includes formulating laws to direct the religious practice of their people. As with the pope, they legislate in accord with divine revelation; they, however, may only fashion laws that conform to those of the universal church. To the extent that bishops act as delegates of the pope and not as prelates exercising their own authority, they, in effect, cede their lawmaking authority to him and act like minor lords in a secular kingdom.

Although bishops delegate to pastors a share in their governing power, in actuality these priests do little more than put operating procedures into effect in their parishes. They do not institute new laws; they, instead, see to it that the provisions of diocesan and universal church law are carried out by the faithful.

In general, the church's hierarchy—from pope to bishop to pastor—treat their people as kings do their citizens: at the most they seek out and weigh their advice; usually, taking their own council, they command and look for immediate results. In governmental practice, they evidence little understanding of their place as servants of the People of God or of the sacramental dignity of that People. Indeed, they more often dictate to it as a parent would to a child. In a democracy the citizenry elects its representatives to construct laws suitable for all citizens; in the church the clerical order derives from the people whom it serves, but that service regularly partakes more of dominance than representation. Nowhere do the people govern, make laws, exercise their own authority; nothing like township rule exists. In theory the principle of subsidiarity might apply to the actions of the pope and bishops. In practice, however, this principle seems rarely operative in the American church. With exceptions noted, monarchical governmental centralization designates church practice.

II. Administrative Oversight in the Enforcing of Laws

When kings legislate, they expect compliance. They maintain a system of intermediaries to communicate their will and to see that it is obeyed. They use members of their family, devotees from their court, and various aristocrats to actualize their rule. These loyal appointees, in turn, employ minor officials and local agents to disseminate the king's directions, to call stragglers back into line, and to punish the seriously errant. In this manner the royal presence is continuously felt in every hamlet and neighborhood throughout the kingdom. The king employs not only governmental but also administrative centralization within the realm. One need only think of the despotic dictatorship of Adolf Hitler—with Gestapo located in every community, with Hitler youth corps members indoctrinated to spy on and report one's own parents to the authorities, with the populace, enthralled by pride and gripped by fear, fanatically carrying out even ungodly wishes—to understand the insidious control of such centralized power.

American democracy knows little of administrative centralization; indeed, "generally, one can say that the salient characteristic of public administration in the United States is to be enormously decentralized."[4] Tocqueville even declares: "...in the United States administrative centralization does not exist. One hardly finds a trace of hierarchy there."[5] This extends down into the states: "In none of the American republics has the central government ever been occupied but with a few objects whose importance attracted its regard. It has not undertaken to regulate secondary things in society."[6]

Indeed, as with its lawmaking so with its administration: both occur only at the level of government and with the people who put laws into effect. Even the federal government acts in that manner. It passes laws that dictate citizen action. It deals directly with the citizen, not through layers of intermediaries, in their execution. For example, the central government passes an individual income tax law. Forms go out from it to the citizen; citizens return them directly to the designated federal agency; payments and refunds pass solely between the citizen and the government. Or again, the federal government passes a selective service act. Young men register directly through local boards that have no relationship to any levels of state or local government. Should a draft occur, all communication and activity happens between the federal selective service system and eligible draftees.

Many signs point to the extreme administrative centralization of the Catholic Church under John Paul II. In his twenty-six year reign he named 232 cardinals and more than 3,300 bishops to run the church. In those selections he showed a strong preference for clerics who shared his conservative views about church policy, even making agreement with him synonymous with orthodoxy. He appointed the overwhelming majority of the 114 cardinals that made Cardinal Ratzinger, Benedict XVI. In John Paul's pontificate, bishops, supposedly possessing their

---

[4]   *Ibid.*, p. 79.

[5]   *Ibid.*, p. 84.

[6]   *Ibid.*, p. 258.

own governing authority, alone or as a national conference, could not even discuss pastoral issues upon which that pope had staked out a position. To do so risked the charge of disloyalty and even heterodoxy. Anthony Padovano calls attention to a glaring example of this debilitating Vatican control:

> In June of 1995, twelve American bishops (with the support of forty other bishops who endorsed but did not sign the document) listed fifteen pastorally urgent issues which the episcopal conference is frightened to discuss because of Vatican intimidation:
>
> 1. presenting the minority position of Vatican II as if it were the majority
> 2. ecumenical issues
> 3. marital annulments
> 4. appointment of bishops
> 5. the relationship of episcopal conferences and Rome
> 6. collegiality in the Church
> 7. the role of women and their ordination
> 8. the shortage of priests
> 9. the morale of priests
> 10. the ordination of married men
> 11. sexual ethics
> 12. contraception
> 13. homosexuality
> 14. abortion
> 15. pedophilia[7]

Should a bishop act contrary to that pope's wishes, he risked the fate of Archbishop Raymond Hunthausen of Seattle. When he allowed Dignity, an organization of gay and lesbian Catholics, to hold its own mass in his cathedral, Rome responded quickly. Within a year it had appointed an auxiliary bishop, Donald Wuerl, to the archdiocese. Bishop Wuerl was given episcopal authority over all areas of diocesan

---

[7]   Anthony T. Padovano, "The American Catholic Church: Assessing the Past, Discerning the Future." Address delivered in November 2003 to the National Conference of Call to Action, Milwaukee, Wisconsin.

life that Rome considered suspicious under Hunthausen. The Archbishop, never censured but deeply hurt by this secret limitation of his episcopal power, openly complained. Although many fellow bishops sided with him, Rome prevailed in the name of Catholic unity and papal primacy. Five years later, in August 1991, this beloved prelate, a man who dared publicly to oppose modern methods of war and who with pastoral sensitivity reached out to all Catholics in his archdiocese, retired. He fell victim to a coalition of conservative Catholic members of his community and their ideological companions in the Vatican.

Administrative centralization courts uniformity. Tocqueville describes it this way:

> Centralization, it is true, easily succeeds in subjecting the external actions of man to a certain uniformity that in the end one loves for itself, independent of the things to which it applies, like those devotees who adore the statue forgetting the divinity that it represents. Centralization succeeds without difficulty in impressing a regular style on current affairs; in skillfully regimenting the details of social orderliness; in repressing slight disorders and small offenses; in maintaining society in a status quo that is properly neither decadence nor progress; in keeping in a social body a sort of administrative somnolence that administrators are accustomed to calling good order and public tranquility. It excels, in a word, at preventing, not at doing.[8]

His words accurately catch the flavor of the 20th Century American church prior to Vatican II. On Sunday, Catholics attended the same mysterious Latin mass. They stood or knelt or sat on cue; they listened to set scriptural readings; they heard the same, sentimental, devotional hymns; they tried to attend to father's sermon on acquiring virtue or avoiding sin; they filed up to the altar rail to receive communion. Finally, released by *ite missa est*, they hurried outside, duty done for another week. At school, Catholic students wore uniforms, said "yes, sister," and did not cause trouble. Families raced through grace before meals and recited the rosary together, and knelt for prayer at bedtime. We all knew the routine, and led the programmed and certain and secure lives of good Catholics. This way we avoided sin and earned heaven. Since we moved in step, we imagined that we were one. In reality, instead of enjoying unity we were practicing uniformity, as we discovered when Vatican II shook up our uniform world.

---

[8]   *Op. cit.,* p. 86.

Tocqueville continues his discussion of administrative centralization and uniformity:

> When it is a question of moving society profoundly or pressing it to a rapid advance, its force abandons it. If its measures need the concurrence of individuals, one is then wholly surprised at the weakness of that immense machine; it finds itself suddenly reduced to impotence.[9]

Vatican II moved our "society profoundly" and called for a "rapid advance." It shattered our uniformity and held out a vision of unity as the People of God. The church challenged us to buy into this new way of being Catholic. Some responded enthusiastically; others dug in their heels defiantly; the "immense machine" of the church found itself "reduced to impotence": it could not give up its reliance on uniformity for the sake of an envisioned higher unity. Its leaders at first selected a cautious bureaucrat in Paul VI on the assumption that he would not move too fast. When he and his ill-fated successor died, the conclave picked a man who gave promise of reestablishing uniformity while letting unity happen as a hoped-for but elusive afterthought.

But John Paul II failed. In the American church we have neither unity nor uniformity. All his intense efforts to enforce uniformity—appointing of conservative bishops, requiring a *mandatum* for university teachers of theology, limiting discussion of contentious issues, enforcing clerical celibacy, maintaining traditional stances in sexual ethics, calling for a return to obedience to the church's teaching magisterium, urging increased vocations to the priesthood and religious life—were doomed from the beginning. Why?—because the agents of uniformity, the legions of sisters and brothers and priests, were no longer available for trench work. With Vatican II they realized that uniformity had long and successfully been parading as unity. At the same time, they caught and understood a vision of unity—between man and woman, between Protestant and Catholic, between cleric and layperson, between humankind and the earth, and, most importantly, between believers and an immanent God. This vision far surpassed all the superficial promises of uniformity now and eternal life hereafter. When the church stopped its pursuit of transformation and backpedaled to the secure boundaries of uniformity, those who understood the direction of Vatican II kept right on going: out of convents and rectories, out of monasteries and schools, out of parishes and churches, and even out of the church itself.

---

[9] *Ibid.*

Given the exodus of these religious professionals, the church has turned in desperation to the laity. Confraternity of Christian Doctrine programs taught by laymen and laywomen have replaced many parochial schools. Lay deacons have stepped in for the missing priests as preachers, as assistants at mass, as eucharistic ministers and visitors of the sick, at baptisms and marriages and funerals. Lay administrators have taken charge of the remaining schools; some have even become substitute pastors. But failure lurks here also. All of these cosmetic changes leave in place the clerical culture and the structure of uniformity. The laity increasingly does the work but its position, at the bottom of the hierarchical pyramid, remains as before. Tocqueville presciently comments:

> Then sometimes it happens that centralization tries, in desperation, to call citizens to its aid; but it says to them: "You shall act as I wish, as long as I wish, and precisely in the direction I wish. You shall take charge of the details without aspiring to direct the sum; you shall work in the darkness, and later you shall judge my work by its results." It is not under such conditions that one obtains the concurrence of the human will. It must have freedom in its style, responsibility in its actions. Man is so made that he prefers standing still to marching without independence toward a goal of which he is ignorant.[10]

If the church continues to seek uniformity at the expense of unity, if it insists on valuing its hierarchical and administrative structure over its sacramental essence as the People of God, if it refuses to shift its focus from a transcendent God served by a monarchical pope to an immanent God enlivening a believing community, then the time is approaching when the laity too will disappear. They will cease being compliant substitutes. They too, the newly minted religious professionals, as they recognize the power charade, will turn their efforts elsewhere to support the democracy of God.

III. The Failure of the Clerical Culture

In their introduction to *Governance, Accountability, and the Future of the Church,* Oakley and Russett summarily attribute the causes of the recent clerical sex scandal:

> ...the acknowledged gravity of the sexual abuse crisis itself and its mishandling by so many bishops at home and abroad is widely seen by

---

10   *Ibid.*

the contributors to spring from the further fact that it is grounded in, builds upon, reflects, and certainly discloses long-established pathologies in the clerical culture, in our modern structure of ecclesiastical governance, and in the well-entrenched and almost instinctive mode of ecclesiological thinking prevalent among so many of our church leaders. That mode of thinking [Francine] Cardman refers to as "the default ecclesiology," an adamantly hierarchical ecclesiology that [Peter] Phan characterizes as one "devoid of any sense of co-responsibility and [downward] accountability." In effect, the clerical sexual abuse scandal is understood as having "ultimately been less about sex than about power" [John Beal] and the crisis it has generated as being nothing less than "an ecclesiological crisis" [Donald Cozzens].

Cozzens himself attempts to pinpoint the heart of what he sees at stake by identifying the persistence within contemporary Catholic ecclesiological (and, certainly, ecclesiastical) discourse of two competing understandings of the nature of the church, both jostling, as it were, for the upper hand. The first of these he characterizes as "static, radically hierarchical, and ahistorical," "fostering a culture of silence and denial." The second, as "organic, communal and respectful of history," fostering in turn "a culture of conversation, consultation, and collaboration."[11]

We have previously discussed most of these issues: "the modern structure of ecclesiastical governance," "hierarchical ecclesiology," "power," and "the nature of the church." However, we have not as yet explored "the long-established pathologies in the clerical culture." Since centralization, both governmental and administrative, creates this culture and spawns its pathology, we should understand it in order to bring about needed transformation.

Let us examine this pathology from three different but complementary standpoints: emotional, political, and organizational. In the following pages I will be drawing on my own professional experience as a psychologist, organizational development consultant, and religious psychotherapist.

Emotional Pathology

In former days, young boys entered minor seminaries instead of attending local high schools. Religious novices regularly joined orders on completing their secondary schooling. Today, most minor seminaries have bolted their doors; dioceses enlist high school graduates; religious orders tend to accept applicants who have

---

[11]   *Op. cit.*, pp. 9-10.

college education or successful adult experience. This upward shift in age reflects a recognized need for candidates to attain a broader emotional development before starting their clerical and religious journeys.

This change addresses only a superficial aspect of the emotional climate of the seminary world. It essentially shifts the burden of emotional development to the secular society before entrance; it does not deal with the clerical milieu and its impact on emotional life.

During the process of emotional growth, a person passes through stages of dependency, independency, and relational interdependency. An emotionally mature adult has the capacity to share his life with another without depletion. This gift, indeed, becomes a wellspring of increased life in the giver. In and through this act of love, the needs of the dependent ego diminish while the energy of the actualized self deepens and expands.

When young men choose to study for the Catholic priesthood, they ordinarily possess only a rudimentary grasp of the indoctrination process. They know that the training will be drawn out and intense. They also expect a regimented lifestyle with strict requirements. They recognize that they are embarking on a formation regime that will shape them into the kind of people the church desires in its priests.

As they settle into their new life, the candidates cannot fail to encounter three salient aspects of their training: others command and they obey; others shape the environment and supply their needs; they relate primarily to God, next to their superiors, then to their companions. Except for occasional visits, they have left their families; except for incidental contacts, they have renounced emotional relationships with women. The required obedience increases dependency on others and removes most responsibility except to conform. The all-male conditions replicate the dependency of youthful teams, or the camaraderie of fraternities. The lack of relationship with women makes all emotional relationship problematic, reinforces male small group dependency, and places individual independence as the emotional goal. That state, one of a securely defended ego, requires distance in relationships, a measuring of others' commitment, and offers little possibility of entering into and sustaining emotionally mature and interdependent relationships.

Because of this formative milieu, religious superiors tend to dismiss emotional growth as, basically, irrelevant; instead, they focus on preventing emotional problems. They warn their charges about solitary meetings with women; they counsel plenty of sleep and exercise to combat solitary sexual urges; they reinforce regulations that cut down the opportunities for homosexual encounters. And they emphasize developing a loving relationship with God as the only allowable substitute for prohibited ones with human beings. This love of God will be made manifest through the development of will power that helps them obey their superiors in all things. As a result, emotional growth, at its best, stays in a kind of limbo, to be pursued later, after ordination; at its worst, the trainees regress to stages of emotional dependency on others or on external signs of achievement.

Having practically ruled out intimate relationships and emotional growth, superiors emphasize intellectual advancement. Students must learn about the church, its foundation and history. They need to understand the demands of a clerical vocation and the tasks entrusted to priests within the church's hierarchical structure. They must study theology and philosophy, scripture and the Church Fathers, conciliar decrees and papal encyclicals in order to remain faithful to church teaching and to be able to guide others responsibly. Intellectual prowess, not emotional maturity, becomes the measure of growth and success; indeed, it regularly substitutes for it.

Although exceptions exist, the typical *ordinandus* presents himself to the bishop as a person well versed in the expectations of the clerical world, with a working-man's knowledge of philosophy and theology, with some liberal education, and, at the most, a level of emotional maturity equal to pre-seminary days. He may have attained some measure of independent intellectual maturity; he probably has scant emotional resources to live as an independent priest in a parish world peopled by children, married couples, single women and single men. His social and relational skills probably peak around male friendship; they certainly do not include interpersonal intimacy. He may have learned to live without emotion; he will have little experience with, or ability in, personal relationships.

The newly ordained priest, if his previous training took, will have developed strong powers of emotional repression; he will be noticeably weak on emotional expression. Since repressed emotions will at some point demand their due, this leaves the young priest in a dangerous situation. As he experiences the ordinary stresses of adult life, as he confronts depression caused by the boring routines of daily existence, as he struggles with emotional needs such as loneliness, he presents as a prime candidate for developing addictive coping habits. In order to blunt emotional disturbance, he may turn to readily available pacifiers like cigarettes, alcohol, food, and sex. He may siphon off a disruptive emotion like anger through the heavy-handedness of the despotic teacher, the dogmatic authoritarianism of the tyrannical pastor, or the power moves of the sexual dilettante with children or young people, mistresses or other men. All of these maneuvers work; they do assuage emotional turmoil for a time. However, they do not solve the problem: emotional expression is not facilitated; emotional repression stays locked in position and sets the conditions for ongoing inner distress; emotional immaturity remains and requires external pacifiers to replace the lack of internal direction and control.

Spiritual directors generally make three disastrous mistakes in preparing aspiring candidates for the priesthood. In the first place, they rely on a structured environment, a culture of obedience, and rewards and punishments to instill group values. From the outset the strategy fails with the independent and the emotionally mature; it works with the emotionally immature as long as they remain in that state; it requires continual reinforcement during training and after ordination. Introjected values, ones imposed from without, do not automatically become internalized personal values. One's own values grow through experience, through free choice, through the risks of personal responsibility, and though an internal recognition that they truly represent the person one is or aspires to become.

In addition, they erroneously think that virtue follows upon knowledge and that will power alone can maintain a virtuous life. As St. Paul commented: "I cannot even understand my own actions. I do not do what I want to do but what I hate. When I act against my own will, by that very fact I agree that the law is good. This indicates that it is not I who do it but sin which resides in me" (Rom. 17:15-17). Virtue demands a vision of the person one may become and an emotional attachment to that vision.

Tragically, they instruct the intellect about Christian morality and a priestly life; they exercise and strengthen the will through the daily challenges of obedience; they treat the emotions as inferior to the intellect and will, as a subset of the unruly body, both of which need to be constantly controlled. Emotions are best avoided, must not be allowed to disrupt a well-ordered life, and require monitoring and discipline. Such directors show scant knowledge of the place of emotions in human life or in the maturing process. Indeed, they value obedient dependency much more than independence, and they equate obedient behavior with love.

In summation, the clerical culture does not prepare young people for adult relationships. Instead, it leaves them prey to emotional needs and dependency.

Political[12] Pathology

In a community of Christian believers, one would hope that leaders would surface who manifest some noteworthy personal qualities. A deeply reflective and seasoned knowledge of revelation built by a habit of union with God in prayer and grounded in a personal relationship with God would top the list. This would be observed in a steady faith in the midst of trials and suffering, in a life noteworthy for the spiritual and corporal works of mercy, and in a Christian presence that inspires others to follow Christ. Such a person could and would lead a community

---

[12]   By "political" is here meant the mode of advancement within the clerical culture.

in heartfelt prayer and explain revelation to that people in understandable terms. He or she would be known for a spiritual wisdom grounded through long personal experience of interiority, would possess a personal knowledge and self acceptance that issues in calmness and humility, and would surround all with a joyful energy while serving the Christian community. Of course, this profile underscores an expectation that Christian leadership concerns itself primarily and essentially with helping others, Christians and non-Christians alike, to discover in their own experience the saving presence of a loving God.

We must presume that over two millennia of the church's existence, some popes were elected, some bishops named, and some pastors selected who lived one or more of these qualities in an outstanding fashion. Many have been officially proclaimed to be saints. We surmise that their holiness shone through their daily occupations, revealing Christ's presence and inviting others to a closer union with him.

Church history and personal experience testify that not all members of the hierarchy exhibit these Christ-like characteristics. Many, indeed, illustrate more obviously the profile of corporate managers, men loyal to the institution and striving to rise within its corporate ranks. Among them, the system itself assumes prime importance: its image in the world, the smoothness of its functioning, its power over its members, its wealth, and its global growth. Power preens over mission; orthodoxy and its preservation become the institution's *raison d'etre*.

Since the challenges posed to its exalted position by the Protestant Reformation and the subsequent spread of other Christian denominations worldwide, fortress Catholicism has ruled. Hierarchical power and absolute authority have trumped Christ's original mission to his followers to "go, therefore, and make disciples of all the nations" (Mt. 28:19). The new mission, shown in the behavior of her hierarchy, could well be summarized as "go, therefore, and preserve the power, authority, and status of the hierarchical Catholic Church."

As all modern executives know, some basic rules guide corporate behavior. Most essentially, they must "keep on task." Whatever else happens, their efforts must, in the case of the Catholic Church, be always and everywhere and untiringly aimed at preserving and maintaining "the power, authority, and status of the hierarchical Catholic Church." Personal issues, community requests or needs, moral conflicts must be considered in light of that overriding goal, and must be dealt with only in a manner to advance its achievement. When Cardinal Law, caught up in the clergy sexual abuse scandal, was forced to resign, he did so because the revolt in the Boston Archdiocese was threatening a major source of American funds for diocesan and Vatican projects. His position was rapidly deteriorating. However, church officials could not allow the perception that the laity somehow had fired a cardinal. Therefore, his eminence was booted upstairs, given the symbolic plum of a Roman cathedral, and church authorities spread about the fiction that Rome, not the people, had engineered Law's removal, reassignment, and advancement.

In a modern corporation all members, from president to foreman to warehouseman, must pull together. They should direct all efforts and energy toward the corporate goal. Internal bickering and disputes must stop. "Rocking the boat" diverts attention, delays action, and challenges the chain of command. Changes may be called for, but they should be initiated from above and happen with the oversight and approval of superiors. Whistleblowers, corporate troublemakers, cause disruption. Deal quietly and unobtrusively with all significant problems. Allow the insignificant ones to continue; addressing them publicly will cause more hassle than they are worth. Many aspiring managers, as a result, overlook problems, minimize them, or even deny they exist. The fabled "elephant in the living room" is hoped just to be passing through. Managers such as these calculate that the beast's passage will leave few telltale traces of its presence.

One has to wonder how many priests chose to ignore the young people entering or leaving a fellow cleric's bedroom. Did they do so in order to avoid creating a fuss, or did they rationalize the evidence away, denying what their eyes and common sense were shouting at them? And what did a bishop say to himself as he avoided reporting a sexually abusive priest to the civil authorities? What was he thinking when he paid off a victim's family on the condition of public silence and then moved the offender to an unsuspecting parish or diocese? One can well imagine phrases like "keep to the task," "don't rock the boat," "avoid scandal," and "but he's such a good priest" figured prominently in the corporate prelate's pathological fantasy world.

The avoidance of scandal must be the Western version of the Oriental saving of face. The Catholic Church projects the image of holiness and dedication to Christ. It furthermore portrays its clerical hierarchy as a cadre of men answering the summons of Christ to embrace "a higher state of life," which means setting aside many of the legitimate pleasures of ordinary Christian life out of a special love for Christ and his followers. Much of their authority, the respect of the people, the honor afforded them in society, and the financial support of their position depend upon this public perception of their saintly sacrifice and selfless charity. Although reasonable Catholics do not expect perfection in their leaders, they do need to know that they too are striving for the Christian holiness that they teach, preach, and command.

What would happen if parishioners found out that their pastor was an active homosexual who enjoyed occasional sexual outings with his boyfriend? What would his people think if they knew that Father spent his evenings traveling from apartment to apartment of his clan of mistresses? Is it not be better for the church if the ordinary of the diocese who loves his secretary did so in secret, instead of resigning from the priesthood to marry her? Given the current shortage of priests, is not the cause of religion better served by secretly paying off pedophilia victims and allowing the clerical perpetrator another chance to be a good priest? If the intact image of holiness means more than truth, humility, and the seeking of forgiveness, then silence and deception might be allowed. But a Christian must hear Christ's condemnation of the Scribes and Pharisees when he, in frustration, exclaimed: "You hypocrites! How accurately did Isaiah prophecy about you when he said: 'This people pays me lip service but their heart is far from me. They do me empty reverence, making dogmas out of human precepts'" (Mt. 15:7-9). Would Christ not condemn the hierarchical employing of a new dogma, "don't cause scandal," constructed in the name of religion, but, in truth, fashioned to preserve a pretense of saintliness?

Human beings use a variety of defenses to protect themselves from the truth:

- A husband explains away his gambling debts by claiming that he just needed a break from work; a priest rationalizes his excessive drinking as being better than keeping a mistress to quiet his loneliness.

- A three-time divorcee dismisses her latest attempt with "he wasn't of my class anyhow"; American bishops minimize the current crisis by assuring themselves that the church has gone through many troubled times in its long history, has always survived, and will weather this storm because Christ himself promised that he would be with them until the end of the world.

- A wife blames her hardworking, salesman husband for her affair with a married man; Rome accuses a bigoted news media for over-blowing the pedophilia crisis in America.

- A frequenter of porn shops leads the civic crusade against a neighborhood adult bookstore; the Vatican keeps up its relentless attack against homosexuality while its seminaries and rectories swell with homosexuals.

- An alcoholic swears that he can, when it comes to liquor, take it or leave it; a bishop refuses to believe that his dear friend, the monsignor, is sexually involved with children.

- A father harshly punishes his teenage son for seeking an explanation after his own boss had lectured him and he could not respond; a bishop refuses to meet with a group of concerned parishioners because a Voice of the Faithful ad in the local paper had criticized his stance on female participation in the liturgy.

- A teenager, afraid of his sexual feelings for a female classmate, becomes addicted to constant and frantic activity; a pope, anxious about the decrease in vocations and falling mass attendance in the United States, rejoices in creating more dioceses, elevating additional cardinals, and naming new bishops for that country.

In every instance, a problem occurs, an action is taken that does not directly address the problem, and the problem remains. When such fruitless behavior permeates the church and is encouraged by its clerical leaders because of its divine mission, this constitutes a glaring example of a religious goal, even the misplaced one of saving orthodoxy for orthodoxy's sake, justifying a host of pathological means. In the long run, the spreading pathology will, by itself, destroy the church's integrity and frustrate even its legitimate enterprises.

Organizational Pathology

When an organization determines that its own continuation should be its principal goal, it closes in upon itself in a defensive reaction. It sidelines, even forgets, its founding purpose in this concentration on self-protection. In addition, it sets up a continuing state of internal conflict over roles and needs.

It chooses directors skilled in organizational politics and proven masters at running a tight ship. They must preach loyalty, demand unquestioning obedience, and emphasize institutional security as a major priority. They will without mercy ferret out the disloyal, mark then as traitors, and punish them through banishment into internal limbo or external darkness. They will need to fashion a network of trusted comrades who practice the party line, demand conformity to party doctrines from subordinates, and help their bosses purge the corporate ranks of the weak, the wavering, and the uncommitted.

This organization lives on its self-importance. Proclaimed the best, it deserves continuity and respect. Its leaders, possessed of uncommon wisdom and blessed with unusual intelligence, do not make mistakes. They will guide the company successfully through the worst of moments and will ultimately prevail over its strongest opponents.

The exhibition of organizational unity comes through remarkable displays of uniformity. All speak as one, preaching a common doctrine. Information from above is received with faith; communications from below contain nothing that contradicts the prevailing corporate doctrines, assessments, or plans. What must be heard will alone be uttered. This sameness of speech issues from identical ways of thinking and produces similar actions. The face painted within the inner chambers nestles repetitively in the dreams of the members and projects with uncanny and predictable accuracy outward to the surrounding world.

What is this closed organization missing? It has lost focus on its goal, the founder's purpose. It attracts politicians, manipulators of people and facts, rather than managers skilled in directing and motivating others. It practices a top-down delivery of corporate dogma and receives back prescribed echoes; communication, in the sense of dialogue, does not exist here, and objective truth is outlawed if it contradicts the company's subjective version of reality. Change, the product of a clash of ideas or a collision of wills or a creative union of images, does not occur. "What was good enough for...", a maxim that stresses sameness, never difference, together, never apart, and the organization's past, never an open and exciting future, replaces independent thinking and substitutes for creative behavior. The fear of corporate displeasure effectively squelches individuality that could bring new and renewed energy to a mutual enterprise. Participation in the network of old boys, and the garnering of special signs of their approval, all at the cost of freedom, become the replacements for a personal life and self-respect.

Such an organization faces an uncertain future. Other organizations, open and creative, may draw away its members to a more promising life. Defectors may deplete the corporate rolls until the organization collapses in on itself, killed by inanition and a debilitating absence of fresh blood. Or a strong opponent may arise, one that can marshal significant enough forces to overcome the closed system or make it exhaust itself in unrelenting defensive efforts. Or again, significant numbers of the corporate faithful, realizing the ultimate fruitlessness of the enterprise, may mount a reasonable and sustained challenge from within that compels change. Forsaking rewards for marching in step, they may refuse to be co-opted by the lure of advancement; instead, they embrace the original vision and, inspired by it, fight for its return. The organization will change, the system will open up, or it will split into parts, some devotees hanging desperately on to pieces of the past, others integrating those pieces into a different and attractive future.

In our days the Soviet Union, the model of a closed society, collapsed. Its lifeblood flowed away, over and around and under the Berlin Wall. Economically and socially starving as it poured its resources into the escalating defensive postures of the Cold War, it finally succumbed to its own seeds of self-destruction.

Before it, Nazi Germany, the product of a fanatical despot, fell before the combined armies of the free world. Its promise of world dominance and racial purity, pronounced by an evil genius and furthered by ruthless denizens of uniformity, could not match the creativity, ingenuity, and determination of self-directed, dedicated, and outraged pursuers of freedom.

During the declining years of the Middle Ages, the Holy Roman Empire, the royal offspring of the marriage of religious and civil societies, flew apart under the internal onslaught of fed-up priests and prelates and monarchs chaffing under the dominance, control, and enforced stability of the feudal world. They preferred freedom to the security of a programmed, inflexible, and overbearing system ruled mercilessly through the double-edged sword of Church and State.

If we could have interviewed the architects and supporters of those massive, closed systems, I am sure that they would have proclaimed their rightness, justified their cruelty, and predicted their ultimate victory over all enemies, within and without. Sure of themselves and their righteousness, they would encourage all to join them in their world-changing enterprise.

The hierarchical Catholic Church gives solid evidence of being a closed system. John Paul II made administrative centralization and church discipline a prime focus of his reign, and he handpicked cardinals to elect a successor formed in his image and likeness. In the meantime, his cabinet secretaries, the cardinals that run Vatican congregations, intimidated conferences of bishops, in America and around the world. Indeed, they seeded those conferences only with episcopal candidates that passed the litmus test of loyalty to Rome. Sitting bishops, moreover, those who desired hierarchical advancement, must act primarily as delegates of the pope, not as ordinaries of their dioceses. So, for example, bishops who entered into dialogue with, or appeared to support, groups like Dignity, Voice of the Faithful, Call to Action, and the Women's Ordination Conference faced censure and threatened diminution of their episcopal power now, and a disregarded life in administrative limbo hereafter. The politically wise bishop silenced priests and religious and organizations that supported shifts in current church discipline. Bishop's conferences, pastoral councils, priests' federations—all urged by Vatican II—exercised no independent power and at best enjoyed only advisory status. Bishops continued to obstruct the work of their own watchdog commission on clergy sexual abuse, still made excuses for their mishandling of the crisis, and still treated victims as the ones causing unnecessary problems. Lay groups seeking dialogue with their bishops routinely crashed headfirst into a stone wall of episcopal intransigence. Some pastors refused to meet with such groups within their parish, especially if they sought greater involvement in parish administration and oversight, even refusing them church space for their meetings. And should a Catholic politician not toe the current party line on morality, some bishops threatened their excommunication and advised their pastors publicly to deny the sacrament to these rebellious offenders of their political-moral agenda.

In summary, we behold a church in which power and authority come from above, communication remains one-sided, change comes, if at all, only glacially, and dissent evokes censure.

Organizational politics, an arena for dialogue and negotiation, become pathological under such conditions. The art of the possible collides with the dictates of the absolute. Problems do not get resolved; rather, they burrow in like persistent sores, at times quiescent, at times festering and inflamed. Life energy pours out in frustration and in fruitless attempts at solutions.

Unresolved problems tend to cluster in six areas. Consider each in turn in the context of the church.

1. Role Invasion

In a complex organization, authority is distributed. Some exercise their own authority; others work with only delegated authority. But each role has its own power, tasks, responsibilities, and accountability. When roles overlap, when someone assumes authority illegitimately in another's area, the problem of role invasion flares. To solve it, all parties must clarify roles, carefully examine gray areas, and negotiate a reasonable separation of responsibilities.

We have glaring examples of role invasion in the American church. As previously discussed, ordinaries of dioceses are prelates who enjoy their own full and proper authority in their diocese to teach, govern, and sanctify their people. Yet Rome, through papal nuncios, Vatican congregations, and metropolitan bishops, uses organizational advancement as a carrot, and threat of censure as a stick, to promote acquiescence to the current demands of orthodoxy and regulations of discipline. As indicated earlier in this chapter, some bishops do not address pastoral problems in their dioceses because of fear of Vatican retaliation.

In Catholicism, some scholars take on the role of theological exploration. It falls to them to consider Christian revelation in light of scripture, tradition, and the faith of the people. They alone illuminate the effect of successive eras in American life on our understanding of the body of the Catholic faith. The church needs their theological training, reflection, scholarship, and research challenging today's boundaries if its wishes reasonably to fulfill its mandate of teaching, governing, and sanctifying the People of God. In recent years, many bishops have usurped the role of theologian. With some exceptions, they do so without any particular training or expertise in theology other than that furnished in the seminary. Instead of being guided by theological expertise, they hamper and restrict professional exploration. They prohibit lines of theological research in the name of their governing power; they cut off the development of Catholic doctrine and compromise the proper functioning of the theologian's role in the community. They lead us to wonder if the position of bishop confers some special knowledge of theology without the requisite scholarly training and pursuit.

Ancillary to this, some American bishops have indicated that their governing and teaching authority make them experts also in various modern academic fields, from politics and current affairs, to medicine and health care, to genetics and human behavior. They act as if they know better how to manage Catholic liberal arts colleges than college presidents do. They demand that, when a speaker who holds an opinion contrary to the bishop's explanation of Catholic teaching is invited to the campus, the engagement should be cancelled. They confuse two separable issues: agreement with a dissenting opinion and freedom of speech, open academic discussion, and the weighing and testing of various sides of significant topics. As experienced teachers know, opposing views stimulate debate, occasion a deeper examination of issues, and develop critical thinking in students and teachers. A liberal arts college, by its very mission, should espouse such free and unrestricted exploration. Bishops who have never taught, who have never been college administrators, who have no more than a journeyman's education in the liberal arts, simply look foolish when they presume to dictate the who and what of academic discussion. Episcopal consecration does not, of itself, bestow intelligence, knowledge, or scholarly expertise. These may be earned only through hard work, not as badges bestowed for loyalty.

2. Competitive Incentive Structures

Organizations have controlling visions about their enterprise. They generate goals and establish pathways to success in relation to them. Managers set up prizes for sustained activity that moves the group toward goals and the realization of self-vision. These rewards, and their corresponding punishments, establish a competitive structure that motivates both employers and employees toward their best efforts. When an organization has an unclear perception of itself, or when it generates contradictory visions, it sets up competitive incentive structures. Members, as a result, may be praised or demonized for the same actions depending upon how one looks upon the activities and the frame of reference placed around them.

Confusion roils the Catholic Church in America concerning its role in the modern world. Questions, such as these, abound:

- Does the church's faithfulness to its founder consist in preserving intact his experience of his Father, or in leading his followers to their own encounter with God?

- Should the church strive primarily to guard its hierarchical administrative structure, or should it concentrate on opening up all nations and peoples to the revelation of Christ?

- Should the church direct its people through obedience now to eternal enjoyment of a transcendent God hereafter, or should it help them through the indwelling Spirit discover in the present the immanent God acting in their lives?

- In essence, is the church a limited monarchy realized in and through its hierarchical structure, or is it a democracy manifested in the People of God?

- Does the church fulfill its mission through obedience that creates uniformity, or through relationships that develop an ever-deepening unity?

Depending upon how one answers these and similar questions, an incentive framework establishes itself. If, for example, we judge that the faithful layperson best acts obediently, without complaint, and without doubt or hesitation, then the bishops and priests who turn out such church members deserve applause. If, on the contrary, we maintain that those who reverence the Spirit of God moving in their lives, and who share that presence with others, are living as exemplary Catholics, then spiritual directors—bishops or priests or laypeople—who assist them should receive our thanks. Or again, if the church and its hierarchy are essentially equated, then its hierarchical administrators merit honor, respect, and obedience simply because of appointed positions. Moreover, good Catholics will resolutely rally to defend them as an essential act of faith. If, on the contrary, the People of God embody the church, then those who respect it, further it, and work for its rightful recognition as the sacrament of God's presence are living more fully their Catholic faith. Who, one may ask, earns today the title of *defensor fidei*: the one who fights the heretics of doubt and disobedience, or the one who battles all usurpers, even ecclesiastical ones, of the role of God's people? In an open system people ask, deal with, and resolve such essential questions; in a pathological one opposing opinions remain unspoken and eat silently away, infectious cancers destroying the Body of Christ.

3. Task Deprivation

Managers of complex corporations assign people with different capabilities to particular jobs. Each task taken alone accomplishes little; linked together, they carry the creative energy of the whole toward desired outcomes. Corporate success depends upon a combination of quality individual performances and smooth, timely interaction of operational networks. When one or more components perform in a shoddy fashion, turning out poor or tardy work, they frustrate the overall endeavor. They pose a task deprivation problem that must be resolved for the sake of everyone. As anyone knowledgeable of sports readily understands, individual performances, no matter how sterling, cannot make up for a lack of reliable teamwork. To address this issue one must unveil the faulty component, understand how it fails, and formulate an effective remedy.

Throughout the pages of this book, we find ample reason for concluding that the Catholic Church in America is in a crisis that could prove fatal. Different authorities, commentators, writers attribute the sad state of current affairs to a range of causes. Few, if any, deny the critical nature of the situation; no one who admits the crisis claims that the church's managers—from pope to bishops to pastors—are performing well and successfully. They alone have governing power; they alone have administrative responsibility; they alone must institute changes for the good of the church. To date, they are managing without significant success.

Let us adopt a simple but illustrative metaphor from sports to illustrate possible options for remedial change. A football team compiles over its season a dismal record of two wins and eleven losses. An unacceptable tally, something must change.

Consider, first, the players: have they the requisite natural skills? Have they passed through the necessary training? If we alter our recruiting guidelines, would we then become a winning team? Applying this to the American church, would altering admission standards to seminaries and novitiates solve the vocational problem? Would the addition of a different formation regime make a substantial difference in the quality and quantity of graduates? Over the past forty years religious directors have implemented both strategies. The numbers of priests and religious continue to tumble; the quality of those remaining suffers from illness, age, overwork, and emotional dependency.

Perhaps, then, we need to design new, more creative plays. Vatican II introduced some different plays. It allowed prayers in the vernacular both at mass and in the sacraments; it opened up relationships to the modern world; it stressed vehicles and practices of communication between groups in the church; it emphasized the collegiality of bishops, among themselves, and in relation to the bishop of Rome. One may argue about the effectiveness, for good or ill, of these changes. Obviously, however, they have not solved the problem; with them in place the condition of the church continues to weaken. One could add yet other plays or revamp the present ones, but we have little evidence to suggest that such alterations would prove sufficient. Bishops add permanent deacons and lay administrators; they do not quiet the desperate need of priests for mass and the sacraments. Bishops merge parishes to save money and to fill the pews; mass attendance still declines. Incidental shifts are not working.

When different plays do not translate into touchdowns, good coaches check out different operating systems; they alter their overall, controlling strategy. They look for one that best fits the talents of their players. At Vatican II the council fathers urged a shift from the hierarchical formation to that of a People of God. But this formation has never been tried. After Vatican II, both Paul VI and John Paul II insisted on advocating the hierarchical formation, and resolutely turned their backs on its possible successor. And the bishops have gone along with Rome. Few, if any, have dared to follow the calling of the Second Vatican Council; they have rather stayed with the time-worn, rewarded hierarchical model. Here, indeed, they fail. Their people, educated and independent, do not comfortably fit into the old system any more. They need and are ready for the new communitarian one. But the bishops act as if all remains the same, instituting cosmetic changes; they design new plays, but keep right on losing. As the bishops prove ineffective as managers and leaders, as religious professionals and laypeople alike abandon them, ignore their dioceses and stream out of their parishes, the situation grows increasingly desperate.

The hiring institution eventually fires the losing coach. The People of God, regrettably, cannot dismiss poor and ineffectual leaders. So they do the next best thing: they do not show up for games, or masses; they give up buying season tickets, or filling collection baskets; and they look around for another team, or church, to whom they may pledge their allegiance. Until the bishops do their job courageously and well, the problem of task deprivation will keep sabotaging the organization they are consecrated to represent and to lead.

4. Differences in Personal Styles

Wherever people congregate, some rub others the wrong way. In organizations, problems between managers and employees at times come down to a conflict of personal styles. What a person does or says becomes incidental; how he acts, or she speaks, and how they relate causes irritation, outright conflict, and even rebellion. When "I can't stand to be in the same room with him" becomes widespread, someone must confront the offensive situation. In an open system direct communication may save the day. The offended one points out the obnoxious mannerisms or behaviors without condemning or belittling the offender; the other listens attentively, making certain about what is stirring up irritation and why. Then he or she explains the situation from the offender's perspective, offering reasons for the problematic style. Finally, together, with deeper understanding on both sides, they explore reasonable compromises as ways of reducing conflict. Sometimes an offensive style changes; more often the airing of the situation makes the style less offensive and introduces increased sensitivity all around.

Closed systems restrict open communication. Managers point out ways of being in the work environment that disturb others. They demand adjustment and point out the negative consequences of inaction. Some employees modify their style, mannerisms, clothing, or behavior so as to fit better into the controlling milieu.

Some leave in anger or desperation. Others remain unmoved but consequently are demoted and isolated. Finally, if that maneuver fails to assuage hostilities, the manager simply fires the incorrigible employee.

Offensive managers within closed systems only face disciplinary action from above. System managers hope that strict oversight will forestall the advancement of personally offensive people. Indeed, they do their utmost to promote people like them and ones they like. A company style develops; employees rise through managerial ranks to the extent they model the personalities, mannerisms, and interpersonal style of superiors. In this way corporate directors assume that interpersonal irritations and complaints from inferiors have scant merit. Managers need not change; they must, however, work effectively to quiet dissenters and stifle disruptive conflict.

The feudal style and lordly manner of Roman popes and Roman/American bishops generate a range of negative reactions among Catholics in the United States. The medieval folderol and courtly pretenses strike some as foolish and archaic, some as inappropriate for successors of the apostles and servants of Christ's body, some as scandalous and unseemly for men purporting to be living witnesses of a meek and humble savior. Bishops whose lifestyle demands jeweled rings, limousines, stately mansions, Bordeaux and Cuban cigars may impress devotees of European monarchies. They will, contrariwise, raise consternation, suspicions, and eyebrows among American Catholics. If bishops could keep to themselves, and display their lordly style only with clerics seeking their own hierarchical advancement, then they could perhaps maintain the fiction that their pseudo-royalty confers dignity and power, that it commands admiration and respect. Sadly, their extravagances reinforce distance, promote isolation, and further the impression that hierarchical appointment means membership in a select and cushy regiment of Vatican-dominated insiders.

No one told John Paul II that within his church he acted more like a Communist commissar than an understanding father. It took intense personal pain and growing societal outrage for the people of the Boston Archdiocese to tell Cardinal Law that he bore responsibility for his corporate mismanagement and imperial removal from the anguish of his people. Few priests dare confront an arrogant and authoritarian bishop. It takes lay-produced journals like *Commonweal*, or an independent lay-owned newspaper like the *National Catholic Reporter,* to expose and challenge pastors who refuse to listen to valid complaints of their parishioners.

From its beginnings, the American experiment occurred in opposition to the self-satisfaction and arrogance of the absolute monarchs of Europe. After emerging victorious from their courageous resistance to royal tyranny, the new Americans decreed that "all men are created equal," and that no one, monarchs or popes, bishops or pastors, have the right to deprive them of "life, liberty, and the pursuit of happiness." In their country they demanded that governing officials be elected by the people, serve at their pleasure, and conduct themselves as "civil servants." If the Catholic Church insists on maintaining its hierarchical administrative structure, it would be wise to realize that allegiance and obedience and a community of effort grow out of a milieu of mutual respect. One may frighten American Catholics through threats of censure or excommunication and the fires of hell into a restless uniformity; fear, however, will never create a Christian community founded by, and nurtured in, respect and love.

The present authorities in the Vatican seem to believe that reining in the unruly Americans will reestablish order, bring peace, and promote stability and growth in the Catholic Church in the United States. They could not be more wrong. The overbearing style of absolute monarchs will stiffen opposition, create dissatisfaction, and stir up rebellion. Americans today, in the face of perceived oppression, will make absolutely clear that they descend from, feel like, and will act in concert with, their freedom-loving forefathers. No matter the sophisticated theological arguments confirming one's position and authority. If a person wants to lead Americans, he must first be seen by them, and accepted by them, as one of them.

5. Personal Need Deprivation

Over the course of his professional life, Abraham Maslow developed a need theory of human motivation. He taught that human beings have a hierarchy of needs. The lower needs must be met to a sufficient degree before higher ones may begin to motivate human behavior.

In his second edition of *Motivation and Personality*,[13] Maslow described the following pyramid of needs:

- Biological and physiological: We require air to breathe, food and water to survive and grow, sex to propagate our species, a balance of warmth and cold to function normally. We need a homeostasis of these elements to sustain our material existence.

- Safety: We seek stability and consistency in a chaotic world. We depend on physical and social structures, civil order and laws, physical and personal limits to protect us, and to free us from fear and anxiety.

- Belongingness and love: Social beings, we search for companionship with, and the acceptance of, others. We congregate in various levels of

---

[13]   Maslow. New York: Harper and Row, 1970.

community: from neighborhood clubs to religious and professional associations, to civic groups and national parties. We chafe under an irritating loneliness, suffer from rejection and ostracism, become depressed when we lack friends, and feel lethargic and unmotivated when we seem isolated.

- Self-esteem: We struggle to achieve a consistent and sufficient level of self-confidence. We garner this through our achievements, through competence in our endeavors, through skilled mastery of materials. To the extent we freely choose the areas of work and the means of pursuing significant projects, to that extent we experience personal satisfaction. In these ways we ward off any nagging sense of social inferiority, personal weakness, and political helplessness. In addition, we require the recognition of others. Success must be appreciated and must be a source of social status, personal importance, and political dominance. We assiduously collect appreciation from others due our successes; we also need their applause.

- Cognitive: From birth we reach out to explore. We strive to understand the self, others, and the world about us. Curiosity drives us to meet new people, to travel to other countries, to search for answers to old questions, and to fashion disparate bits of information into networks of meaning. Knowledge gives us a sense of solidity and purpose in our otherwise fleeting existence.

- Aesthetic: Discreet stimuli constantly bombard us. If we could not shape them into recognizable patterns, we would be overwhelmed. We require order to know, to act, and to control. When that order moves regularly in symmetry with others, or when it fits with others in harmony, we feel delight and appreciation. This recognition of beauty soothes us out of chaos and mirrors the intricacy of our own lives. It also stimulates us to search more attentively and with focused penetration through the omnipresent diversity that surrounds us to the underlying unity that supports everyone and everything.

- Self-actualization: We experience an inbuilt desire for, and capacity for, growth. We recognize seeds of ability that, through care, attention, discipline, and nourishment, may realize their potential. We seek fulfillment that may quiet our restlessness, a yearning, in the deepest center of the self. We may know who we are; we may only guess at who we may become. Being, though necessary, cannot carry the excitement of discovery and the satisfaction of realizing an ever-expanding, ever-deepening becoming.

- Transcendence: (After doing considerable research with self-actualizing subjects, Maslow added this peak to his hierarchical pyramid.)[14] Human beings, social beings, seem destined to reach beyond themselves to others in love. They need to establish themselves; they must find independence in their own ego. But then they must move outward, connect, and realize enhanced life and being in that connection. The self itself arises in and through such enlivening relationships.

This brief overview of Maslow's theory offers a basis for exploring this area of organizational pathology arising out of administrative centralization: personal need deprivation.

A closed system depends upon structure and order, law and limits as guarantors of continued existence. It seeks its own continuity and relies on the stability it imposes to assure it. In the midst of a rapidly changing world, its fears only change. For it, anxiety comes from the possibility of overwhelming and unpredictable forces sweeping over it and upsetting its institutional security.

From the Council of Trent to the Second Vatican Council, the Catholic Church operated as a closed system. It strove to ward off all challenges to its stability and continuity through a hierarchical structure and by pervasive control over its members. It established sacramental gateways at major life transitions and demanded their utilization as a sign of, and continuance in, church membership. Within its laws and regulations, it insinuated itself into every aspect of human life: from sexual and familial relationships, to interpersonal and social obligations, to ecclesial expectations and spiritual pathways. The church assured the obedient of belongingness and acceptance within a community of holiness now, and promised eternal security with God in heaven hereafter. For the disobedient, it threatened excommunication, ostracism and rejection now, followed by the eternal devastation of hellfire. In Maslow's terms, the Catholic Church functioned out of a safety need. At the same time it relied on a combination of its members' belongingness and safety needs to establish, reinforce, and maintain their compliance and its own continuity. As long as the church's institutional needs and its members' personal needs were in harmony, personal need deprivation presented no more than an occasional and essentially isolated problem.

---

[14]   Cf. Maslow, Abraham. *Religion, Values, and Peak Experiences*. Viking Press: New York, 1970; *The Farther Reaches of Human Nature*. Viking Press: New York, 1971.

6. Incompatible Personal Needs

By the era of Vatican II, American Catholics had, predominantly, as a people moved beyond the basic needs of physiology, safety, and belongingness. They now occupied the middle and upper middle class brackets of American society. They were well represented in the country's professional and managerial ranks: one of their own, John F. Kennedy, was serving as president. Catholic men were earning competitive salaries; they were transplanting their families into newer and safer suburban neighborhoods. They felt confident and accepted in their workplaces both as Catholics and as citizens. They were sending their children on for a college education; they themselves with their wives were drawn to the symphony, concerts, theater and other expressions of high culture. In Maslow's terms, they had sufficiently satisfied their lower needs; they now were engaged in meeting their self-esteem, cognitive, and aesthetic ones.

Vatican II moved in harmony with the state of the American Catholic people. It offered the laity ways of being more involved in their church and more responsible for bringing the message of Christ into the modern world. It counseled all its members to become part of this era, to connect with, share with, and listen to, others outside our faith. It even opened up the liturgy to rituals and celebrations more in sync with today's aesthetic tastes, and set to the side liturgical actions suitable for a feudal society but inappropriate for a democratic one. It de-emphasized hierarchical controls while it insisted upon the development of a knowledgeable, capable, and engaged People of God.

The retrogressive pontificates of Paul VI and John Paul II refocused the church on its own security. They stressed the evil of modern secularization; they urged the faithful to return to the forms, rituals, and practices of a church isolated from today's destructive influences, and safe within its own confines. When the faithful did not respond obediently and with alacrity, these popes and their bishops and pastors fell back upon the threats of exclusion and the ominous judgments of a wrathful God. But such misplaced strategies clearly failed. A constantly diminishing number of Catholics care whether the church authorities exclude them, and fewer than ever equate hierarchical fulminations with a prediction of divine punishment.

American Catholics (except, perhaps for the more recent waves of immigrants) need a sense of self-esteem and dignity within their own church. They do not seek community harmony based on obedience to church authorities. Nor can they be threatened into compliance. As educated adults, they need to know the truth about their church, how it operates, its honest strengths and real weaknesses. They yearn for theological understanding far more sophisticated than easy spiritual platitudes and barely veiled moral teachings aimed at compliance. Most of all, they seek spiritual instruction that may open up personal ways of finding, touching, relating to, and living with an immanent God.

In their liturgies they seek transforming symbols, a chain of images and movement, prayers and songs that can function as doorways into the experience of God's presence. They want to meet together the God in whom they believe, by whose life they live, and through whose love they grow. They want to be and to celebrate the sacrament of Christ's presence that they are.

Diverse needs may motivate a person simultaneously. One may eat a sandwich, listen to Mozart, and read a newspaper, attending alternatively more to one, then another. This demands, however, that the lower needs in Maslow's hierarchy are in reasonable balance: A student, pulling an all-nighter before a crucial exam, may collapse before finishing a necessary review of test-preparation materials. In that instance a physiological requirement effectively trumps any self-esteem-enhancing grade.

Political organizations routinely attempt to motivate others to cooperate with them by accentuating lower needs through threats or punishing behaviors. In warfare an enemy surrenders to save his life; to elicit necessary information interrogators deprive captives of physical necessities; torturers challenge a prisoner's physiological and safety needs to such an extent that they override loyalty to a group or self-esteem as a soldier. A hero dies rather than reveal data that compromises his companions; a martyr endures cruel torture and brutal death rather than renounce her religious faith.

In the Middle Ages the Catholic Church, united to feudal monarchies, sanctioned torture and even killing as means of uprooting heresies or stimulating conversions. It also employed excommunication to enforce obedience and to exact contrition. Today, the church only threatens everlasting torture in hell as delayed punishment for sinners; in effect, it leaves the bloody mess to the righteous justice of God. It still employs various levels of banishment to compel orthodoxy: the Vatican silences a controversial theologian; a bishop threatens a Pro-Choice politician with excommunication; a public dissenter cannot receive a Catholic burial; because of dangerously liberal views Rome passes over a bishop in line for advancement; the appearance of a speaker who supports a married clergy is cancelled by a Catholic university after an episcopal complaint; a pastor refuses to meet with parishioners pushing for change and excludes them from all parish committees. In these instances, and numerous others like them, we find painful examples of incompatible personal needs clashing together.

The hierarchical church furthered by John Paul II exhibits, from top to bottom, some clearly defined needs:

- to preserve the hierarchical structure (safety);

- to squelch dissent (safety);

- to continue the status quo (safety);

- to hide and deny its own failings (safety);

- to blame others for its own failings (safety);

- to compel orthodoxy (belongingness);

- to equate obedience to the hierarchy with being a good and faithful Catholic (belongingness, self-esteem);

- to maintain clerical control (self-esteem);

- to promote its own conservative loyalists (self-esteem);

- to equate the Catholic Church with its hierarchical structure (self-esteem, cognitive).

All of these needs motivate members of the hierarchy to act in concert to preserve, promote, and enhance the church's present administrative structure. We see hierarchical administrative centralization in a determined effort to preserve itself, for itself. Except for the words "church" and "Catholic," nothing distinguishes this list of prominent needs from that of any absolute monarchy, any struggling modern corporation, or the armies of a secular power. It deserves notice that the higher needs—cognitive (except once), aesthetic, self-actualization, and transcendence—do not appear. The ecclesial enterprise in its founding, its theology, its spirituality, and its preaching purports to be primarily about these higher needs; in practice, however, orthodoxy has turned in on itself, and orthodoxy has become hierarchy.

Church members who identify with the hierarchy, for whatever reasons, probably have needs similar to it. At least, when dissension threatens, these needs will come to the fore. Since the 1960's, in an American Catholic Church split between advocates of Tridentine uniformity and Vatican II unity, the former have taken upon themselves the battle for orthodoxy, the banishing of dissent, and the return to an obedient, ordered Catholicism. This puts a decided emphasis on religiosity, the performance of required activities because they are expected, and much less on religion, a community's relationship to its God. For them Catholicism reduces to obedience to the hierarchy and marshaling forces for its defense. Party loyalty, in them, triumphs. These Catholics and their clerical superiors rarely manifest needs in conflict as together they must defend themselves and the church from the incursions of the modern world, and from their own community.

Those Catholics, however, be they bishops or priests or laity, who do not identify their faith in this fashion, find themselves constantly motivated by needs in
conflict with the present hierarchical powers. Consider a few examples.

A young pastor, hoping for assignment to the cathedral parish and someday to
his own diocese, would not dream of making any decision that could raise episcopal suspicions. For him the church has become the clerical brotherhood; he belongs
to it and treasures its acceptance of him.

A group of his parishioners, upset by the clergy sexual abuse scandal, in response
to worries of some mothers for their own children, meet together and forward an
oversight plan to the pastor for his consideration. Judging their plan a threat to
clerical power, he refuses to meet with the people and orders them to disband. But
the parishioners, needing each other's support and acceptance, resist. They regard
the pastor as uncaring; he dismisses them as intruders on his authority.

A new pastor fires, without any explanation or warning, a seasoned and beloved
religious education director. In his own mind he maintains that he has the authority as pastor to make whatever administrative decisions he wishes. The parish
belongs to him; he answers to no one except the bishop. As might be expected, a
committee of long-time parishioners, among them a number of professionals and
corporate managers, come to see him. They also feel ownership for their parish,
a community to which they have over the years contributed much. They need to
assume an active role in the parish in order to feel good about themselves and the
community. When the committee asks the pastor for his reasons behind the dismissal, he shuts them out, resolutely stating: "it's a personnel matter and nobody
else's business." The RCIA director, a prominent local attorney, keeps pressing.
To the astonishment of the delegation, the pastor summarily fires him also, and
abruptly terminates the meeting.

Father began mass ten minutes late: he had to finish his conversation with the
plumber about necessary repairs in the rectory. It didn't matter; he could recoup
the time. He knew the ordinary by heart, he could read the prayers of the day
quickly, and they would sing only one verse of the opening and closing hymns. As
they began processing to the altar, he instructed the deacon to make his sermon
brief and to the point. He had also decided to skip all formal singing of mass
prayers: no one would notice; he had a mediocre voice anyway.

All went as planned. He did wish that the deacon would quit beginning his
sermons with a joke and ending with a sentimental, pious poem. Aside from
that, he missed the preacher's point as he found himself wondering why so few
parishioners had showed up for mass. With attendance down this meant fewer
communions and a too-meager collection. Moreover, community singing really
falls flat when only a scattered few chime in. Perhaps he should get back to using
the children's choir. Well, anyhow, he made up the ten minutes. This meant the

parking lot would be clear before other parishioners started congregating for the next round.

The young woman trudged to work. She felt unsatisfied and rather sad. Her husband had stayed home with their two babies. The eight o'clock Sunday mass afforded her a quiet space before her 10:00 A. M.-6:00 P. M. shift at the hospital where she worked as an occupational therapist. Today, however, mass had been especially un-nourishing. Community and community participation were practically non-existent. Father had seemed hurried and distracted; his prayers flew out like recitations, not attempts to address the divine. As he was mumbling away, she found herself kneeling, eyes closed, hands over her ears, trying to find her own prayer room inside. When she did watch the liturgical action, she imagined the celebrant to be an ungainly puppet pulled about by uncoordinated strings. And her eyes kept going to father's shoes protruding out from under his alb. They held center stage under the altar. She could just make out the Nike label. Couldn't he, at least, have left his tennis shoes for later? So much, she sighed, for the symbolic power and beauty of the liturgy.

In a healthy and open church these and legions of other mismatched needs would be dealt with directly. Together, pastors and parishioners would unburden themselves, bringing needs and problems forward as the necessary first step toward satisfactory solutions. But in a church wedded to hierarchical control, imposed order, and member obedience, the hard truth rarely gets voiced. Instead, roles play out, duties get performed, requirements are satisfied, and life drains away in an endless cycle of irritation and anger, complaints and recriminations, resignation and external compliance. Thus does the organizational pathology develop, spread, and eventually kill, even among the followers of Christ.

IV. Disengagement: The Sad Result of Administrative Centralization

Before concluding this chapter, let us consult Tocqueville once again as he points to unintended results of this questionable organizational strategy.

A leader who micromanages his organization must maintain a cadre of active agents checking out every secluded corner. Others within the group lack responsibility for its overall success. In this regard they remain essentially disengaged: "oversight belongs to the boss's men; we just do as we're told." Tocqueville comments on the debilitating effect on these passive members:

> But I think that administrative centralization is fit only to enervate the peoples who submit to it because it constantly tends to diminish the spirit of the city in them. Administrative centralization, it is true, succeeds in uniting at a given period and in a certain place all the

disposable strength of the nation, but it is harmful to the reproduction of strength. It makes [the nation] triumph on the day of combat and diminishes its power in the long term. It can therefore contribute admirably to the passing greatness of one man, not to the lasting prosperity of a people.[15]

When people exercise no claim outside their particular duty, they lose sense of the total project. It concerns them solely as the excuse for their employment or membership.

People, in such countries, act as citizens by obeying the laws and living in accord with local norms of conduct. They know little about the body politic, care nothing for politics and politicians, and contribute only incidentally to the corporate welfare. Tocqueville poignantly describes this marriage of passivity and disinterest:

There are nations of Europe where an inhabitant considers himself a kind of colonist, indifferent to the destiny of the place that he inhabits. The greatest changes come about in his country without his concurrence; he does not even know precisely what has taken place; he suspects; he has heard the event recounted by chance. Even more, the fortune of his village, the policing of his street, the fate of his church and of his presbytery do not touch him; he thinks that all those things do not concern him in any fashion and that they belong to a powerful foreigner called the government. For himself, he enjoys these goods as a tenant, without a spirit of ownership and without ideas of any improvement whatsoever. This disinterest in himself goes so far that if his own security or that of his children is finally compromised, instead of occupying himself with removing the danger, he crosses his arms to wait for the nation as a whole to come to his aid.[16]

Could he have described better the situation of most Catholics when the council fathers gathered at Vatican II? How many church members had more than a superficial sense of the historic and life-changing discussions about to take place in Rome? Indeed, like tenants, most simply let a faraway Vatican shape their corporate life, with little care shown by them and scant input from them expected or given.

---

[15] *Op. cit.,* Tocqueville, p. 83.

[16] *Ibid.,* p. 88.

This state of affairs bodes ill for any group, including churches. Compliance is obtained at the cost of freedom, and allegiance eventually disappears. Tocqueville remarks further about the father waiting upon his nation's aid:

> Yet this man, although he has made such a complete sacrifice of his free will, likes obedience no more than any other. He submits, it is true, at the pleasure of a clerk; but it pleases him to defy the law like a defeated enemy, as soon as force is withdrawn.
>
> When nations have arrived at this point, they must modify their laws and their mores or they perish, for the source of public virtue is almost dried up; one still finds subjects in them, but one no longer sees citizens.[17]

Obedience follows upon ominous signs of vigilance and cautionary displays of force; remove them and chaos ensues.

In the name of good order, acceptance of its regulations, and obedience to God's laws, the Catholic Church has given the task of preserving orthodoxy and overseeing community behavior to its clerical hierarchy. It alone has the authority and responsibility to maintain faithfulness according to the dictates of Rome—the Vatican and reigning pontiff. This oversight sifts down through the organization even to the internal confines of the individual conscience. God's forgiveness in confession awaits those who display contrition for disobedience and promise assent to ecclesiastical mandates. This has created a church membership, as Tocqueville would say, composed of subjects but increasingly devoid of citizens.

In the Tridentine church in America prior to Vatican II, the hierarchy relied on vast numbers of priests and religious to be agents of order. They established uniform standards across the nation, parish by parish, grade school to high school, in urban congregations and rural communities. They translated the teachings of Rome into local situations and enforced the papal will. As noted in the introduction, an exodus of these purveyors of uniformity began with Vatican II, accelerated during the papacies of Paul VI and John Paul II, and their ranks continue to shrink. Just as Tocqueville might have predicted, as the clerical and religious enforcers disappear, the hierarchical control over the people weakens. No longer compelled to obey out of anxiety over ecclesiastical disapproval, the people opt quite naturally for freedom. And, made passive by centuries of blind obedience, they do not automatically step in to save the organization, either through becoming substitute agents of the hierarchy, or through acting forcibly to correct the illness sapping

---

[17]   *Ibid.,* pp. 88-89.

the lifeblood of the community. After all, like the threatened man, they expect the hierarchy to save the day; responsibility resides with it, not them.

Nobody loyal to the church wishes its state to be as described. Nor need it be so. If the church relinquished self-identification with its administrative structure, if it espoused unity over uniformity, it could then generate the allegiance and assistance of its members. Tocqueville pictured the situation of the new American nation, one that dared democracy and democratic disorder, as one filled with the energy of citizenship:

> What I most admire in America are not the *administrative* effects of decentralization, but its *political* effects. In the United States the native country makes itself felt everywhere. It is an object of solicitude from the village to the entire Union. The inhabitant applies himself to each of the interests of his country as to his very own. He is glorified in the glory of the nation; in the success that it obtains he believes he recognizes his own work, and he is uplifted by it; he rejoices in the general prosperity from which he profits. He has for his native country a sentiment analogous to the one that he feels for his family, and it is still by a sort of selfishness that he takes an interest in the state.[18]

Who would not wish such civic pride to exist in, and give life to, our parishes, our communities, our dioceses, and our church?

A stark choice confronts the church in America today: do we want a well-regulated, well-ordered organization with the ruling hierarchy presiding over passive subjects and emptying parishes, or will we accept the relative disorder of democracy as the price of creating a people fired with love of, and energy for, a church the whole membership owns and for which each one assumes responsibility? Recognizing the pluses and minuses attendant upon both positions, Tocqueville comes out forcefully for the democratic one as holding out the possibility of exciting growth:

> Democracy, even if local circumstances and the dispositions of the people permit it to be maintained, does not present to the eye administrative regularity and methodical order in government; that is true. Democratic freedom does not execute each of its undertakings with the same perfection as intelligent despotism; often it abandons them before having received their fruit, or it risks dangerous ones: but in the long

---

[18]   *Ibid.*, p. 90.

term democracy produces more than despotism; it does each thing less well, but it does more things. Under its empire, what is great is above all not what public administration executes but what is executed without it and outside it. Democracy does not give the most skillful government to the people, but it does what the most skillful government is often powerless to create; its spreads a restless activity through the whole social body, a superabundant force, an energy that never exists without it, and which, however little circumstances may be favorable, can bring forth marvels. Those are its true advantages.[19]

And so we choose: a well-greased organization or the restless response to the Spirit of God?

Tocqueville drives in one last nail that consigns administrative centralization to the realms of failure and eventual dissolution. It does not work. Despots lure subjects to follow them "as the mender of all ills suffered...the sustainer of the oppressed, and the founder of order. People fall asleep in the bosom of their temporary prosperity to which it gives birth; and when they awake they are miserable."[20] Why this misery? Tocqueville explains:

What does it matter to me, after all, that there should be an authority always on its feet, keeping watch that my pleasures are tranquil, flying ahead of my steps to turn away every danger without my even needing to think about it, if the authority, at the same time it removes the least thorns on my path, is absolute master of my freedom and my life, if it monopolizes movement and existence to such a point that everything around it must languish when it languishes, that everything must sleep when it sleeps, that everything must perish when it dies?[21]

This organizational gambit fails because it demands loss of freedom as the price of security. In addition, only self-deception and continuing propaganda can maintain the fiction that overall, centralized control can micromanage successfully the life of a nation. Tocqueville puts the case bluntly: accept the truth, live with the messiness of freedom, or die of fruitless exhaustion:

---

[19] *Ibid.*, p. 234.

[20] *Ibid.*, p. 229.

[21] *Ibid.*, p. 88.

But I also think that when the central administration claims to replace completely the free cooperation of those primarily interested, it deceives itself or wants to deceive you.

A central power, however enlightened, however learned one imagines it, cannot gather to itself alone all the details of the life of a great people. It cannot do it because such a work exceeds human strength. When it wants by its care alone to create so many diverse springs and make them function, it contents itself with a very incomplete result or exhausts itself in useless efforts.[22]

The Catholic Church in the United States is balancing, precariously, on the fulcrum of destiny. Continued inaction will lead to a withering away into irrelevancy and psychological death. Its bishops must move. Will they shift their weight backward, opting for the orderliness and security of centralized monarchies? A betting man would place his wager here: Rome certainly supports that direction. And many American Catholics, anxious in a dangerous world, yearn for safety, certainty, and security. Or will the bishops dare to step forward, releasing their time-hardened grip on the politics of power, and offer back to the People of God their church?

---

[22] *Ibid.*, p. 86.

Chapter Five: An Ecclesial Bill of Rights

I. A Vision of Equality for All

At a defining moment of our history, the American colonists declared:

> We hold these truths to be self-evident, that all Men are created equal, that they are endowed by their Creator with certain unalienable Rights, that among them are Life, Liberty, and the Pursuit of Happiness.[1]

In abandoning Europe they broke the restrictive bonds of feudalism imposed by princely rulers in Church and State. Now—

> All the English colonies [therefore] had among them, at this period of their birth, a great family resemblance. All, from the beginning, seemed destined to offer the development of freedom, not the aristocratic freedom of their mother country, but the bourgeois and democratic freedom of which the history of the world had still not offered a complete model.[2]

They had ample experience of monarchical domination that controlled every aspect of life, including the internal realms of conscience and religious belief. They rejected this political intrusiveness; instead, they constructed individual freedom as their goal. Although raised in the structured milieu of inequality, they embraced a vision of equality as the one, firm guarantor of a fledging democratic freedom.

As Tocqueville explains the relationship of freedom and equality:

---

[1] *Declaration of Independence*, July 4, 1776.

[2] *Op. cit.*, Tocqueville p. 30.

It is not that peoples whose social state is democratic naturally scorn freedom; on the contrary, they have an instinctive taste for it. But freedom is not the principal and continuous object of their desire; what they love with an eternal love is equality; they dash toward freedom with a rapid impulse and sudden effort, and if they miss the goal they resign themselves; but nothing can satisfy them without equality, and they would sooner consent to perish than to lose it.[3]

Our forefathers left ancestral homelands, endured dangers of perilous seas and hostile wilderness, and challenged the martial might of the Old World's premiere army, in order to secure for themselves, their families, and their descendents "Life, Liberty, and the Pursuit of Happiness." Somehow they realized that one person could possess these inestimable goods only if the opportunity were indiscriminately available to all. Their democracy would pursue freedom; it would, however, be founded upon equality.

Fifty-five years after their world-altering assertion, Tocqueville attested to its enduring existence in the new nation:

The social state of the Americans is eminently democratic. It has had this character since the birth of the colonies; it has it even more in our day.

I said in the preceding chapter that a very great equality reigned among the emigrants who came to settle on the shores of New England. Not even the seed of aristocracy was ever deposited in this part of the Union.[4]

Today, conservative proponents of structured societies, both political and religious, rail against democratic associations as seedbeds of licentiousness, as gatherings without order that generate communities of chaos, and deify the individual at the expense of the common good. They mistakenly equate democracy with freedom. They fail to understand that freedom does not define democracy, but that it flows from the democratic exercise of equality. As the framers of our Declaration of Independence recognized, a God-given equality embeds inalienable rights in human nature. Those rights, enjoyed by all, practiced by each in respect to every other, create the societal structure that protects life, guarantees liberty, and enables progress toward happiness for all.

---

[3]   *Ibid.*, p. 52.

[4]   *Ibid.*, p. 46.

II. Inequality and Discrimination in America

While Tocqueville lauds the wisdom and endurance of the American democratic experiment, without hesitation he points to its deplorable inconsistency regarding two other races sharing the American homeland. One, the Indian race, either rejected American citizenship or perished in accepting it.[5] The other, black men and women from the African continent, intermingled with their white masters but were denied citizenship.[6] If "all Men are created equal," does this not include the American Indian and the African American? If all men "are endowed by their Creator with certain unalienable Rights...to Life, Liberty, and the Pursuit of Happiness," do Indians have to forfeit their way of life to torrents of white Europeans or disappear from the face of their land, or do blacks have to embrace servitude or die? In Tocqueville's era white Americans kept equality, rights, life, freedom and opportunity from both races through the self-serving fiction that these fellow inhabitants, to them wild savages and mere slaves, were not human.

The Roman Catholic Church is undoubtedly Caucasian, western, and European.[7] That being said, no canon law demands white ascendancy nor prohibits the ecclesiastical advancement of other races. Nor do any formal declarations of church councils or popes dictate any species of western or European jingoism. The church reaches out around the world and invites all human beings of whatever race or color, nation or condition to join it.

Women

Yet the church's hierarchy stubbornly maintains the unequal status of women within its organization. No woman can enter the hierarchical ranks; no woman can receive the grace of ordination; no woman can assume sacramental leadership of the Catholic community.

---

5   *Ibid.* cf. pages 307-325.

6   *Ibid.* cf. pages 326-348.

7   This statement raises a further question: for how long will the church remain Caucasian, western, and European? The available evidence suggests that after the New Reformation of Vatican II, John Paul II, a man from Poland, on the Eastern edge of Europe, was brought into the papacy to spearhead a second Counter-Reformation. He appears to have written off Europe and North America, locations championing and trying to follow the directions of Vatican II, in favor of the hierarchically conservative churches of Africa, Asia, and South America. John Paul's death could have brought about the ascendancy of a non-European, non-Caucasian pope from the Southern Hemisphere. It did not. If not now, then soon. Cf. Philip Jenkins, "The Next Christianity," *The Atlantic Monthly, October 2002, pp. 53-68.*

Previously, I have discussed the reasons pro and con for this clerical decision; we need no repetition of those arguments. However, it does seem both appropriate and necessary to indicate in the present context why the Vatican's stance vis-à-vis women in the church gravely troubles American Catholics.

As Americans, we resolutely accept that all human beings, no matter their race or sex or condition, are created equal. We, furthermore, hold it as a basic fairness that every person must be given the opportunity to make of self whatever each desires and is willing with energy and talent to pursue. Educated Americans, and especially those of developed conscience and sensitivity, recognize with deep pain the searing gap between these foundational principles of our democracy and the history of America's treatment of its indigenous Indians and its enslaved, segregated blacks. We do not witness ethnic cleansing in Serbia as a unique 20th Century horror; we have already wept with the Cherokees on the "Trail of Tears" from Georgia to Oklahoma in the winter of 1838-1839. We cannot be with astonishment heartsick at the slaughter of innocent Vietnamese peasants at My Lai; our hearts already lie broken with three hundred Sioux men, women, and children gunned down at their encampment on Wounded Knee Creek. Nor can we feign a special shock on witnessing the brutal torture and humiliation of Muslim insurgents at Abu Ghraib military detention center near Baghdad; we know all too well the stories of rape and sexual humiliation, whipping and branding, terror and lynching that broadcast the horrid sins American Christians committed against innocent black men and women.

The Vatican instructs Americans to accept women's role as that of second-class citizens of the church. Why? Perhaps, like the American Indians, they cannot be allowed ecclesial leadership because of moral inferiority: they did, according to western scriptural tradition, bring sin into human experience through the lure of a forbidden apple. Or, perhaps, like American blacks they constitute a demeaned sub-species, not fully human, people capable of serving but never leading. Whatever the reason, every time the pope claims that women cannot represent Christ because of their sex, every time a papal directive silences discussion of women priests, every time a bishop places narrow restrictions on women and girls in liturgical settings, obedient American Catholic men collude in a non-democratic judgment of inequality; they call up a history of white American Christians, staunch advocates of democracy, acting hypocritically. Sure, all *men* are created equal: but no women...and even not all men if they happen to be other than Caucasian.

When American Catholics open the morning paper and read about another perceived Vatican denigration of women, intentional or not, they have to wrestle with the exposure and shock, emptiness and embarrassment, chagrin and shame, loneliness and guilt of persons shown to the world to be hypocrites, sinners, and saboteurs of democracy. We do not need the notorious scandals of clerical pedophilia to wish we belonged to another church. We live, year after year, with the shame that drives many to churches that would not think, in some god's name, to discriminate against women.

The Laity

Previously, we saw how Western history pushed the church into defining itself by its hierarchy. If "hierarchy" and "Catholic Church" are synonymous, then only members of that hierarchy may validly claim to be the church. This excludes all women as they are barred from entering the clerical order. In effect, it also denies that identification to any man who, unwisely, it would appear, chooses not to become a cleric. The conclusion passes astonishment: no layperson, man or woman, lives and loves, prays and serves, suffers and dies as Christ's presence on earth. Such a theological stance directly contradicts Vatican II's assertion of the church's identification with the People of God. Moreover, it mistakenly teaches that ordination, not baptism, brings about the church community and its sacramentality.

In this understanding of the church, laypeople *belong* to the church but they *are not* the church. They exist in it analogously to black men and women in slaveholding America. Slaves worked on plantations they could not possess, lived with and served white families not their own, and only suffered white acceptance through constant dedication and faithful obedience. In the larger picture, they dwelt and worked and died in America, but they had no rights as American citizens. They exercised no say in the shape, government, or the future of the political entity that possessed them.

Given the current identification of *church* with *hierarchy*, laypeople cannot shape the governing structure; they cannot even voice their preferences about whom they wish as their pastor, their bishop, or their pope. They can register their agreement with, or opposition to, directions being taken by ecclesiastical authorities through compliance or disobedience, but their actions always remain, at best, advisory. In sum, the good slave was expected by its master to "love, labor, and let be"; the good Catholic layperson is meant to "pray, pay, and obey."

The church hierarchy may well learn from the experience of Southern plantation owners. Their slaves loved them with a loyalty born of necessity. But that bond rarely transformed into true love because of the slave's resentment over a loss of freedom and an all-enveloping inequality. Slaves, for the most part, labored dutifully and without noticeable complaint. Indeed, plantations flourished through their efforts. Relatively few of them fled, daring to risk severe punishment and even death as the price of freedom. Even fewer rebelled until they had behind them the military might of firmly aroused northern states. Many former slaves, then free, fought with valor and fierce determination against their erstwhile masters.

The church touts itself as a community of love. To the extent that laypeople belong to but are not the church, that love, in truth, probably reflects loyalty born of necessity. Baptized as unknowing children, raised as obedient Catholics, warned constantly against "losing the faith," threatened with eternal fire should one dare to "fall away from the church," many stay as members because they must: family pressure keeps them in line as does the persistent threat of punishment hereafter. Those who remain obey their priests, and do what they can to placate parents, pastors, and a punishing deity. But authorities would foolishly expect ownership of church endeavors from laypeople deprived of ownership of the church itself. Only the foolhardy would bank on equal responsibility from those suffering under an officially sanctioned inequality. Many, finally, will abandon the church, fed up with an ecclesial life of subordination and subservience.

One must ask the pope and his bishops the following, directly, and with the expectation of a clear, non-evasive answer: "Who, then, do you say that the church is?" If they reply, "the hierarchy," then they should, in prudence, expect from their laity responses born of inequality. Should they respond, "the People of God," then they must renounce monarchical ways and now, former masters, embrace their role as servants of that People.

Prior to Vatican II, the social hierarchy of the church stood firm, immobile, and rarely challenged, at least from within. The council fathers in emphasizing the community of the church and de-emphasizing any hierarchical hegemony, brought into the open the underlying dissatisfaction of democratic, educated, and adult laity. Sensing what was occurring, the hierarchy subsequently attempted to contain the perceived damage to their status by electing, first, Paul VI, and more importantly, a strong-willed and monarchical John Paul II. Over the past twenty-five years a massive struggle has convulsed the church: on one side, the pope and his bishops and conservative followers have striven to regain the monarchical structure fortified by the Council of Trent and reinforced by Vatican I; on the other, democratic voices among the clergy and laity have cried out for the equality of the People of God. The outcome has been stasis, at least in America, until the scandal of sexual and organizational malfeasance. In a clerical take on the old proverb concerning a naked emperor, the cassock has been lifted and the sins of the master revealed. Hierarchical dominance, with the leaking away of the remaining vestiges of moral authority, has numbered days before change or death.

When John Paul II died, the world's bishops appointed a successor molded in that pontiff's image and likeness. In so doing, they hope to win the battle John Paul fought with righteous valor. But this new pope will also fail. Democratic people in the church have caught the scent of freedom and are realizing the truth of equality under God. In Tocqueville's experienced counsel we may reasonably expect the following if the American church is to survive:

Democratic peoples love equality at all times, but in certain periods, they press the passion they feel for it to delirium. This happens at the moment when the old social hierarchy, long threatened, is finally destroyed after a last internecine struggle, and the barriers that separated citizens are finally overturned. Then men rush at equality as at a conquest, and they become attached to it as to a precious good someone wants to rob them of. The passion for equality penetrates all parts of the human heart; there it spreads, and fills it entirely. Do not say to men that in giving themselves over so blindly to an exclusive passion, they compromise their dearest interests; they are deaf. Do not show them that freedom escapes from their hands while they are looking elsewhere; they are blind, or rather they perceive only one good in the whole universe worth longing for.[8]

Homosexuals

White Christians have discriminated against members of other races; males of diverse religious faiths have separated men and women in worship and have treated women as morally and religiously inferior; the Catholic Church still condemns as a group men and women who live out their homosexual orientation. One may reasonably ask what explains this ongoing ecclesiastical condemnation. In doing so, let us, as a first task, discard the false explanations.

In 1973, the American Psychiatric Association removed homosexuality from its classification of mental disorders. It had based the previous negative judgment on data received from people engaged in psychotherapy. With new research methods and an examination of a broader population, investigators could not establish any consistent causal link between homosexuality and mental illness. For certain, some people with a homosexual orientation suffered from mental disorders, just like some with a heterosexual one. But others of both orientations were leading normal and balanced psychological lives. Two years later, the American Psychological Association formally concurred with the decision of the psychiatric profession. Today, virtually every professional association of mental health providers rejects any blanket theory equating a homosexual orientation with mental illness.

The American Psychological Association describes sexual orientation as "an enduring emotional, romantic, sexual or affectional attraction to another person." This orientation develops gradually, with some indications occasionally present even in childhood, but it noticeably "emerges for most people in early adolescence without any prior sexual experience." Although no causal factor can be definitely

---

[8]   *Ibid.,* p. 481.

singled out, "most scientists agree that sexual orientation is most likely the result of a complex interaction of environmental, cognitive and biological factors." As to the role of choice, the Association asserts: "human beings can not choose to be either gay or straight." [9] If one accepts this professional judgment, then a person's sexual orientation has no relationship to personal sin. It develops without conscious attention or choice.

Mental health experts dismiss any condemnation of homosexuality because of mental disorder or personal culpability. The church, however, insists on declaring any deliberate homosexual behavior sinful. This judgment stems immediately from the church's moral position that forbids any deliberate act of sexual behavior between non-married people. Since it strictly maintains that marriage may be validly contracted only between a man and a woman, it, therefore, holds that homosexuals may never licitly engage in deliberate sexual activity. A homosexual, either gay or lesbian, even though he or she does not choose a homosexual orientation, must live a non-sexually-expressive, celibate life.

One must look more deeply to understand the church's acceptance of deliberate sexual activity only in marriage. It teaches that sexual behavior leading toward intercourse has, according to human nature, two essential goals: the conception of children and the growth in the mutual love of the sexual partners. Only in a marriage between a man and a woman may *both* of these goals be met. Neither gay nor lesbian couples may through sexual intercourse conceive together a child; therefore, they may not morally engage in deliberate sexual activity with a person of the same sex.

No reasonable basis exists for asserting that homosexual couples cannot grow in mutual love through interpersonal sexual activity. No one may validly claim that homosexual partners cannot establish a stable, lasting, growing, and healthy relationship. And should they adopt children, they have shown themselves capable of being as loving and effective as parents of a heterosexual persuasion. The home of a homosexual couple may be as healthy and happy an environment for children as that provided by a man and woman. Only with misinformation and through blatant prejudice do people assert otherwise.

Church moralists insist on an essential relationship between deliberate sexual activity and the conception of children. They maintain that human sexuality exists for the good of, the continuation of, the human species. An individual, therefore, has no right to place any obstacle to conception during sexual activity; to do so would be to act selfishly, and to take to oneself behavior meant for the common good of humankind. It is with this argument that the church prohibits homosexual couples from deliberate sexual activity.

---

[9]   Cf. http://www. apa. org. pubinfo/answers. html

Some difficulties make questionable the church's position. Let us consider them in turn.

Is ordinary marital sexuality directed toward the conception of children? In actual fact, in desire, and in intention the response is no. For purposes of illustration, allow me to speak about my own marriage.

I married at age thirty-seven; my wife was nearing her thirty-fourth birthday. She had potentially twelve years of fertility ahead of her. At the most she could actually conceive on fourteen days during a given fertility cycle; therefore, all told, she might conceive about half the time, or six years out of the twelve. We have now been married for thirty-three years. For the last twenty years my wife could no longer conceive. Therefore, in our marriage, calculating time alone, we could not have conceived a child twenty-seven out of our thirty-three years together. Moreover, because of financial and emotional reasons we had no desire for children or intention of conceiving them the first three years of our marriage. Because of the dangers of mongolism affecting infants, the first-born of a mother over forty, we did not wish children during the five years between her ages of forty to forty-five. This leaves four years, half of which she could not conceive, that we actually hoped to have children. Therefore, in two out of our thirty-three years we worked at, and were capable of, producing children. In our sexual relationship, the conception of children has had little influence.

Does ordinary marital sexuality necessarily anticipate sexual intercourse? For anyone who has lived in a sexual relationship, the time spent in sexual intercourse, the activities leading up to it, and the together time afterwards, is relatively brief compared to the rest of one's life. For most healthy adults nine or ten hours a day are consumed by work, traveling to and from it; another six or seven hours are spent sleeping; already fifteen to seventeen hours of a day are unavailable for other activities. When one adds the required time used for meals, for household chores, for caring for the family, for keeping contact with friends and relatives, for evening meetings associated with school or work or volunteer activities, the actual occasions when a married couple could be alone and quiet together become markedly infrequent. And even during those too rare moments tiredness, preoccupations and worry, as well as lack of immediate desire, may derail sexual interaction leading to intercourse.

Does this mean that the sexual relationship and its expression necessarily flags and lessens as the opportunities for intercourse decrease? By no means must that be so. Passing touches, loving glances, a brief kiss, a hug, moments just holding each other before going to sleep or arising, an expression of love, an experience of the day shared and enjoyed together—all of these and numerous other such moments make up the ongoing fabric of a sexual life together. Nor do any of them depend on sexual intercourse, either as a substitute or in anticipation or preparation. These actions, all part of a sexual life, relate intrinsically to that shared life and not neces-sarily to intercourse. Indeed, most deliberate sexual activity in marriage does *not* focus upon intercourse or the conception of children.

Are the two proposed ends of marriage—the love of the partners and the conception of children—co-equal? In addition, do they adequately describe the reality of married life? The love of the spouses, the nourishment of that love, and the deepening of the relationship certainly hold special importance for the peace, happiness, and shared life of the spouses, their home and family. In addition, the sexual relationship of the spouses as described, not sexual intercourse and not the conception of children, essentially binds the couple together physically and emotionally, creatively and spiritually. When church moralists equate a sexual relationship with sexual intercourse, and then go on to equate marriage with the conception of children, they make a fateful mistake. One need only think of those periods when age or infirmity, work or absence, or the demands of a busy life make sexual intercourse either impossible or impractical. Does one really believe that in those situations the sexual relationship of the spouses necessarily weakens and diminishes? On the contrary, it often strengthens and deepens.

The church teaches, as if chiseled in stone, that marriage has two essential and equal ends, the love of the spouses and the conception of children. For anyone living a married life, these assertions fall distressingly short of common experi-ence as such equates marriage with intercourse and conception. Actual married life dictates otherwise. The end of marriage is the sexual shared life of the spouses; all other goods of life and family flow from it.

If one agrees with the preceding analysis, then the church's basis for denying both marriage and deliberate sexual activity to homosexual partners vanishes. Such couples may love each other and grow in that love; these partners may live vibrant sexual lives together with no intention of producing children; these lovers may establish homes and families that further their own life and growth, and con-tribute to a healthy community.

In our American democracy, homosexuals have not achieved equality with, nor enjoy equal rights with, their heterosexual neighbors. This discrimination flies in the face of America's declaration that "all Men are created equal" and have "unalien-able Rights" to "Life, Liberty, and the Pursuit of Happiness." Homosexuals cannot marry; except in rare instances, they do not enjoy the protections and privileges connected with a civilly recognized union; in many states they cannot adopt children. This undemocratic civil situation stems largely from the prevalent con-demnation of homosexuality by Catholicism and other Christian denominations.

In the Nineteenth Century, Christian churches strongly influenced the outlawing of black slavery. This prepared for a democratic acceptance of that race in our society. In the nineteenth and twentieth centuries Christian missionaries and their sponsoring denominations led the Caucasian community to reevaluate the social fabric of the tribes, the history, and the ongoing life situation of America's Indians. In a democratic Catholic Church, in America's 21st Century may we find a way to accept our homosexual brothers and sisters as honored members of our church? May we, indeed, once again lead our country into a fuller, richer, truer equality for all Americans, including, especially, our gay and lesbian fellow citizens? For this to happen, our bishops must shoulder the task of breaking through the entrenched moralism of Rome. It promises to be difficult. They will need perseverance and much patience. The discoveries and understandings of the social and behavioral sciences may lend scientific assistance, and the American dedication to, and appreciation of, human equality may offer a vision and a purpose. Equality does not come from monarchical societies, political or religious; it flows out of the perceived blessings and rights of democracy.

III. A Bill of Rights for American Catholics

Having considered the general areas of equality and inequality in the Catholic Church in the United States, let us zero in on more specific examples of both. Taking a cue from the *Declaration of Independence*, we may turn our attention to the "unalienable Rights...of Life, Liberty, and the Pursuit of Happiness."

Tocqueville speaks somewhat glowingly of the topic of rights: "After the general idea of virtue I know of none more beautiful than that of rights, or rather these two ideas are intermingled. The idea of rights is nothing other than the idea of virtue introduced into the political world."[10]

He contributes a unique perspective by joining virtue and rights. In context, virtue appears to have this meaning:

> A strong leaning, a certitude of soul, which leads to doing good and avoiding evil....
>
> It is also said of those tendencies that belong to one or another kinds of duties or right behaviors: Christian virtue, moral virtue...civil virtues, private and public and domestic virtues, stoic virtue.[11]

---

[10]   *Ibid.*, p. 227.

[11]   *Dictionnaire De L'Académie Française.* Sixième Édition, 1835, 2:927. "Disposition ferme, constante de l'âme, qui porte à faire le bien et à fuir le mal...Il se dit aussi des dispositions particulières propres à telle ou telle espèce de devoirs ou de bonnes actions. Vertu chrétiennne. Vertu morale...Vertus civiles. Vertus privées, publiques, domestiques. Vertu stoïque."

This differs from the generally accepted idea that virtue exists only as an accomplishment. As recently as 1965, the German theologian Karl Rahner defined virtue in this fashion:

> In the broad sense, any fully developed capacity of the human will or intellect (for example, in the sphere of knowledge, wisdom or science); in the strict sense, the power (competence) to accomplish moral good, especially to do so gladly and with constancy, even against opposition without and within and even at considerable sacrifice.[12]

For Tocqueville, an inalienable right would have the following characteristics. It is—

> The ability to do something, to possess it, to dispose of it, to demand it, to have a legitimate claim to it, whether this power follows naturally upon relationships established between persons, or whether one holds that only from a social compact, positive laws, or particular conventions: the rights of man in society...a right that cannot be prescribed.[13]

For him rights flow from virtue, a natural inclination of the human being toward truth and goodness, an inalienable quality of the human spirit that contributes to the growth and perfection of human life. In stressful situations, people grant rights readily and steadfastly to their neighbors; democracies, indeed, protect them as natural possessions of their citizens.

Democracies inculcate in their citizens the idea of rights, at first through parents with their children, then through teachers in schools with young people, and finally through laws that instruct all citizens. As Tocqueville comments, people gradually accept the responsibility of paying attention to, being sensitive to, respecting and protecting others' rights, because to do so creates a social milieu in which one may freely enjoy the same personal rights:

---

[12]   Karl Rahner & Herbert Vergrimler, *Theological Dictionary.* New York: Herder and Herder, 1965, p. 483.

[13]   *Ibid.,* 1:587. "Faculté de faire quelque chose, d'en jouir, d'en disposer, d'y pretender, de l'exiger, soit que cette faculté résulte naturellement des rapports qui s'établissent enter les personnes, soit qu'on la tienne seulement du pacte social, des lois positives, des conventions particulières. Les droits de l'homme en société.... Droit imprescriptible."

I wonder what, in our day, is the means of inculcating in men the idea of rights and of making it, so to speak, fall upon their senses; and I see only one, which is to give the peaceful exercise of certain rights to all of them: one sees that well among children, who are men except for force and experience. When the child begins to move in the midst of external objects, instinct brings him to put to use all that he encounters in his hands; he has no idea of the property of others, not even of its existence; but as he is made aware of the price of things and he discovers that he can be stripped of his in his turn, he becomes more circumspect and ends by respecting in those like him what he wants to be respected in himself.[14]

Personal rights expand with a person's adulthood into political rights. "In America the man of the people has conceived a lofty idea of political rights because he has political rights; so that his own are not violated, he does not attack those of others."[15] These rights "descend to the least of citizens…. There is one of its greatest merits in my eyes."[16]

Only with experience and maturity do citizens come to respect the rights of others, to expect the same rights for themselves, and to accept the responsibilities attached to them. Children and young people, in general, obey their superiors out of necessity; they conform to the demands of family, childhood friends, and classmates out of fear of retaliation and the desire to earn a fair shake for one's self. Some adults never move past such immature motivations. They obey laws, not because laws protect the rights of all, but because they fear being caught. People without rights or without the habit of living out of them fall into this category.

Tocqueville recognizes the difficulty of getting citizens to live out of civic virtue rather than fear: "I do not say that it is an easy thing to teach all men to make use of political rights. I say only that when that can be done, the resulting effects are great."[17]

Mature citizens hesitate to drive under the influence of alcohol because they respect the rights of others to life and health; nor do they wish at any time for themselves or their family to be at the mercy of a drunken driver. They comply with car emission regulations, not for fear of a ticket, but because citizens deserve a clean and healthy environment. Democracies aim to develop citizens who obey

---

14　*Op. cit.*, pp. 227-228.

15　*Ibid.*, p. 228.

16　*Ibid.*, p. 228.

17　*Ibid.*, p. 228.

laws enacted by their representatives because they respect their own and their fellow citizens' rights. Monarchies employ force, surveillance, and fear to further the king's will; subjects comply, not because of self or civic virtue, but because of the ruler and his minions. One's motivation may include loyalty, even excitement over the direction of the king's rule, but it rarely becomes love; usually fear of royal displeasure and its consequences lurk just below even the most positive surface.

The amendments to the United States Constitution spell out the rights that belong to American citizens. Government agencies may not abridge, deny, or curtail them. The Catholic Church has formulated no document approximating a bill of rights for its members. The *Code of Canon Law*"[18] mentions rights here and there; most however, deal with the church's hierarchy. This omission does not sit well with democratic peoples who instinctively distrust monarchical governments and their bureaucracies. When human rights are persistently violated in the name of ecclesiastical discipline and control, they have even less reason to entrust themselves, their families, their religious and spiritual lives to the hierarchy.

We have already considered how Bishop John England, in his day, wrote a diocesan constitution for his diocese in South Carolina. He knew the American system of government, the needs of the American people, and he adapted ecclesial practice so as to be both practical and effective. His successors in the American episcopacy, in our day, could well follow his example.

Since Vatican II, with its initial hope and subsequent non-application, and with a never-ending cascade of human rights scandals touching on church governance, here and abroad, the American Catholic has diminishing faith in the moral authority of the episcopacy. As has been discussed elsewhere, educated Catholic adults today listen to their clergy but then make up their own minds as to the wisdom and prudence, or lack thereof, of the clerical position. This book purports to offer an understanding about the reasons for the loss of episcopal authority, as well as suggestions for regaining it. One such action would entail the United States Conference of Catholic Bishops, as a body, writing a bill of rights for the People of God in America. That would spell out for American Catholics where the bishops stand in relation to its own bureaucracy. To regain trust, the bishops must show that they hear their people, recognize their needs, and affirm their rights before the world.

In the wake of human rights abuses that characterized the Second World War, the General Assembly of the United Nations formulated, agreed to, and disseminated a *Universal Declaration of Human Rights*. Its *Preamble*, altered to fit the current discussion, offers a starting point and model for America's Catholic bishops:

---

[18]   *Code of Canon Law*. Washington, D.C.: Canon Law Society of America, 1983.

Whereas recognition of the inherent dignity and of the equal and inalienable rights of all members of the *People of God* is the foundation of freedom, justice, and peace in *our church*,

Whereas disregard for human rights have resulted in *shameful* acts which have outraged the conscience of the *People of God*, and the advent of a world in which human beings shall enjoy freedom of speech and belief and freedom from fear and want has been proclaimed as the highest aspiration of *that People*,

Whereas it is essential, if members of the *People of God* are not compelled to have recourse, as a last resort, to rebellion against *religious* tyranny and oppression, that *their rights* should be protected by the rule of law,

Whereas it is essential to promote the development of friendly relations between *peoples of religious faith*,

Whereas the *People of God* reaffirms *its* faith in fundamental human rights, in the dignity and worth of *each of its members*, and in the equal rights of men and women, and has determined to promote social progress and better standards of life in larger freedom,

Whereas a common understanding of these rights and freedoms is of greatest importance for the full realization of this pledge,

Now, therefore, the *United States Conference of Catholic Bishops* proclaims this *Declaration of Human Rights of the People of God in the United States.*

Here would be a clarion call within the Catholic community announcing a church founded on the essential dignity of a people created by God and formed, each and every one, into the sacrament of Christ on earth. The bishops would, then, need to follow this proclamation with rights that flow naturally from it.

The American *Bill of Rights* and the United Nations' *Universal Declaration of Human Rights* supply ample material that bishops could adapt. Given the experience of periodic disregard of human rights in the past forty years within the church, specific rights deserve emphasis in any attempt to restore the people's trust in their religious leaders:

Article 1: All human beings are born free and equal in dignity and rights. They are endowed with conscience and should act towards one another in a spirit of brotherhood.

Article 2: Every Catholic has the right to recognition in the Church as a person before the law.

Article 3: The rights of members of the People of God shall not be denied or abridged by Catholic Church authorities in the United States on account of race or color, sex or sexual orientation, or age.

Article 4: Every Catholic has the right to freedom of thought, conscience and religion; this right includes freedom to change his or her religion or belief, and freedom, either alone or in community with others and in public or private, to manifest that religion or belief in teaching, practice, worship and observance.

Article 5: Every Catholic has the right to freedom of opinion and expression, this right includes freedom to hold opinions without interference and to seek, receive and impart information and ideas through any media and regardless of community boundaries.

Article 6: Catholic Church authorities in the United States shall make no law respecting an establishment of religion or an attempt to do so, or prohibiting the free exercise thereof; or abridging the freedom of speech, or of the press; or the right of the Catholic people peaceably to assemble, and to petition their bishops for a redress of grievances.

Article 7: All Catholics are equal before Church law and are entitled without any discrimination equal protection of that law.

Article 8: No Catholic shall be subjected to arbitrary interference by Catholic Church authorities with one's privacy, family, home or correspondence, or to attacks upon one's honor or reputation. All Catholics have the right to the protection of Church law against such interference or attacks.

Article 9: In the exercise of personal rights and freedom, every Catholic shall be subject only to such limitations as are determined by Church law solely for the purpose of securing due recognition and respect for the rights and freedom of others and of meeting the just requirements of morality, public order, and the general welfare of a democratic society.

Article 10: In all religious prosecutions, the accused shall enjoy the right to a speedy and public trial, by an impartial jury of the diocese and parish wherein the alleged violation shall have been committed; to be confronted with the witnesses against him or her; to have a compulsory process for obtaining witnesses for the defense, and to have the assistance of counsel for that defense.

An analysis of these proposed rights would show that they fall into the three categories announced to be inalienable in the *Declaration of Independence*: Articles one to three address an equal right to life in the Catholic community; articles four, five, and six speak of the freedom of the People of God; and articles seven through ten detail the legal protections Catholics may expect as they pursue the growth and development of their faith.

One may reasonably inquire why the church in America needs such a bill of rights. Does this not appear to be contrary to the Catholic religion?

Tocqueville takes up the question of the compatibility of Catholicism and democracy:

> I think that it is wrong to regard the Catholic religion as a natural enemy of democracy. Among the different Christian doctrines, Catholicism appears to me, on the contrary, one of the most favorable to equality of conditions. Among Catholics, religious society is composed of only two elements: the priest and the people. The priest alone is raised above the faithful: everything is equal below him.
>
> In the matter of dogmas, Catholicism places the same standards on all intellects; it forces the details of the same beliefs on the learned as well as the ignorant, the man of genius as well as the vulgar; it imposes the same practices on the rich as on the poor, inflicts the same austerities on the powerful as the weak; it compromises with no mortal, and applying the same measure to each human, it likes to intermingle all classes of society at the foot of the same altar, as they are intermingled in the eyes of God.
>
> If Catholicism disposes the faithful to obedience, it does not prepare them for inequality. I shall say the contrary of Protestantism, which generally brings men much less to equality than to independence.

> Catholicism is like an absolute monarchy. Remove the prince and conditions are more equal in it than in republics.[19]

If he reasons correctly, then inequality among Catholics functions only as a hierarchical artifact attached to administrative position. As regards the state of believers, equality rules. A bill of rights would formalize that equality, giving firm notice of its existence and practice within the church. The church as hierarchy posits and depends upon inequality; the church as the People of God proclaims the equality of those baptized into the body of Christ. We lack a bill of rights in the church, not because of inequality there, but because of the historical identification of the hierarchy and its structural inequality with the church itself. Correctly seen, rights and equality partake of the essence of Catholicism.

As discussed previously, the practice of virtue in community depends upon rights within that community. The church's clergy, from pope to bishop to priest, constantly extol virtue and urge its growth among the faithful. Yet virtue disconnected from rights usually portrays compliance, a kind of obedience dictated by loyalty born of fear of displeasing the powerful: in this instance, the hierarchy here, and a Divine Judge hereafter. To the extent the hierarchy preaches and maintains inequality within the church, to that extent its sabotages the development of virtue within it. Rights point to and maintain equality; together they construct a home for the practice of virtue, a habit born of respect and meant to flourish in love.

The church needs a formal declaration of rights because, in its hierarchical expression over the centuries since the Council of Trent, church leaders have emphasized duties and responsibilities; at the same time, they have neglected and downplayed rights. Catholics have been told in minute detail what to do and what to avoid; they still wait in vain to hear what they may expect as their due from the priests ordained to serve them.

IV. Current Rights in the Catholic Church in America

In the remaining pages of this chapter, let us consider the "Unalienable rights…to Life, Liberty, and the pursuit of Happiness" as they exist in America's democracy and as they find scant presence in America's Catholic Church.

Life

Every human being has a right to life, to its nourishment and its protection. Every American citizen, therefore, as long as he or she meets necessary health standards,

---

[19]   *Op.cit.,* pp. 275-276.

has the right to marry a person of choice and they to give birth to children together. The couple and their family need a suitable dwelling in which to make a home; they may choose one according to their means or they may expect government to provide shelter that meets its own health specifications. It must be located in a safe environment, or, if not, must be protected by local agencies assuring the family's safety and health. In order to live, all people need clean air and water, healthy food, appropriate clothing, sanitation facilities, and medical assistance as required. Government must see that these are available to all within legal guidelines. Since the human being needs to grow intellectually, children must receive standard school instruction; to develop emotionally they require a supportive and non-abusive interpersonal environment; to realize some degree of moral and spiritual maturity, they must have the opportunity to receive the influence of, and to practice, a religious faith: our government must assure that all may exercise these rights. Since many of life's necessities depend upon family income, breadwinners have a right to a job and to at least a minimum wage for their efforts; otherwise, the government must provide a sufficient substitute. Many of the issues stirring political discussion in our time revolve around these rights and the government's part in securing them: a fixed minimum wage, universal health care coverage, affirmative action, the right to work, welfare reform, penal code reform, separate and equal education, and low income housing—to list just a few.

In general, the Catholic Church in the United States supports the rights to life guaranteed by the government to its citizens. It, however, refuses, as does the government, to take any firm moral stance against modern warfare or against capital punishment. It staunchly allies itself with the opponents of abortion, but its political campaign to outlaw the destruction of fetuses while condoning the just killing of its parents and siblings rings hollow. As previously mentioned, decisions in line with the late Cardinal Bernardin's plea to stand for the "seamless garment of life" would lend credibility to the bishops' supposed moral stance in defending human life.

In its *Code of Canon Law*", the church affirms the right of the faithful to spiritual nourishment. Canon 213 declares: "The Christian faithful have the right to receive assistance from the sacred pastors out of the spiritual goods of the Church, especially the word of God and the sacraments."[20]

The word translated as "right" is "*jus*," the Latin term for "law," as in *Codex Juris Canonici*, the *Code of Canon Law*". This right to spiritual nourishment comes to Catholics according to the *Code* as a legal benefit determined to be owed them.

---

[20]   *Op. cit.*, pp. 71-72. *Jus est christifidelibus ut ex spiritualibus Ecclesiae bonis, praesertim ex verbo Dei et sacramentis, adjumenta a sacris pastoribus accipiant.* Cf. *Op. cit.*, "*Dogmatic Constitution on the Church*," p. 64.

It does not, therefore, exist as an inalienable right flowing from their nature as members of the People of God. It could, indeed, be revoked in any future edition of the *Code* as determined by the then-reigning pontiff.

The canon recognizes the central place of the Word of God and the seven sacraments in the furthering and maintaining of the Catholic faith. It seeks to assure their availability to the Catholic people. It does not, however, include any sort of quality control: sermons must be preached, but who sees that they deserve a hearing; prescribed prayers and rituals surround particular sacraments, but what happens when prayers spew forth as hurried, unintelligible mumbles or when rituals are enacted with the grace of programmed robots? The church, rather lamely, stands behind the validity, *ex opere operato* (by the act itself, no matter the intention or quality of performance), of these ecclesial actions; they say nothing about their effectiveness, or ineffectiveness, as spiritual nourishment.

Further threatening this right is the distressing decrease in priestly vocations. Many parishes have no resident pastor; many have only the occasional services of a circuit-riding, overworked priest; many others are closing, being consolidated with neighboring parishes because of the shortage of priests as well as diminishing attendance at, and involvement in, church activities. We know that this situation can only worsen unless remedial action occurs. A large pool of potential ministers of the word and sacrament awaits the summons to ameliorate the crisis. As of now, this availability continues to go unutilized; the substitutes, sadly, happen to be a pool of women barred from the sacramental priesthood, and married men, many of them inactive priests, rejected in a chimerical defense of clerical celibacy. One wonders how America's bishops conscientiously balance this right of the People of God, a right battered by infrequency and irregular quality, with papal restrictions, unnecessarily and stubbornly held without open and universal discussion and consultation, that are exacerbating the decline in parish life in their dioceses.

Two other canons speak of the nourishment of Christian life through education. Canon 217 enunciates "the right to a Christian education" [*jus habent ad educationem christianam*] while Canon 229 declares: "Lay persons are bound by the obligation and possess the right to acquire a knowledge of Christian doctrine…" [*obligatione tenentur et jure gaudent*]. The former emphasizes that such education is necessary "to develop the maturity of a human person and at the same time come to know and love the mystery of salvation"; the latter flows from the laity's obligation to live, announce, defend, and spread the Catholic faith. Canon 217, therefore, points to a true right while Canon 229 simply posits Christian education as a necessary condition for being a lay Catholic.

In actual practice, most Catholics experience religious education as an obligation difficult to avoid. Students in Catholic grade and high schools must attend religion classes; pastors impress upon parents of Catholic students in public schools the duty to get them into regular Confraternity of Christian Education classes. Some Catholic colleges still require Catholic students to take a set minimum of philosophy and theology courses. And all laypeople face a lifetime of Sunday sermons, willingly or not, but inevitably.

Since Vatican II, a growing number of laypeople have chosen to pursue degrees in theology, religious studies, religious education, and comparative religion. For the most part, they do so in order to take over positions once filled by priests and religious: as lay deacons, directors of religious education programs, chaplains in hospitals and colleges, retreat and spiritual directors, and even parish administrators. Many of these people do so, not simply as the path to a church job, but "to develop the maturity of the human person." They, indeed, accept their Christian education, no matter the church's intention, as a right belonging to them as members of the People of God.

Lay people so employed by the church have a right, in justice, "to a decent remuneration" that allows them "to provide decently for their own needs and for those of their family," which should include "pension, social security and health benefits."[21] In a church community long accustomed to the contributed services of teaching religious and pastoral support furnished through the collection basket, the paying of professional salaries, including benefits, has been slow in coming. Lay professionals in parishes and schools and hospitals regularly complain of starvation wages that barely keep them alive now, and offer little hope for a financially secure future. "Decent remuneration" often depends more on the wealth of the religious employer than upon the needs of employees and their families. Simple justice demands that dioceses make up for the poverty or niggardliness of its institutions.

The church declares no other rights to life, natural or legal, either in its *Code of Canon Law*" or in documents generated by Vatican II, affirming the equality of church members. The bill of rights proposed above, specifically articles one through three, could cover the deficit.

Liberty

In the United States citizens enjoy two types of civil liberty: freedom from government intrusion, and freedom to participate in the life of the community.

From their experience of European monarchies, our ancestors knew painfully the arbitrary power of the State. They, consequently, decided that, even though the individual could rarely marshal the physical forces required to resist law enforcement officers, as the source of the government's legitimacy, the citizen has the moral

---

[21] *Op. cit.,* Canon 231, #2.

and civic right to resist any and all unlawful actions of those agents. These rights protect citizens from slavery and involuntary servitude, from cruel and unusual punishment upon being found guilty in a court of law. They shield individuals from self-incrimination, from having to testify against another when that would violate a close personal or legal relationship, and from continued accusation and trial after the dismissal of charges. Most importantly, they build a fortress around one's home, family, and personal effects: no one without a legal warrant may violate another's personal space in unreasonable and illegal searches and seizures.

Americans freely consent to engage in a common enterprise: to join with their fellow citizens in forming, maintaining, and growing the body politic. They elect representatives, inform them of their concerns as citizens, and periodically review their representatives' actions taken on their behalf. To exercise these civic duties well, Americans rely on a free press to inform them truthfully of important facts, and upon their own unimpeded right to share opinions with fellow citizens. They meet together, work, worship, and share their lives and homes and families freely with one another. They recognize that their corporate existence demands reasonable laws and a dependable order. They expect every citizen to have equal rights under the law in case of disputes, and all the advantages of a fair, open review of relevant facts in the presence of their peers.

The Catholic Church has come far from its identification with civil power during the Middle Ages. Religious police or government agents carrying out the joint will of Church and State no longer use fear and force to compel belief or to combat heresy. For that reason current church documents contain next to nothing concerning freedom from coercive power.

Three exceptions may be noted. Canon 219 states straightforwardly: "All the Christian faithful have the right [*jure gaudent*] to be free from any kind of coercion in choosing a state of life."[22] This means that no one, even for the good of the church, may unduly influence a young person to enter a religious order or to study for the priesthood. Nor may anyone force a person to marry in order to obtain the services of expected offspring. Parents, teachers, or pastors who apply moral or psychological pressure in these regards violate the legal rights of the church member affected.

Canon 221 assures the faithful that they may exercise the legal opportunity to defend their rights before an ecclesiastical court that must judge them fairly, according to canon law, and, should they be found guilty, punish them according to legal norms.[23] This canon offers small comfort to the laity as they have only a scarcity of rights to defend; legal actions would most likely charge them with

---

[22]   *Ibid.*, p. 73.

[23]   *Ibid.*

failing in their responsibilities rather than defend them over the deprivation of their rights. Moreover, ecclesiastical courts operate under the purview of the hierarchy; yet members of the hierarchy are the most likely instigators, prosecutors, and judges of the legal action. The canon includes no guarantee about a speedy and open trial, one conducted in the presence of one's peers, nor one in which the defendant is confronted in public by accusers. American Catholics bridle at papal investigators gathering secret information, compiling damaging dossiers against bishops or theologians or church activists, and then instigating repressive and punitive measures against them. This seems an unfair exercise of power that insults a democratic people and deprives church members of a fair and impartial hearing by their peers. American bishops, acting as Americans rather than monarchical princes, must be sensitive to their parishioners' insistence on the right to a fair trial. They should resist, and not cooperate with, papal investigations that re-create the era of the Two Swords when Church and State united in an often-abusive authority.

Canon 220 joins a legal proscription to a moral obligation.[24] Persons sin when they slander or libel others, thereby harming their good name in the community. This canon threatens to prosecute any Catholic who sets out to destroy publicly, through lies, another's reputation. Although this protection extends to all the faithful, one must wonder whom, in reality, it protects. Can we envision a parishioner summoning another parishioner before an ecclesiastical tribunal on the charge of spreading public falsehoods? Every day someone rebuts false accusations in state courts; I, personally, have never heard of such an action by a layperson in a church court. It seems much more likely that this canon seeks to shield the good name of the hierarchy from public embarrassment. Should Catholics dare to challenge a cleric's reputation, let them beware: this outrage may constitute a private sin and a public scandal deserving prosecution in both secular and ecclesiastical forums.

In addition, this canon protects all the faithful from self-incrimination. A church employer—a pastor, a principal, or a bishop—may not legally make public confession a necessary condition for continued employment. Nor may a confessor expect such as requisite for absolution.

By implication, and more broadly, the canon condemns any invasion of another's privacy. This right protects one's personal space [*jus cuiusque personae ad propriam intimitatem*]. This would include one's actions, the friends with whom one associates, vacations taken and entertainments enjoyed, or any lavishness surrounding one's personal life. For the most part, these protections seem unnecessary for private persons: who really cares what they do anyway? They do create a wall of privacy around public figures. In the church, the hierarchy, principally, hold

---

[24]   *Ibid.*

public office. This calls up the ongoing debate about the privacy owed public persons versus the information a community deserves and requires about its leaders. Should the extravagances, indulgences, and expensive lifestyle of many clerics be nobody's business but their own, or should the people be kept aware of their private peccadilloes and personal failings along with their proclaimed public stances? One need only be reminded of the secretive assaults of some clerics on innocent children to settle upon an answer. The people deserve to know when and if their leaders are hypocrites. In America, citizens enjoy rights that protect them from the intrusions of overreaching government agents; this canon, in effect, bestows on its governing clerics a legal justification for hiding themselves from the inquiring eyes of the Catholic people.

The freedom to express oneself and one's opinions is enshrined in the First Amendment to the United States Constitution. As Tocqueville explains, this freedom flows directly from the sovereignty of the people:

> In a country where the dogma of the sovereignty of the people reigns openly, censorship is not only a danger but also a great absurdity.
>
> When one accords to each a right to govern society, one must surely recognize his capacity to choose among different opinions that agitate his contemporaries and to appreciate different facts, the knowledge of which can guide him.
>
> The sovereignty of the people and freedom of the press are therefore two entirely correlative things: censorship and universal suffrage are, on the contrary, two things that contradict each other and cannot be found in the political institutions of the same people for long. Among the twelve million men who live in the territory of the United States, there is not *a single one* who has yet dared to propose restricting the freedom of the press.[25]

Although he is speaking specifically about freedom of the press, his point holds for freedom of speech. Clearly, our founding fathers thought so also: the First Amendment addresses as one the freedom of speech, association, the press, and petition of government concerning grievances, all means of sharing information, facts, and opinions with one's fellow citizens.

The lawmakers at Vatican II in the *Dogmatic Constitution on the Church* equated the church with the People of God. In its fourth chapter, entitled "Laity," they

---

[25]   *Op. cit.,* pp. 173-174.

acknowledged the duty and the right of laypeople, as the occasion demanded, to share their opinions with church leaders:

> An individual layman, by reason of the knowledge, competence, or outstanding ability which he may enjoy, is permitted and sometimes obliged to express his opinions on things which concern the good of the church. When occasions arise, let this be done through the agencies set up by the church for this purpose. Let it always be done in truth, in courage, and in prudence, with reverence and charity toward those who, by reason of their sacred office represent the person of Christ.[26]

In this statement the Council Fathers echoed Canon 212, #3:

> In accord with the knowledge, competence and preeminence which they possess, they [the Christian faithful] have the right and even at times a duty to manifest to the sacred pastors their opinion on matters which pertain to the good of the Church, and they have a right to make their opinion known to the other Christian faithful, with due regard for the integrity of faith and morals and reverence toward their pastors, and with consideration for the common good and the dignity of persons.[27]

In neither instance do the lawmakers posit the source of this right. However, given its position in the document on the nature of the church, one may surmise that the writers at least had in mind the sovereignty of the People of God as the ground out of which this right grows.

If censorship appears absurd, as Tocqueville says, in a democracy, it has become a noticeable irritant in the American church. Once upon a distant time, the *Index of Forbidden Books* flourished; it provided a bulwark against opinions that "would confuse the people." In our era of universal education and in a country where large numbers of Catholics have undertaken to earn a college degree, confusion stems more from "what are they afraid I'll find out" than "this writer makes me doubt my faith." Anyway, attempts at censorship, in the long run, usually fail.

Let me share two brief vignettes from my own life that illustrate the absurdity and fruitlessness of ecclesiastical attempts to shield the faithful from heterodox explorations.

---

[26] *Op. cit.,* p. 64.

[27] *Op. cit.,* p. 71.

In 1959 I was engaged in a masters program in philosophy at the Jesuit house of philosophy in Spokane, Washington. I came upon a reference to a Jesuit-priest-author, Teilhard de Chardin. Attracted by a brief sketch of his work and his thinking about human existence, I attempted to borrow his *Phenomenon of Man* from our library. I was rebuffed with the curt indication that "that book" was located in "Hell," the locked room in which forbidden volumes languished. Chardin's writings had been sentenced there because of controversial and suspicious theories.

That weekend, my sister, a sophomore at nearby Gonzaga University, paid me a call. I mentioned this irritating prohibition that was preventing me from deciding for myself the truth or falsity of a fellow Jesuit's theology of man and of God's presence in material creation. At a subsequent visit, she brought me a copy of Chardin's *Phenomenon* that she had readily picked up at her Jesuit school's bookstore. I read it during that summer's retreat. I liked it enough to ask her then to get me his *Divine Milieu*.

By 1969 Vatican II and its hope-filled reforms seemed increasingly remote. Paul VI had dismissed the views of his expert commission on birth control in favor of hoary tradition. His curia was exerting itself in an attempt to reign in still further the freedom of the sons of God unleashed by John XXIII and his Council.

I received a notice from Rome via the Jesuit Order concerning the training center for Latin, Central, and South American missionaries in Cuernavaca, Mexico. Fr. Ivan Illich, a New York secular priest, something of an exile, directed it. All priests and religious were hereby warned to avoid his place because of its openness to liberation theology, a suspect mixing of theology and Marxism. The communiqué arrived just as I was searching for a likely "intercultural experience," a requirement of a doctoral course in "Intercultural Sensitivity." I recognized Illich's name; I knew zero about his center; I had read a couple of books by Gustavo Gutierrez; I had caught tremors issuing from the episcopal conference in Medellin, Columbia, the year before. I made arrangements to spend a month in Cuernavaca.

During my days there, I studied Spanish and took short courses in the culture of Latin America; at night I practiced my halting language skills on the Mexican family with whom I was boarding. In free minutes I attended seminars by Illich and Paulo Friere. One evening, I heard a talk by the Canadian theologian, Gregory Baum, on his book, *Man Becoming*; on another, I joined a crowd listening to Erich Fromm, a local resident, an exciting social psychologist (I had recently devoured his *Escape From Freedom*). Other moments, I met many Spanish-speaking young people from around the Americas; they were energized by the stirrings of social change sweeping the continent and even beginning to transform their church. Late one night, fifteen or so of us engaged in an earnest and emotional conversation about

Cuba, its revolution, the place of socialism in South America, and the response of the United States to people-based liberation movements.

I met other religious there, priests and sisters and brothers. They had not let the sour rumblings from Rome deter them. Many were destined for various mission fields; they needed the perspective and information the center afforded. On St. Ignatius' feast day, July 31ˢᵗ, I had sauerbraten and potatoes with the only other Jesuit in residence: Fr. Gordon George, the English assistant to the Jesuit general, Pedro Arrupe. He, too, was taking a summer study vacation at this off-limits intellectual resort. He inquired about my work in religious psychology, especially about the use of group dynamics with religious communities. As a fruit of that discussion, I spent the month of January in 1971 in the Alban Hills outside of Rome: my erstwhile dinner companion invited me to be on a leadership development team for English-speaking Jesuit provincials from around the world. So much for the obstructive merits of censorship.

Although Paul VI abolished the *Index of Forbidden Books* in 1965, the church still clings tenaciously to episcopal control over books touching upon Catholic faith and morals. Canon 823 makes this position clear:

> In order for the integrity of the truths of the faith and morals to be preserved, the pastors of the church have the duty and the right to be vigilant lest harm be done to the faith or morals of the Christian faithful through writings or the use of instruments of social communication; they likewise have the duty and the right to demand that writings to be published by the Christian faithful which touch upon faith or morals be submitted to their judgment; they also have the duty and right to denounce writings which harm correct faith or good morals.[28]

In carrying out this legal prescription, bishops require that priest-authors, prior to publication, submit their manuscripts to church censorship. "In undertaking the office, the censor, laying aside any respect for persons, is to consider only the teaching of the Church concerning faith or morals as it is proposed by the ecclesiastical magisterium." [29] Upon reviewing the manuscript, the censor either returns it to the author with indications of required emendations, or, judging favorably, he or she grants a *nihil obstat* ["nothing stands in the way of publishing this book"] and forwards it to the bishop, who may review it further or, in turn, may issue his final *imprimatur* ["let it be published"]. If the author happens to be a religious,

---

[28]   *Ibid.,* p. 307.

[29]   *Ibid.,* canon 830, #2, p. 311.

the approval of the appropriate major superior is also required and the superior's *imprimi potest* ["it is able to be published"] obtained.[30]

When this review happens between the Christian faithful and a bishop, not between a priest or religious and a superior, the situation involves conflicting rights. As previously indicated, Canon 212 states explicitly that the Christian faithful "have the right and even at times a duty to manifest to the sacred pastor their opinion on matters which pertain to the good of the Church"; and "have a right to make their opinions known to the other Christian faithful." At the same time, Canon 823 affirms that bishops "have the duty and the right to demand that writings to be published by the Christian faithful which touch on faith or morals be submitted to their judgment." How may these rights be reconciled?

Canon 212 places four conditions on the right of the Christian faithful to share their opinions publicly: they must exercise "due regard for the integrity of faith and morals." At the same time they must manifest "reverence toward their pastors," respect the "dignity of persons," while considering "the common good" of the church community. Catholic authors need to follow these guidelines. In their own consciences, they must be at peace that their actions satisfy them.

On their part, bishops must respect the right of the Christian faithful to share their opinions. They will show this in action by appointing censors known "for their knowledge, correct doctrine and prudence,"[31] and by making certain that their own judgments and those of their censors "laying aside any respect for persons...consider only the teaching of the Church concerning faith and morals."[32]

In the current state of the American church, the true problem lies in complying with teachings as "proposed by the ecclesiastical magisterium."[33] For reasons detailed extensively throughout this book, trust between the American hierarchy and American Catholics has been shattered. Bishops behold a people in revolt who do not manifest "reverence toward their pastors"; laypeople see a hierarchy that does not respect them and that rules primarily for its own advancement. Bishops must censor because they distrust their people; laypeople do not accept episcopal interpretations of faith and morals because they do not trust the honesty of the bishops or the truth of their interpretations.

The impasse seems evident: bishops consider themselves to be leaders of the Catholic people, but many Catholics regard them, not as leaders, but as self-serving Roman bureaucrats set on maintaining personal power and privilege.

---

[30]   *Ibid.*, canon 832, p. 311.

[31]   *Ibid.*, canon 830, #1, p. 311.

[32]   *Ibid.*, canon 830, #2, p. 311.

[33]   *Ibid.*

If this divide continues, one may reasonably expect the following as it touches upon publications and censorship:

- Priests and religious, people who know the church and its hierarchy intimately, will only write books that fit into the current perception of the church as held by the episcopal hierarchy.

- Lay Catholics, if they wish to publish with Catholic presses and with episcopal approval, will imitate clerical and religious authors.

- Lay authors daring to challenge the current hierarchical administration and its interpretation of Catholic faith and tradition will not submit their writing for episcopal review and will seek out secular presses.

- The bishops and their conservative followers will not listen to, or wrestle with, the opinions of Catholics challenging church management.

- The rights of laypeople to be heard and bishops to review publications will not be honored.

- Distrust between hierarchy and laity will continue to grow.

American bishops could at once draw off this unpleasant struggle. Publish the bill of rights proposed above; underline especially articles four through six. Moreover, let it be known to Catholic authors, lay and religious and clerical, that they may write books critical of church administration, and that the bishops will allow them to be published in Catholic presses. At the same time, serve notice that such opinions and criticisms will be publicly challenged and debated in the same presses. Encourage an ongoing and fervent dialogue between opposing viewpoints in the presence of the whole Catholic community. The worst result would be that everyone would grow through a difficult, but terribly necessary, exchange. It takes no courage to talk to oneself...or to the already converted.

We have considered how the Catholic Church gives its people scant rights to free speech and the press, or the right to petition. Does it recognize the right to assembly?

One canon, 215, affirms the freedom of the Christian faithful to initiate associations *outside* the organization of the church with the purpose of furthering its mission to the world:

> The Christian faithful are at liberty to found and to govern associa-
> tions for charitable and religious purposes or for the promotion of the

Christian vocation in the world; they are free to hold meetings to pursue these purposes in common.[34]

An adjacent canon, 214, acknowledges the right of the people "to worship God according to the prescriptions of their own rite...and to follow their own form of spiritual life...."[35] Of course, these rights may only be exercised as they conform to the teachings and practice of the church.

Nowhere does canon law pay attention to any rights of Catholics to form associations *within* the church organization. Dioceses and parishes abound with special gatherings of the faithful—from the Altar Society and the Holy Name Society to the Knights of Columbus and the Diocesan Council of Catholic Men—but all operate under the aegis of pastors and bishops. Catholics are allowed no freedom to associate in any way outside of clerical control. The church does not recognize any right of teachers in Catholic schools or nurses in Catholic hospitals to unionize. It discourages the association of laypeople concerned with lobbying for change in the church itself: groups such as the Women's Ordination Conference, Dignity, and CORPUS are virtually outlawed in some dioceses. It maintains an official neutrality regarding political issues like the annual protests at the School of the Americas, before the Supreme Court building in Washington denouncing Roe vs. Wade, outside state prisons leading up to and during state-performed executions. Yet many priests and sisters, many students from Catholic colleges, and some bishops, participate in those demonstrations as individuals as long as the issue involved does not contradict positions formally taken by the church's hierarchy. Around controversial issues, like the wars in Vietnam and Iraq, the church supports the government, does not want its disapproval, and leaves to fringe groups like CALCAV and Pax Christi the task of non-sanctioned protest.

Tocqueville remarks: "In America, the freedom to associate for political goals is unlimited."[36] The church does not recognize that right within its boundaries, nor does it seem to understand its vital place in American life. Tocqueville leaves no doubt about this:

America is, among the countries of the world, the one where they have taken most advantage of association and where they have applied that powerful mode of action to a greater diversity of objects.

---

[34] *Ibid.*, p. 73.

[35] *Ibid.*

[36] *Op. cit.*, p. 182.

Independent of the permanent associations created by law under the names of townships, cities, and counties, there is a multitude of others that owe their birth and development only to individual will.

The inhabitant of the United States learns from birth that he must rely on himself to struggle against the evils and obstacles of life; he has only a defiant and restive regard for social authority and he appeals to its power only when he cannot do without it.[37]

When the current clerical scandal rocked the American Catholic community, abuse victims gathered together to push for justice and for protection; they did not petition church leaders in some vain hope of an official ecclesiastical remedy. At the same time, concerned laypeople set up Voice of the Faithful chapters across the country to enforce a demand for lay oversight of dangerous clerics and negligent bishops. The United States Conference of Catholic Bishops, feeling the outrage of the people, bowed to public opinion and appointed a watchdog commission of lay experts to monitor diocesan compliance with its own sexual abuse policies. In each instance, coming together into a free association was the automatic response of American Catholics faced with immorality and organizational mismanagement.

The hierarchy, wary of lay associations arrayed to confront it with its failings, responded typically. Since lay people have no ecclesial right to associate, and since they properly petition church leaders and then leave all remedies to them, it sought to keep all control within its ranks. It apologized to victims in the name of the church while softly chiding them for breaking silence and creating scandal; it warned Voice of the Faithful participants against invading governance reserved to the clergy, refused to meet with them, and even barred them from associating on church property; it bestowed halting oversight authority upon its national lay commission only to obstruct its work and gradually drain away its authority over individual dioceses. The bishops acted predictably for managers within a monarchical system. No matter the heartfelt apologies, their actions betrayed weightier concerns: How do we contain the damage? How do we vindicate ourselves? How do we maintain our authority and preserve our positions? How do we salvage the reputation of the clerical order and restore dignity to its operations in the face of public opinion?

The hierarchy failed to lead the people because each group had contrary concerns: for the people, the hierarchy should pay for its crimes and negligence; for the hierarchy, the victims should accept the official concern and promises of future preventive action so that the church could get on with its important mission to the world. Some might say that church leaders operate so far ahead of their people

---

[37] *Ibid.*, p. 180.

that they can no longer lead them; others would maintain they cannot lead the people as their directions have radically diverged; most would urge that the hierarchy must radically transform itself if it wishes to lead effectively the American Catholic community.

The Pursuit of Happiness

The American colonists abandoned a European world in which Church and State constructed happiness by definitions that laid out, not only the goal that constituted it, but also the mode of reaching it. The Church, both Catholic and Protestant, envisioned the goal as eternal union with a pleased and loving God in heaven. Both preached that the way to attain heavenly bliss came through following faithfully directions given by church leaders. The specific teaching only diverged as to the essential core that must be believed and obeyed: humble and consistent obedience constituted the way to the goal. The State, monarchical and aristocratic, defined the goal as union with the ruling monarch who loved, valued, blessed, and supported his loyal followers. One achieved this through obedience to the king's law, service in his endeavors, tested loyalty to the king's will, and success that redounded to his fame. In both the religious and political spheres, the goal of happiness remained forever clear, certain, and fixed. The path itself, though generally staying the same, admitted of adjustments to fit the historical moment as well as the level of advancement attained. Neither goal nor means ever changed: believers become holier, not different, and citizens become courtiers, but always as citizens.

In the Europe still emerging from the Middle Ages, one had various means of measuring happiness. Title immediately distinguished the successful from the ordinary. The Catholic Church honored its cardinals as "princes of the church," just as secular princes elicited respect by their closeness to the king. Title indicated position, the proximity to power, and the allegiance it requires. The pope, presumed holy, undoubtedly had authority from God, and exercised it over a worldwide congregation; a king's minister, in his name, demanded obedience to his laws and could command royal forces to compel compliance. With position, one gained the appurtenances of power: ecclesial and royal mansions, decorated with old masters, scenes of lavish ceremonies and celebrations, with participants resplendent in sumptuous and bejeweled robes. A churchman could not, with certainty, know God's final judgment about his eternal destination; no matter, he definitely could gauge his ascendancy in the church on earth, much as secular lords do in earthly kingdoms.

Our founding fathers decided that government had no place in defining the life goals of its citizens. That must remain a private task, one carried out between the individual and his or her creator. They recognized that human beings, by nature, have an inbuilt urge to change, to grow, to develop their unique abilities. They must assess their possibilities and their talents, select those that hold out promise and delight, and make the decisions and take the actions that may actualize them.

Tocqueville spells out the deep philosophical differences between these two positions. He speaks first of the task within monarchical and aristocratic systems:

> When citizens are classed according to rank, profession or birth, and all are constrained to follow the track to the entrance to which chance has placed them, each believes that he perceives the furthest boundaries of human power near himself, and none seeks any longer to struggle against an inevitable destiny. It is not that aristocratic peoples absolutely deny man the faculty of self-perfection. They do not judge it to be indefinite; they conceive of improvement, not change; they imagine the condition of coming societies as better, but not different; and all the while admitting that humanity has made great progress and that it can make still more, they confine it in advance within certain impassable limits.
>
> They therefore do not believe that they have arrived at the sovereign good and the absolute truth (what man or what people has ever been senseless enough to imagine it?), but they like to persuade themselves that they have attained nearly the degree of greatness and knowledge that our imperfect nature permits; and as nothing around them is moving, they willingly fancy that everything is in its place. It is then that the legislator claims to promulgate eternal laws, that peoples and kings want to raise only monuments [lasting] for centuries, and that the present generation takes on the charge of sparing future generations the care of regulating their destinies.[38]

When the early Americans struggled on to our shores, they not only rejected the set piece of Europe; they also opened themselves, albeit unwittingly, to a wholly different mode of living. Tocqueville continues:

> As castes disappear, as classes get closer to each other, as men are mixed tumultuously, and their usages, customs, and laws vary, as new facts come up, as new truths are brought to light, as old opinions disappear

---

[38] *Ibid.,* p. 427.

and others take their place, the image of an ideal and always fugitive perfection is presented to the human mind.

Continual changes then pass at each instant before the eyes of each man. Some worsen his position, and he understands only too well that a people or an individual, however enlightened [it or] he may be, is not infallible. Others improve his lot, and he concludes from this that man in general is endowed with the indefinite faculty of perfecting himself. His reverses make him see that no one can flatter himself with having discovered the absolute good; his successes inflame him to pursue it without respite. Thus, always seeking, falling, righting himself, often disappointed, never discouraged, he tends ceaselessly toward the immense greatness that he glimpses confusedly at the end of the long course that humanity must still traverse.[39]

Americans, as Americans, seek happiness, but they define it subjectively rather than objectively. Self-interest propels them as they seek to develop their abilities and grow as persons through the pursuit of those interests. They need a certain level of their society's goods to maintain themselves and their families reasonably in respect to their fellow citizens. But they require above that only the titles and power, positions and material resources requisite for their own dreams. The dreams motivate them, not societal recognitions that may differentiate them from others. One need only recall the thousands upon thousands of Americans who annually run through the boroughs of New York chasing only their dream. An infinitesimal few will earn a monetary reward, gain a victory, secure commercial endorsements, or enjoy even a brief, spotlighted moment; most will have only their private exultations: I finished the course; I didn't give up; I lowered my time by some glorious seconds or unlikely minutes; I feel so good about myself. Self-interest alone drove them along that exhausting, yet exhilarating, track.

No country had previously made the goal of its union the self-interest of its people. Indeed, this individualism seems contradictory to the good of the whole. It should spawn selfishness, an everyone-out-for-self mentality that fractures community.

Tocqueville, looking at American society, beholds unity in spite of individualism. He explains it this way:

> I have already shown in several places in this work how the inhabitants of the United States almost always know how to combine their own

---

[39]   *Ibid.*

well-being with that of their fellow citizens. What I want to remark here is the general theory by the aid of which they come to this.

In the United States it is almost never said that virtue is beautiful. They maintain that it is useful and they prove it every day. American moralists do not claim that one must sacrifice oneself to those like oneself because it is great to do it; but they say boldly that such sacrifices are as necessary to the one who imposes them on himself as to the one who profits from them....

Long ago Montaigne said, "When I do not follow the right path for the sake of righteousness, I follow it for having found by experience that all things considered, it is commonly the happiest and most useful."[40]

Self-interest, so understood, does not militate against community. Indeed, in our time, given the advances of modern psychology, we have come to recognize that humans, by nature beings in relationship, cannot separate their own growth and development from their way of relating to others. People may accumulate all the goods the world offers, but without a positive mutual relationship to that world the riches soon turn to ash.

Tocqueville contrasts the morality of sacrifice and of a valued self-interest that includes others in this fashion:

When the world was led by a few powerful and wealthy individuals, these liked to form for themselves a sublime idea of the duties of man; they were pleased to profess that it is glorious to forget oneself and that it is fitting to do good without self-interest like God himself. This was the official doctrine of the time in the matter of morality.

I doubt that men were more virtuous in aristocratic centuries than in others, but it is certain that the beauties of virtue were constantly spoken of then; only in secret did they study the side on which it is useful.[41]

Americans, on the contrary, are pleased to explain almost all the actions of their life with the aid of self-interest well understood; they complacently show how the enlightened love of themselves constantly brings them to aid each other and disposes them willingly to sacrifice a part of their time and their wealth to the good of the state.[42]

---

[40] *Ibid.,* p. 501.

[41] *Ibid.,* pp. 500-501.

[42] *Ibid.,* p. 502.

Catholicism preaches that human life has one goal: everlasting union with God in heaven. That blessed state constitutes the only final and true happiness worthy of humankind's utmost and constant effort. If the "pursuit of happiness" means the right to search for the personal goal that will bring happiness, for Catholics the church defines that goal, and leaves no room for further search. Human nature in its essence is directed toward, yearns for, and finds completion in, divine union. Catholics enjoy no right to pursue that happiness; rather, they have the responsibility to do so.

No one seriously expects the Catholic Church to change its vision of the purpose of human life. Neither a monarchical nor a democratic ecclesial structure would require it. Democracy simply demands that government stay away from the definition because the task belongs to the individual conscience. Moreover, it preserves the right of individuals to form their own consciences. No government, nor church, nor person—not even a parent—may alienate that right.

As the Catholic layperson seeks God in this life, he or she does have two inalienable rights that flow from baptism into the Body of Christ. They turn out also to be responsibilities. No body, ecclesial or governmental, may lawfully deny them, as long as the rights of others are respected.

In the *Decree on the Apostolate of the Laity*, the fathers of Vatican II clearly state the first of these rights and its theological basis:

> Since it is proper to the layman's state in life for him to spend his days in the midst of the world and of secular transactions, he is called by God to burn with the spirit of Christ and to exercise his apostolate in the world as a kind of leaven.
>
> The laity derive the right and duty with respect to the apostolate from their union with Christ their Head. Incorporated into Christ's Mystical Body through baptism and strengthened by the power of the Holy Spirit through confirmation, they are assigned to the apostolate by the Lord himself. They are consecrated into a royal priesthood and a holy people (cf. 1 Pet. 2:4-10) in order that they may offer spiritual sacrifice through everything they do, and may witness to Christ throughout the world.[43]

This conciliar affirmation fills out and expands on a legal right recognized in the *Code of Canon Law*:

---

[43]   *Op. cit.,* p. 492.

All the Christian faithful have the duty and the right to work so that the divine message of salvation may increasingly reach the whole of humankind in every age and in every land.[44]

Further on in the same conciliar document, the fathers enunciate with some passion the second right, one that obviously flows from the first:

It has always been the duty of Christian couples, but today it is the supreme task of their apostolate, to manifest and prove by their own way of life the unbreakable and sacred character of the marriage bond, to affirm vigorously the right and duty of parents and guardians to educate children in a Christian manner, and to defend the dignity and lawful independence of the family.[45]

Canon 226, #2 gives the reason for this particular right:

Because they have given life to their children, parents have a most serious obligation and enjoy the right to educate them; therefore Christian parents are especially to care for the Christian education of their children according to the teaching handed on by the Church.[46]

As regards the exercise of these rights, American Catholics, at times, run into conflict with hierarchical bureaucracy. It does not allow any individual right to pursue life goals, relative to this earthly life or a heavenly one to follow, if one's actions contradict its teaching or demands. One may engage in the "pursuit of happiness" but only "my way." Obedience trumps rights. In the proposed bill of rights for American Catholics, articles seven, eight, nine, and ten seek to put boundaries on ecclesiastical intrusion into the right to pursue one's own way to a full and happy life.

A personal life experience illustrates the conflict. I was attending the sixth grade in our parish school. Within the rapidly expanding Catholic population following upon the Second World War, a single sister was attempting to teach sixty, sixth-grade students at one time. She divided the class into two sections: the well behaved and studious sat in the back of the room; the rambunctious and slow were confined together directly under her nose. Sister routinely assigned reading

---

[44] *Op. cit.*, canon 211, p. 71.

[45] *Op. cit.*, p. 502.

[46] *Op. cit.*, p. 75.

or writing to the self-educating group; we did as directed while she spent most of her time, effort, and actual teaching with the problem students. I found the assignments easy and the class boring. Although I earned straight A's that first semester, I knew little more in January than I did the previous September.

My mother, a former grade school teacher, could no longer abide the crowded situation. She spoke with the principal of the grade school in our town's other Catholic parish who agreed to accept me into its sixth grade class. When my mother informed our pastor of her decision, he exploded in anger. She had no right to take me out of his parish and his school. As members of the parish, we owed it our loyalty, our presence, and, of course, our tuition. If she persisted in her disobedience, he would excommunicate our whole family. Needless to say, I transferred to the other school forthwith.

Setting aside whether the pastor had church law behind him in support of his threat, his handling of the problem eloquently highlights the conflict between a democratic people blessed with the right of the pursuit of happiness, between a member of the People of God assured by the church of her parental right to educate her children, and a pastor raised in a monarchical system that demands humble acquiescence from the laity. My mother could educate me her way just as long as this did not conflict with his authority; when that happened, her right diminished while his authority swelled.

In the name of obedience the church hierarchy routinely tells the Catholic people, not only what constitutes happiness, but also what it must do to attain it. In a self-serving fashion, it often conveniently forgets that its teaching and governing roles do not negate nor override the right of the individual conscience. The believer must listen to, and seriously consider, the directions of church leaders; in the last analysis, however, the final prudential decision belongs to the individual. Although I never asked her, I am certain that my mother, understanding our pastor's objections, decided that she must conscientiously place me where I had a reasonable opportunity to grow as a student and person. How many Catholics, every day, make decisions that run contrary to the explicit teaching of the hierarchy—they practice birth control, they divorce and remarry, they live together with a sexual partner who might or might not become a marriage partner—with a clear conscience? Church moralists would like to pass this off as the spoiled fruits of an erroneous conscience; perhaps it rather constitutes the expressed right of a prudential one. A monarchical hierarchy commands compliance; a democratic one teaches, helps to explore relevant angles and options, and then leaves the decision to the person seeking his or her God.

V. The American Church Needs a Declaration of Independence

The opening lines of the *Declaration of Independence* frame this chapter:

> We hold these Truths to be self-evident, that all Men are created equal, that they are endowed by their Creator with certain unalienable Rights, that among them are Life, Liberty, and the Pursuit of Happiness.

To conclude this chapter, it seems appropriate to summarize how the Catholic Church in America stands in relationship to that founding document. Taking the phrases one by one, what judgment does it earn?

"We hold these *Truths*": As Immanuel Kant argued, objective reality may exist, but no human being can view it other than subjectively. Ever since the Protestant Reformation the "truth" of the Catholic Church was identified with its hierarchy. Indeed, the "hierarchical" Catholic Church differentiated it from the Christian churches and ecclesial communities born of that Reformation. For over five centuries the Catholic gestalt placed its hierarchy in the foreground and relegated the Catholic people to the contextual background out of which the hierarchy ordained, consecrated, taught, governed, and blessed.

Vatican II attempted to shift the gestalt. The council fathers, perhaps unwittingly, most likely by inspiration, moved the People of God into the foreground. "Catholic" for them meant membership in that People, the sacrament of Christ's continuing presence on earth. The hierarchy, born of the church in order to serve it, has meaning and purpose to the extent it furthers the life of the Christian faithful.

Since Vatican II, under the pontificates of Paul VI, John Paul II and, now Benedict XVI, the hierarchy fights to regain the foreground, its accustomed place. It attempts to take back to itself the identification of "Catholic" and "hierarchical," at the same time displacing the People of God into the pre-Vatican II background. The recent clerical sexual abuse scandal in the United States has aroused that People, and exacerbated the struggle for the truth of the church.

"To be *self-evident*": From a hierarchical perspective, God chooses the head of the church, and bestows upon him God's own power and authority. Through this papal instrument, God dispenses the authority of teaching, governing, and sanctifying his people to bishops in all lands and around the world. They, in turn, ordain priests who may bring God's sacramental grace to all who believe in Christ and his church. With that grace, the Christian faithful seek God in this life by loyally and constantly following the way illuminated for them through the teachings, directions, and laws laid out by the church's magisterium. Nothing could be clearer, more certain, or more self-evident.

Until recently, the People of God automatically accepted this hierarchical version of the church. Vatican II changed that. Many realized that their church had been taken from them over the centuries in the name of protecting orthodoxy, preserving the faith, and securing the power and positions of the hierarchy.

Since Vatican II, some other truths about the church have become self-evident to the attentive People of God. Subsequent popes, their curiae, and the whole hierarchical apparatus have sought to negate the actions of that church council. The hierarchy refuses, in practice, to act as part of the People of God; it rather places itself over that People. Orthodoxy has become its own reason for existence: preserving it, protecting it, has displaced the ongoing encounter with a living and immanent God. The maintenance and enhancing of hierarchical authority has become the sign of loyalty and the secure coin of eternal salvation. The People of God hunger to taste the presence of God in their lives; instead, the hierarchy gives them laws to be obeyed, directions to be followed, and obeisance to be offered. The hunger for God remains and only increases.

"That *all* Men are created equal": In his letter to the Galatians, Paul asserts: "All of you who have been baptized into Christ have clothed yourselves with him. There does not exist among you Jew or Greek, slave or freeman, male or female. All are one in Christ Jesus (Gal. 3:27-28)."

Moreover, in our modern world, and especially in the United States, the movement for women's rights and their equality with men is changing society. Yet John Paul II hung stubbornly onto the cultural artifact of female subordination. His theological arguments against the ordination of women, based as they are on a Mediterranean culture of two thousand years ago in which women were socially subordinated, seem archaic and foolish. One wonders if he was not fighting humankind's perennial battle of the sexes, a conflict between a threatened patriarchy and a strengthening matriarchy.[47] The Catholic Church has in recent times showered honors upon Mary, the Mother of Jesus, in a silent recognition that it has excluded femininity from the Godhead. For all that, she still remains "the handmaid of the Lord," the servant of, not the equal of, God. Theologians speak of the Holy Spirit as Sophia, Wisdom, and Wisdom as feminine; some even call God "Mother." Still, that pope demanded that the feminine belongs neither in the Godhead nor before God's altar.

In a church defined as hierarchical, clerics and religious, embracing a higher state of life, are raised above the laity. Yet, as Paul says, "All are one in Christ Jesus." We have here the absurdity that George Orwell underlined in his *Animal Farm* when he observed that in that community "all animals are created equal, but

---

[47]   Cf., for the sake of discussion, Eisler, Riane. *The Chalice and the Blade*. New York: HarperCollins, 1987.

some are more equal than others." True equality exists only in the church understood as the democracy of God.

"That they are endowed...with *unalienable Rights*": With two exceptions, the
hierarchical church understands rights as alienable. They come from the pope and
his bishops as legal grants; they may be reversed according to the will of that
hierarchy. Only the right to bring the Christian message to others, including one's
children, comes to the layperson directly through incorporation into the Body of
Christ. In a church understood to be the People of God, inalienable rights would
inevitably and necessarily flow from the transformed nature of Christian existence, not from any kindness or attention or political largesse on the part of the
hierarchy.

The Code of Canon Law ascribes surprisingly few rights to the Christian faithful. Nor do the decrees of Vatican II do more than enlarge upon rights already
established. Catholics are everywhere told of obligations and warned against trans-
gressions. Duties are described, responsibilities fixed, rewards and punishments
detailed as the special fruits of obedience or the terrifying wages of sin. As a result
of a paucity of rights, the Catholic faithful tend to practice virtue out of compliance or to quiet fear. Preachers eulogize virtue flowing from love, but how may one
love without the freedom that comes from rights? Equals may love; non-equals
may in loyalty obey, but never truly love. Christians stand in awe before the eternal
majesty; they love the Christ who "Though he was in the form of God, he did not
dream equality with God something to be grasped at. Rather, he emptied himself
and took the form of a slave, being born in the likeness of men (Phil. 2:6-7)."

"Unalienable...right to...*Life*": Once baptized, the Christian lives with the life
of Christ. As Paul declares: "...the life I live now is not my own; Christ is living
in me (Gal. 2:20)." That life is nourished by the sacraments, the Word of God,
and by Christian education. Just as no one has an inalienable right to baptism—it
comes as a free gift from God—so one only has the right to its nourishment as a
gift of the church. It bestows the gift and demands that it be utilized. Rights and
responsibilities entwine: sacraments shall be offered and received; sermons shall be
preached and heard; the Christian faith shall be explained and accepted. Nothing
enforces the quality of these ecclesial actions; nothing assures the actual nourishment of the people's faith. The right to life often reduces to the responsibility just
to be in attendance.

"Unalienable...right to...*Liberty*": Paternalism restricts the freedom of the
People of God. Bishops, intent on preserving orthodoxy, dictate the flow of information about the church that reaches Catholics from Catholic sources. They control
diocesan newspapers and discourage lay newspapers and periodicals; they censor
books written by priests and religious while they reserve the right to review lay
publications; they frown upon, and even outlaw, lay associations formed to lobby

on disputed issues within the church. They and their pastors even refuse to meet with lay groups disturbed by malfeasance within clerical ranks that negatively affect the church. Nothing like the United States Constitution's First Amendment exists within the church.

The American hierarchy—its bishops and priests—still treats its people like the unlettered, newly immigrated, often helpless, and theologically unsophisticated parishioners of yesteryear. It harkens back to the eras when father, the educated figure in the Catholic community, knew best. It thinks that the freedom of the *sons and daughters* of God should be taken literally, but today's adult Catholics do not require or want paternalism. They resent being treated like children unable to think for themselves and to make prudent decisions about their lives as Americans and Catholics. Most certainly, they reject any inference that their church belongs to the hierarchy and that they have no active voice within parish and diocesan life. Although the church acknowledges the laity's right to petition their pastors and bishops, that right languishes in disuse when the petitioner addresses the management or mismanagement, governance or lack thereof, in the church itself.

"Unalienable...right to...the *Pursuit of Happiness*": As it is understood in the American democracy, this right does not exist in the Catholic Church. The church determines both the goal of life and how that goal is to be achieved. It leaves little room for exploration, doubt, or individuality. Catholics, as Catholics, must love God and their neighbor. The way of that love is spelled out in the Ten Commandments, the Precepts of the Church, the theological and cardinal virtues, the Sermon on the Mount, and the laws and regulations of the Church. The hierarchy defines, explains, controls, and dictates the moral and religious and spiritual lives of the Catholic people.

In psychological terms, the Church fails to understand the essential difference between the personal self and a person's ego. Because of this, self-interest is made equivalent to egocentricity, a selfish state of separation from others, the world, and God. The church does not grasp that the self, being-in-relationship, encompasses the love of self and neighbor commanded by Christ. For one to pursue his or her own self-interest, to seek to realize unique abilities and develop as a self-initiating and responsible adult is the preeminent task of every human being, every American, and every Catholic. Such is enshrined in the American "pursuit of happiness."

The Catholic Church in America operates under a writ of dependence based on compliance, not rights. It would take a major transformation within the management of the church for that writ to approach anything like a declaration of independence. In a hierarchical church, equality suffers; in the democracy of God, the equality that Tocqueville found irrepressible among the citizens of the United States lives.

The church in the United States stands at a momentous crossroad: will its leaders cling to the monarchical status quo, or will they grasp a God-given opportunity to transform, in the spirit of Archbishop Carroll and Bishop England, into an *American* Catholic Church?

Conclusion

I completed the body of this book in late February 2005. On April 2nd Pope John Paul II succumbed to illnesses that had plagued his declining years. He died surrounded by the attention and affection of the Catholic people, and with the general respect of the non-Catholic world.

Many immediately proclaimed his holiness, petitioning for his canonization. Indeed, his successor, in one of his first papal acts, waived the ordinary five-year period after one's death in order that an official inquiry into John Paul's sanctity might begin. In the end, of course, the state of his soul, holy or not-so-holy, rests between him and God.

Although time and the judgment of history will eventually assess his effect upon the church he ruled and the world stage he trod, few today doubt that he strongly impacted both. For the past twenty-eight years he moved among the world's leaders. They courted him in Vatican City; he traveled to 129 of their countries where he brought the message of Christ to each nation's leaders and crowds of ordinary citizens. He asserted his influence throughout the Catholic world through his writings, by his concentrating of power in the Vatican, through his persistent defense of traditional Catholic morality and ecclesiastical discipline, and his fashioning of a hierarchy molded in his conservative image. Indeed, as events would show, he elevated to the College of Cardinals 114 of the 117 men who would pick his successor: even in death he would continue to shape his kind of church.

In a summary statement, Ronald Modras, a theology professor at St. Louis University, concluded that in 1978 John Paul II "inherited a polarized church. His job was to be a bridge builder. He left it far more polarized today."[1] A group of American scholars spelled out the papal positions that contributed to this divided community:

---

[1]   Arthur Jones, "Another side of John Paul II," *National Catholic Reporter*, April 15, 2005, p. 21.

- The pontificate's suppression of theological discussion;
- The corresponding muting of academic freedom;
- The pope's muzzling of liberation theology through his episcopal appointees, many of them bishops with little pastoral experience;
- John Paul's "from the top down" Christology;
- His use of Vatican II language to impose a return to a Vatican I concepts;
- His endorsement, in a move against enculturation and inclusivity, of a revanchist approach to liturgical translation;
- His re-clericalization of a church that had already embraced the laity as the People of God in the church of the people;
- His treatment of women in the church.[2]

Shortly after this pope's demise, Thomas Cahill, an American Catholic author, briefly assessed John Paul's legacy. Recognizing a diversity of papal traditions over the centuries, he characterized this one as follows:

Despite his choice of name, John Paul II shared little with his immediate predecessors. John Paul I lasted slightly more than a month, but in that time we were treated to a typical Italian of moderating tendencies, one who had even, before his election, congratulated the parents of the world's first test-tube baby—not a gesture that resonated with the church's fundamentalists,...

John Paul II has been almost the polar opposite of John XXIII, who dragged Catholicism to confront 20th century realities after the regressive policies of Pius IX, who imposed the peculiar doctrine of papal infallibility on the First Vatican Council in 1870, and after the reign of terror inflicted by Pius X on Catholic theologians in the opening decades of the 20th century. Unfortunately, this pope was much closer to the traditions of Pius IX and Pius X than to his namesakes....

But John Paul's most lasting legacy to Catholicism will come from the episcopal appointments he made. In order to have been named a bishop, a priest must have been seen to be absolutely opposed to masturbation, premarital sex, birth control (including condoms used to prevent the spread of AIDS), abortion, divorce, homosexual relations, married priests, female priests and any hint of Marxism. It is nearly

---

[2]   Ibid.

impossible to find men who subscribe wholeheartedly to this entire catalogue of certitudes; as a result the ranks of the episcopate are filled with mindless sycophants and intellectual incompetents. The good priests have been passed over; and not a few, in their growing frustration as the pontificate of John Paul II stretched on, left the priesthood to seek fulfillment elsewhere.

The situation is dire. Anyone can walk into a Catholic church on a Sunday and see pews, once filled to bursting, now sparsely populated with gray heads. And there is no other solution for the church but to begin again, as if it were the church of the catacombs, an oddball minority sect in a world of casual cruelty and unbending empire that gathered adherents because it was so unlike the surrounding society.

Cahill concluded trenchantly. He declared that John Paul II "was not a great religious figure. How could he be? He may, in times to come, be credited with destroying his church."[3]

Cahill uttered some tough words. In the context of this book, what effect has the papacy of John Paul had on the Catholic Church in America? On April 3rd, the day after the pope's demise, *The New York Times* presented some summary statistics derived from research undertaken by CARA. It noted these changes over the twenty-eight years of his reign:

- Number of priests: -26%
- Number of sisters: -48%
- Number of brothers: -37%
- Number of graduate-level seminarians: -38%
- Number of parishes: +3%
- Number of parishes without a resident pastor: +350%
- Percentage of Catholics attending mass at least weekly: from 48% to 27%
- Percentage of Catholics favoring abortion: from 34% to 38%
- Percentage of Catholics who regard homosexuality as morally acceptable: from 15% to 39%
- Percentage of Catholics with confidence in religious leaders: from 45% to 18%.[4]

---

[3] "The Price of Infallibility," Op Ed Section, *The New York Times*, April 5, 2005.

[4] "American Catholics in John Paul's Time." *The New York Times*, April 3, 2005, p. 5.

One could add the overwhelming majority of American Catholics who disagree with John Paul II's insistence on the immorality of birth control (80% in a 1990 Gallup Poll), and on the steadily growing acceptance of both married and women priests.[5]

Clearly, the late pope has failed to convince Catholics in America to follow his vision. He sought to re-clericalize the church, yet the numbers of priests and seminarians, sisters and brothers plummeted during his pontificate. He insisted on the tradition of clerical celibacy and on an all-male priesthood; a strong majority of American Catholics wish both church regulations removed. He demanded that Catholics stay faithful to his conservative stances regarding sexual morality, but they use birth control, have abortions, divorce and remarry, enjoy premarital sexual interaction to a degree virtually indistinguishable from their non-Catholic neighbors. He urged them to attend mass, receive communion regularly. Almost three-fourths report that they disregard his advice. One may argue about who is wrong, the pope or the people; no one may reasonably assert that American Catholics, as a whole community, either accept his version of the Church or follow without hesitation his dictates.

During John Paul's tenure seminaries emptied, religious houses closed, parishes merged, increasing numbers of parishes lacked a resident pastor, mass attendance dramatically decreased. On his watch, one stream of priests married and another of disillusioned, incensed women abandoned his Church to become ordained in welcoming Protestant communities. At his direction, national councils of bishops became subordinated to the Vatican bureaucracy while an embarrassment of his episcopal appointees sexually abused children or collaborated in allowing their victimization to continue and spread. No matter his intentions, the late pope has bequeathed to us a church divided between Latin masses and underground masses and empty masses, between traditional Catholics and non-practicing Catholics and former Catholics, between righteous conservatives and a disgusted majority and a dispirited body of progressive priests and laity.

Given the evidence, one may, with more than a tinge of sadness, conclude that Thomas Cahill has a serious, considered, and telling point.

---

[5]   Cf. William D'Antonio, James Davidson, Dean Hoge, Mary Gautier, "American Catholics from John Paul II to Benedict XVI," a survey conducted in 1987, 1993, 1999, and 2005. *National Catholic Reporter*, September 30, 2005, p.15. In response to the statement "Church leaders have final say on birth control," Post-Vatican II Catholics showed 11% agreement, Vatican II Catholics 13% agreement, and Pre-Vatican II Catholics 20% agreement. In the same survey, p. 11, only 29% of all respondents said that a celibate male clergy was very important to them.

On April 19th, seventeen days after the former pope's death, his cardinal appointees elected a new pontiff. Cardinal Joseph Ratzinger, Dean of the College of Cardinals and Prefect of the Congregation for the Doctrine of the Faith, was presented to Church and World as Pope Benedict XVI. Arguably, no one in the hierarchy is more identified with the policies and directions and centralization of the previous pontificate than Cardinal Ratzinger. Since 1981, for the last twenty-four years, he had enforced John Paul's conservative vision within the Church's hierarchy, across the Church's institutions, and upon professors and theologians thinking and writing and speaking about dogma, morality, and ecclesiastical discipline. In the glow of funeral adulation, warmth and respect demonstrated toward the expired pontiff, the conclave eschewed anything that smacked of newness, difference, or reform. Instead, the loyal electors queued up behind an old warrior on whom they could count to carry on the legacy of their departed boss. In doing so, they delighted Catholic traditionalists, outraged Catholic progressives, and shocked into silent waiting the body of the Catholic faithful. Unless God should intervene with the most telling of miracles, this choice could only reinforce, and even exacerbate, the ecclesial fissures widened under John Paul's rule.

The new pope began predictably. Following a pope famous, or notorious, for canonizations, he greased the way for his predecessor's saintly elevation. Carrying on John Paul's embrace of the young as the hope of the Church, he made his first papal foray to Cologne in August to address the World Youth Day convocation. Responding to the pedophilia scandal in the United States and John Paul's condemnation of it, he appointed Archbishop Levada of San Francisco to carry on his watchdog role at the former, and aptly named, Holy Office. And he has put American seminaries on notice: a papal commission will visit them to ferret out any vestiges of heterodoxy and homosexuality. Aberrations, both doctrinal and sexual, shall not be countenanced.

The seminary investigation attempts to link the clergy sexual abuse scandal with homosexuality. "A study commissioned by the American bishops found last year that nearly 80% of the abused were boys."[6] At least some ecclesiastical officials seem to conclude from this that homosexuality leads to pedophilia. They are wrong. While a correlation might exist in a given population, no causality has ever been established. Certainly, some homosexuals, as some heterosexuals, sexually abuse young boys. Many, however, do not nor do they have any inclination in that direction.

Benedict XVI's Vatican, faced with a persistent public uproar over clerical victimization of Catholic children, is demonstrating a strategy not unlike that

---

6   "Gay Men Ponder Impact Of Proposal by Vatican." *The New York Times*, September 23, 2005.

taken by the United States Defense Department after the torture abuse revelations at the Abu Ghraib prison in Iraq. At first, military authorities blamed the illegal activity on a few rogue military police, all reservists, whom they determined to punish summarily. To date, nine have been charged; six have pleaded guilty; three, including Pfc. Lynndie England and her former boyfriend, Corporal Graner, have been convicted for their part in the torture practices. Since then, however, "the Army has opened more than 400 inquiries into detainee abuse in Iraq and Afghanistan, and punished 230 enlisted soldiers and officers."[7] However, only one commanding officer, a reserve brigadier general, Janis Karpinski, has been relieved of her command. No action has been initiated against any of her superiors, from the commander of military police brigades to Secretary of Defense Donald Rumsfeld.

Vatican authorities would like to blame the pedophilia scandal on a few sinful priests, especially gay ones. If clerical superiors remove them from the ministry and take forceful measures barring homosexuals from ordination, the Vatican hopes that the Catholic people, recognizing its firm intentions and determined leadership, will quiet down. The former pope did accept the resignation of Cardinal Law, the Church's own General Karpinski, because he, as she, governed at the eye of the storm. But no other bishop or cardinal has been removed for collaborating in, allowing, or failing to stop, the distressful decades of the abuse of children.

A reasonable citizen may conclude that the military system—from the White House to the Pentagon, from the Joint Chiefs of Staff to regional commanders—bears responsibility for policies that allowed detainee torture to occur in the field. A reasonable Catholic may judge that a clerical culture of silence and a monarchical governing structure wedded to maintaining its unchallenged power should be held accountable for at least mismanagement, if not also a callous disregard of the abuse in our parishes. Benedict XVI had better care less about Church image and more about the Catholic people.

During his time as prefect in charge of doctrinal obedience, Cardinal Ratzinger struck out an all-star lineup of theologians. When his friend Hans Kung questioned papal infallibility, the Vatican revoked his license to teach Catholic theology. Charles Curran, an American priest teaching at Catholic U., contended that Catholics had a right publicly to dissent from Church teaching on sexuality. He now professes at Southern Methodist University. Leonardo Boff, a Franciscan and professor of theology in Petropolis, Brazil, questioned whether Christ intended a centralized, hierarchical church. Twice he was silenced for a year. After leaving the Franciscans in 1992, he became a professor at the State University of Rio

---

[7]   "Private Found Guilty in Abu Ghraib Abuse." *The New York Times*, September 27, 2005, p. 12.

de Janiero. Liberation theologian Gustavo Gutierrez argued that Jesus promised not only a spiritual, but also a political liberation to his followers. Therefore, Christians have a duty to create a just and communal society. Between 1983-1986 Cardinal Ratzinger's congregation examined into and criticized Gutierrez's writings. Dominican Matthew Fox attempted to reconcile Catholic, non-Catholic, and modern beliefs. The Vatican imposed a year of silence; then his Order dismissed him. He now serves another Christian people as an Episcopal priest. A Sri Lankan, Tissa Balasuriya, argued that the Catholic Church must acknowledge the legitimacy of other faiths. After refusing to sign a profession of faith that included barring women from ordination, the Vatican engineered his excommunication. The humbled priest reconciled with authorities the next year.[8] And as late as February 2005 the Congregation for the Doctrine of the Faith denounced Jesuit father Roger Haight's book, *"Jesus: Symbol of God."* He described his work "as an attempt to express traditional doctrines about Christ and salvation in a language appropriate to a postmodern culture." He wrote because "my fear is that educated Catholics will walk if there isn't an open attitude toward other religions...." He may not teach Catholic theology "until his positions have been corrected so as to be in full conformity with the doctrine of the church."[9]

The new pope barely had time to settle into his papal quarters before his administration struck into silence yet another intelligent Catholic voice. On May 6th, the Reverend Thomas Reese, editor of the Jesuit magazine *America*, resigned under orders from the Vatican. As the direction came from the Congregation for the Doctrine of the Faith in mid-March, it may be viewed as the last act of Prefect Ratzinger, or a chilling portent of the authoritarian papacy of Benedict XVI, or, indeed, both. After his election, Vatican commentators used every opportunity to re-invent "God's Ratweiler" into a kinder, gentler, all-embracing Holy Father. Image-makers and spin-masters surround us with their managed view of reality. But even children know full well that "actions speak louder than words," no matter how cleverly encomia are packaged.

Although the process leading to Reese's dismissal remains cloaked in obscurity, he happens to have earned the Vatican's displeasure because he presented in his magazine current issues in the Church as topics to be explored rather than positions to be defended. *Our Sunday Visitor*, a weekly Catholic newspaper, in its editorial about Reese's dismissal, states clearly the probable Vatican expectations about Catholic journalism:

---

8   "Off the Reservation." *The New York Times*, April 24, 2005, The Week in Review, p. 4.

9   John Allen, "Vatican denounces Fr. Roger Haight's book, bars him from teaching." *National Catholic Reporter*, February 18, 2005, p 10.

As editor of *America*, Father Reese pursued a point-counterpoint style with regard to some of the most controversial issues of the day. It is a model of journalism that is deeply American: Its assumption is that every issue has two sides, and if we hear what advocates of each side say, we can make up our own minds about the issue. This model assumes not objective truth, but rather that decisions are best made by weighing various arguments and coming to our own conclusions,..."

What they [Catholics] need is for the Catholic press to be faithful to its mission: To engage society itself in debate about the critical questions of human existence and offer Catholics the tools to intellectually challenge the culture while defending Catholic teaching and the Gospel.[10]

Not everyone agrees that Catholic journalism should be reduced to the role of passing on Church positions as does, for example, *Observatore Romano*, or of presenting an apologetic for official declarations. In its editorial about Reese's dismissal, the *National Catholic Reporter* stresses the place of dialogue as an ally of truth:

Apologetics certainly have their place, but thoughtful Catholics also need spaces where they can think through the hard questions that faith inevitably generates. Denying them that space does little to protect the truth, and much to foster alienation and intellectual sterility....

If, in previous eras, Catholic thinkers and activists remained unquestioning of church teachings and the presumptions that undergirded them, we Catholics might still believe that the earth is the center of the universe....

The point is clear. Church teaching changes considerably over time as the institution, often with great reluctance, takes in accumulated knowledge, some of it developed in its own institutions, and allows previous understandings of the world, of nature, of humans and of the church itself to be revised.[11]

Whatever position one takes, the secretive and high-handed use of ecclesiastical authority causes serious concern about the directions being espoused by the new pope. On its website, *Commonweal* posted its response to the Vatican action:

---

[10]   Arthur Jones, "Ouster troubles prominent Catholic journalists," *National Catholic Reporter*, May 20, 2005, p.6.

[11]   "A priest to celebrate, not sack," *National Catholic Reporter*, May 20, 2005, p. 24.

Those calling for the strict regulation of Catholic discourse argue that public dissent from church doctrine creates scandal, confusing or misleading the "simple faithful." What really gives scandal to people in the pews, however, is the arbitrary and self-serving exercise of ecclesiastical authority. What the CDF has done to Thomas Reese and *America* is the scandal. Is it possible that not one bishop has the courage to say so? That too is a scandal.[12]

When John Paul II died in April, I decided to wait some months before writing this conclusion. Should his successor begin fashioning a different kind of pontificate, I would need to make significant changes in various parts of the book. It has become clear to me that Benedict XVI's reign will be no more than a continuation of the one just concluded. I have seen nothing in Joseph Ratzinger's past behavior as a member of the hierarchy and of the Vatican bureaucracy that indicates some radical departure is lurking, waiting for the right moment to surface. Moreover, the first six months of his papacy gives no sign of departing from John Paul's version of Catholicism. We will most certainly experience now a Wojtyla—Ratzinger continuum. We will, of course, witness a stylistic difference, such as between a young and energetic former athlete and an old scholar in his late seventies, between a charismatic crowd charmer and a shy professor, between a combative Pole and a retiring German. Contrasting styles, indeed; divergent visions of, and aspirations for, the Church and how it should be governed, no. I, therefore, need rewrite nothing. Whatever I have ascribed to John Paul II regarding Catholic doctrine, traditional morality, internal ecclesiastical discipline, and hierarchical control, I may safely attribute to Benedict XVI.

The situation of the American Church altered little in 2005. The following chart dramatically shows the continuing crisis:

	1962	2004	2005	Total Change
Priests	55,181	44,212	43,404	-21%
Newly Ordained Priests	944	441	364	-61%
Seminarians	49,254	4,330	4,735	-90%
Sisters	173,351	71,468	69,963	-60%
Brothers	11,502	5,504	5,517	-90%[13]

---

12   Cf. www.commonwealmagazine.org

13   *Op. cit., The Official Catholic Directory Anno Domini 1962, 2004, 2005.*

The slight increase in seminarians and brothers represent a leveling off that is almost insignificant in the overall picture. One wonders, also, what the recently released decree on homosexuality in the priesthood will mean for the population figures of both seminarians and priests.

Church membership stays fixed at 23% of the overall population. The hierarchy advanced predictably, adding six archbishops and two bishops. To fill the gap in parishes and schools the Church added a total of 334 permanent deacons and 747 lay teachers in 2005.

Catholic elementary schools continue to decline, showing a decrease of 117. High schools fared a trifle better, showing a decrease of only thirty-one. Colleges and universities remained essentially the same as last year.[14]

A profusion of groups still divide the ecclesiastical scene. On the left they coalesce around a variety of issues: CORPUS and FutureChurch and the Women's Ordination Conference lobbying for a more inclusive priesthood; Dignity seeking respect and equality for gay and lesbian Catholics; Voice of the Faithful demanding a cessation of clerical violence against children, and Pax Christi petitioning for a definitive end to modern warfare. At the opposite extreme many groups still agitate to regain the order, obedience, and predictability of the Tridentine version of Catholicism: Marcel Lefebvre's Society of Pius X refuses to accept the reforms of Vatican II, the Legionnaires of Christ seeks to turn back the priesthood to pre-Vatican II days, Catholics United for the Faith fights vigorously against perceived encroachments from the left on the integrity of Catholic doctrine and life, and Opus Dei strives to bring traditional Catholicism into daily life and to be a conservative evangelizing force in modern society. The silent majority, the mass of American Catholics, avoids the politics of Church membership. If they belong to any parish groups, they tend to be of a devotional nature, like the Holy Name Society and the Blue Army, an altar society or a sodality. Yet underneath the familiar surface of parish life uncomfortable emotions roil. The pedophilia scandal generates shame and disgust, parish and school closings cause deep sadness and loss, and vanishing priests and religious make Catholic life strangely unfamiliar and uncomfortably empty. What is happening to the Church? What will become of it?

Two likely scenarios loom on the horizon. In the first, the Church in America continues on the path of the last forty years. Priests and religious depart, their ranks deplete until lay administrators run parishes and lay teachers staff schools. Mass and the sacraments of Confession and Holy Eucharist become sometime occasions. As clerical presence wanes so does lay allegiance to the hierarchical church. Mass attendance diminishes further, the sacraments tend to be special appearances: the baptism of a baby, the marriage of young adults, the burial of parents and

---

[14]   *Ibid., Anno Domini 2005.*

grandparents. Parishes close or merge; a parish home becomes little more than a memory and a wish. Progressive Catholics, finding themselves blocked by an intransigent hierarchy, give up in disgust. They seek community in the somewhat familiar Episcopalian tradition or the lay polity of Congregationalism, in civic, charitable, and humanitarian organizations, or simply in the spiritual fellowship of their own family. Traditional Catholics stick to the Church like glue. They wear themselves to a frazzle ferreting out traitors to their religious vision and berating others' betrayal of their Catholicism and them. At the same time, the community fades way under their noses. A once vibrant church lives on only as an interesting, if archaic, medieval museum.

This depressing scene flows from three causes. In the first place the pope and his Vatican pour their efforts into preserving control over the worldwide Catholic community, and do nothing to heal the ecclesial crisis in the United States. Meanwhile the American bishops, considering themselves to be little more than the pope's agents and resident overseers, sit and wait for non-existent directions from Rome. They measure the success of their episcopates by juicy promotions and Vatican plaudits, not by effective management. The laity, to their distress, either sit silently in the pews praying somebody will do something constructive, or they choose political sides, denouncing their opponents, and prefer righteous rectitude to the health of the community.

The present pope has spoken about the need to purify the Church. He stands ready for its membership to decrease substantially if such is required. In this second scenario, Rome attempts to reconstruct a pre-Vatican II church. It silences and removes independent or disobedient bishops and priests. It exhibits no tolerance for theological debate over issues of ecclesiastical discipline. It ejects troublesome theologians from universities, contentious editors from journals and magazines and newspapers, and bars questioning preachers from pulpits. It demands that women keep silent in church, that homosexuals live as celibates, and laypeople observe strict obedience to their hierarchical masters. It forces priests and religious, or at least their remnant, back into cloisters, medieval garb, and monastic separation from the modern world.

Rome could pull this off. The American Church would shrink as intelligent and mature members—bishops and priests, religious and laity—abandoned it. It would become, in Cahill's words, "an oddball minority sect...unlike the surrounding society." But it would not recreate the early church of the catacombs, a community bound together in faith and love "in a world of casual cruelty and unbending empire." No, it would be a community consumed by fear under the critical gaze of a cruel and unbending theocracy. Each member would, then, have to decide whether life is possible in such a situation. To those earnestly lobbying for the restoration of a Tridentine church in America: beware of what you dream.

Your dreams might just get realized. It would not, however, be the church you remember, though it would share some outward appearances. Its interior would be shriveled up and barely able to sustain life.

Thomas Cahill, in *The New York Times* article quoted previously, offered a third possible scenario. He proposed that the Catholic Church should start over. It must go back to its original roots in a loving community celebrating the life, death, and resurrection of Jesus. It must forget about popes and bishops, cathedrals and parishes, medieval pomp and clerical power.

For Cahill's vision to be realized, the Catholic Church in America would have to die first. Then, the worldwide Church would have to implode in the equivalent of 9.0 earthquake, a towering tsunami, or a stage five hurricane. Although the Church in America is visibly declining, its death, if coming, still lies below the horizon. The worldwide Church, though losing membership and vitality across developed nations, is growing in the developing world, especially in Africa and South America. Ecclesiastical disaster, if such should occur, threatens only in the unforeseeable future.

This book describes yet another vision of Catholicism in America. Unlike for Cahill, it does not flow out of ecclesial death but rather from ecclesial transformation. Nor does it demand separation from the legitimate authority of popes and bishops. However, it insists that the core of the Church, indeed the living presence of Christ on earth, is the People of God. It refuses to accept as theologically correct the interpretations of Vatican II espoused by Paul VI, John Paul II, and Benedict XVI. The hierarchy *is not* the Church. The essence of Catholicism *is not* obedience to its pope and bishops. A Tridentine church held that view; the Vatican II church replaced it with the faith of the People of God.

The Vatican II church does not reject a papal, episcopal, and clerical polity. It simply shifts its position from monarchical authority to democratic service. The clerical caste rises out of the organizational and administrative needs of the Catholic People. It receives its power and legitimacy from God and through that People. The People of God calls for and expects its service. A Tridentine church emphasized ordination as the path to positions of power; the Vatican II church points to baptism as the source of Christian life and dignity. Baptism makes the community. It erases distinctions between clerics and laypeople, men and women, heterosexuals and homosexuals, between majority and minority. It leaves intact the difference between baptized and non-baptized, between believers and non-believers, buts it does not presume to judge the relationship of a loving God to anyone outside the visible body of the Catholic people. It prizes above all the unity realized in and through a relationship to God; its does not equate uniformity with unity.

Can this vision be realized in our Church? Vatican II has furnished us with the blueprint; the church, however, remains to be built. It cannot be constructed by a European pope and Vatican: they know about medieval kingdoms; they have no clue about the shape of, life in, or faith of a democracy based on equality and freedom, rights and a mature independence. Only a community born into democracy, steeped in its tradition, and loyal to its vision can bring to life a renewed, transformed, and democratic church.

We stand at a God-presented crossroads. To stop now presages a pining away, perhaps unto death. The path to the right is paved with cobblestones, a Roman road smoothed by centuries of Catholic armies bent on conquering the world and extending a Vatican hegemony around the globe. To the left, a road less traveled beckons. Under bright blue skies it passes through waving fields of grain, over majestic mountains, across vast and fruitful plains, until it links sea to shining sea. It begins in baptismal waters; in the Spirit of God it charts a path across a young landscape toward the realization of divine life. We cannot expect others to initiate this journey; it is ours to explore as an American and democratic church. Go in peace, then, to love and serve our God.

References

Abbott, Walter M. (ed.). (1966). *The Documents of Vatican II*". New York, New York: The America Press.

Agonito, Joseph. (1988). *The Building of an American Catholic Church: The Episcopacy of John Carroll*. New York, New York: Garland Publishing, Inc.

Ahlstrom, Sidney. (2004). *A Religious History of the American People*. New Haven, Connecticut: Yale University Press.

Allen, John. (February 18, 2005). "Vatican denounces Fr. Roger Haight's book, bars him from teaching." *National Catholic Reporter*. St. Louis, Missouri.

American Psychological Association website:
http://www.apa.org.pubinfo/answers.html

Cahill, Thomas. (April 5, 2005) "The price of infallibility." *The New York Times*. New York, New York.

Carey, Patrick. (1982). *An Immigrant Bishop: John England's Adaptation of Irish Catholicism to American Republicanism*. Yonkers, New York: United States Catholic Historical Society.

Catholic Diocese of Spokane website: http://www.dioceseofspokane.org. "A Short History of the Diocese." Spokane, Washington.

Center for Applied Research in the Apostolate (CARA). (2004). "Frequently Requested Church Statistics." Washington, D.C.

Code of Canon Law". (1983). Washington, D.C.: The Canon Law Society of America.

Commonweal website: http://www.commonwealmagazine.org

Dictionnaire De L'Académie Française. (1835). *Sixième Edition*.

D'Antonio, William, Davidson, James, Gautier, Mary, & Hoge, Dean. (September 30, 2005). "American Catholics from John Paul II to Benedict XVI." *National Catholic Reporter*. St. Louis, Missouri.

Dolan, Jay P. (2003). *In Search of An American Catholicism: A History of Religion and Culture in Tension*. New York, New York: Oxford University Press.

Eisler, Riane. (1987). *The Chalice and the Blade*. New York, New York: HarperCollins.

Eliot, T.S. (1943). *Four Quartets*. New York, New York: Harcourt, Brace and World.

England, John. (1810). *The Religious Repertory for the Year of Our Lord 1809*. Cork, Ireland: J. Haley, Publisher.

England, John. (c.1822). *The Constitution of the Roman Catholic Church of North Carolina, South Carolina, and Georgia*.

Guilday, Peter. (1922). *The Life and Times of John Carroll, Archbishop of Baltimore (1735-1815)*. Volumes I & II. New York, New York: The Encyclopedia Press.

Guilday, Peter. (1927). *The Life and Times of John England, First Bishop of Charleston (1786-1842)*. Volumes I & II. New York, New York: The Encyclopedia Press.

Hanley, Thomas. (1976). *The Letters of John Carroll*. Volumes I & II. Notre Dame, Indiana: Notre Dame Press.

Hughes, Thomas. (1907). *History of the Society of Jesus in North America, Colonial and Federal*. Volume I. London, England: Longmans, Green.

Jenkins, Philip. (October 2002). "The Next Christianity." *The Atlantic Monthly.* Boston, Massachusetts.

Jones, Arthur. (April 15, 2005). "Another side of John Paul II." *National Catholic Reporter.* St. Louis, Missouri.

Jones, Arthur. (May 20, 2005). "Ouster troubles prominent Catholic journalists." *National Catholic Reporter.* St. Louis, Missouri.

Maslow, Abraham. (1970). *Motivation and Personality.* New York, New York: Harper and Row.

Maslow, Abraham. (1970). *Religion, Values, and Peak Experiences.* New York, New York: Viking Press.

Maslow, Abraham. (1971). *The Farther Reaches of Human Nature.* New York, New York: Viking Press.

McElrone, Hugh P. (ed). (1894). *The Works of Right Reverend John England.* Volumes I & II. New York, New York: P. J. Kenedy and Sons.

Morris, Charles R. (1997). *American Catholic.* New York, New York: Vintage Books.

National Catholic Reporter. (May 20, 2005). "A priest to celebrate, not sack." St. Louis, Missouri.

New Catholic Encyclopedia. (1967). Editorial staff of the Catholic University of America. New York, New York: McGraw-Hill.

Oakley, Francis & Russett, Bruce (eds.). (2004). *Governance, Accountability, and the Future of the Catholic Church.* New York, New York: Continuum Press.

O'Connell, John (ed.). (1867). *The Life and Speeches of Daniel O'Connell, M. P.* Dublin, Ireland: James Duffy.

O'Leary, Arthur. (1787). *Miscellaneous Tracts.* Dublin, Ireland: John Chambers.

Padovano, Anthony. "The American Catholic Church: Assessing the Past, Discerning the Future." Address given to the National Conference of Call To Action, Milwaukee, Wisconsin, November 2003.

Rahner, Karl & Vergrimler, Herbert. (1965). *Theological Dictionary*. New York, New York: Herder and Herder.

Rouse, W. H. D. (trans.). (1956). *Great Dialogues of Plato*. New York, New York: New American Library.

Steinfels, Peter. (2003). *A People Adrift*. New York, New York: Simon and Schuster.

The New York Times. (April 3, 2005). "American Catholics in John Paul's Time." New York, New York.

The New York Times. (September 23, 2005). "Gay Men Ponder Impact Of Proposal by Vatican." New York, New York.

The New York Times. (September 27, 2005). "Private Found Guilty in Abu Ghraib Abuse." New York, New York.

The Official Catholic Directory, Anno Domini 1962. New York, New York: P.J. Kenedy and Sons.
...*Anno Domini 2002.*
...*Anno Domini 2004.*
...*Anno Domini 2005.*

Tocqueville, Alexis de. (2000). *Democracy in America*. Mansfield, Harvey & Winthrop, Debra (trans. & eds.). Chicago, Illinois: University of Chicago Press.

United States Continental Congress. (1989). *Journals of the Continental Congress 1774-1789*. Washington, D.C.: Gales and Seaton.

Vance, William L. (1989). *America's Rome*. New Haven, Connecticut: Yale University Press.

Weigel, George. (2002). *The Courage to be Catholic: Crisis, Reform, and the Future of the Church*. New York, New York: Basics Books.

Willis, Robert. (1994). *Transcendence in Relationship: Existentialism and Psychotherapy*. Norwood, New Jersey: Ablex Publishing Company.

Author Index

A

Abbott, Walter 80, 115, 233
Agonito, Joseph 23, 26, 29, 34, 233
Ahlstrom, Sydney 50, 55, 233
Allen, John 233
American Psychological Association 181, 233

C

Cahill, Thomas 220-222, 229-230, 233
Carey, Patrick 39, 41-42, 233
Carroll, John 15-17, 20-22, 24-27
Code of Canon Law 188, 193-195, 210, 215, 233, 241
Commonweal 8, 161, 226-227, 234, 244

D

D'Antonio, William 222, 234
Davidson, James 22, 234
Dictionnaire L'Académie Française 185, 234

E

Eisler, Riane 214, 234
Eliot, T.S. 77, 234
England, John 37-39, 41-42, 44-49, 234

G

Gautier, Mary 222, 234
Guilday, Peter 26, 28, 32, 42, 50-51, 53, 234

H

Hanley, Thomas 17, 20-24, 26, 29, 31-32, 34, 234
Hoge, Dean 222, 234
Hughes, Thomas 21, 234

J

Jones, Arthur 219, 226, 235

K

Kenny, Kevin 58

M

Mansfield, Harvey 236 *see* Tocqueville
Maslow, Abraham 162-166, 235
McElrone, Hugh 15, 50, 52, 235
Morris, Charles 6-7, 235

Subject Index

About the Author

A Jesuit from 1953-1972, Robert Willis holds master's degrees in philosophy and theology, and a doctorate in psychology. He has documented these years as a Catholic religious and priest in his recently published *Breaking the Chains: A Catholic Memoir* (iUniverse, July 2005).

His interest in political science grew, originally, under the tutelage of his father, Judge Robert J. Willis, superior court judge for Yakima County in the State of Washington. During his master's work in philosophy, Willis concentrated his efforts on the relationship of ethics and law, both in his thesis and in political science courses at Gonzaga University in Spokane, Washington. This carried over into political activism with Pax Christi in opposition to the war in Vietnam and with Common Cause in demanding honest and accountable government. At the same time he volunteered as a member of the Civilian Review Board for the Selective Service System in New Jersey, served as a member of the Regional Review Board of the Central New Jersey Health Planning Council, and presided as chairman of the Board of Psychological Examiners for the State of New Jersey. As a visiting fellow, he participated in a military/civilian program at the Army War College in Carlisle, Pennsylvania.

Willis studied psychology at the United States International University in San Diego, California, while working with Dr. Carl Rogers and colleagues at The Center for Studies of the Person in nearby La Jolla. He emphasized, both academically and in professional practice, the building of a positive relationship between traditional religion and modern psychology.

As a licensed psychologist, Willis built a career as a consultant with religious institutions—dioceses and orders, colleges and hospitals—as a professor of pastoral counseling and religious psychology, and as a psychotherapist for priests, brothers and sisters struggling to integrate their personal and religious lives in our modern world. From 1991 until his retirement in 2000, he directed the Pastoral

Counseling Center of West Hartford, Connecticut. In this capacity, he trained younger therapists to work effectively in religious and psychological contexts; in addition, day in and day out he counseled both Catholic and Protestant clients conflicted with personal, familial, and societal issues.

Willis has written on psychological practice: *Transcendence in Relationship: Existentialism and Psychotherapy* (Ablex, 1991). Many of his articles about therapy appear in professional journals: *The Psychotherapy Patient, Psychotherapy in Private Practice*, and *Voices: The Art and Science of Psychotherapy*. In religious psychology he contributed chapters to books in the field: *The Ministry of Governance,* James K. Mallett (ed), Canon Law Society of America; *Quality of Work Life,* Ken Buback and Mary Kathryn Grant (eds), Catholic Health Association, and *Proceedings: Mercy Sponsorship Seminar,* Mercy Health Conference. He also has articles in Catholic publications: *Sisters Today, Spiritual Life, America, Commonweal, American Catholic—Northeast, The Barat Review,* and *Human Development.*

For more detailed information, visit the author's website: <robertjwillis.com>.

Dr. Willis lives with his wife, Patricia Cannon Willis, in Hamden, Connecticut.

978-0-595-37922-4
0-595-37922-2